Volume **2**

Essays from HORIZON

PERSPECTIVES IN
WESTERN CIVILIZATION

WILLIAM L. LANGER, *Editor*
Coolidge Professor of History, Emeritus   *Harvard University*

AMERICAN HERITAGE PUBLISHING CO., INC.   *New York*
HARPER & ROW, PUBLISHERS, INCORPORATED   *New York, Evanston & London*

Perspectives in Western Civilization: Essays from Horizon   Volume 2

Library of Congress Catalog Card Number: 79–185243
ISBN: 06–043835–5

INTRODUCTION

WILLIAM L. LANGER

I t is now roughly a century and a half since historical research and writing ceased to be the occupation of retired statesmen or gentlemen scholars. The rigorous, systematic training thenceforth given to professional students has improved the quality of historical literature immeasurably. But it has also increased the quantity of the product to the point where only the specialist can master even a restricted segment. The days when all cultured society awaited the next volume of Macaulay, Thiers, or Michelet have gone beyond recovery. No man is nowadays competent to write the whole history of a nation or a period on the basis of original research. At best he can draw together the vast specialized literature and supply his own interpretation of the synthesis.

With so extensive a knowledge of historical events it stands to reason that the textbooks used by students can never be more than the merest distillation of the data. Indeed, the material must be compressed to the point where it may become lifeless or at least colorless. Only a more detailed treatment can convey something of the flavor of past events.

It is exactly this function that the present selection of essays from *Horizon* magazine is intended to fulfill. These articles cover the gamut of European history, though not in any systematic way. One might say that they sample the events of the past, providing for selected topics the detail necessary for better appreciation and acquainting the student with problems and solutions that have of necessity to be omitted from a general text. These essays are all written by people of competence in their field. They are fully abreast of modern knowledge of their subjects and serve to put flesh on the bare bones of historical fact. Anyone with an interest in the past should enjoy the scope and variety of this collection, while the student should find it stimulating and provocative as well as informative.

CONTENTS

Even the Spanish historians of today tend to devote their attention and energy to the study of Spain's golden age, that is, to the sixteenth century when Spain, having discovered and conquered huge empires in the New World, employed the resources of those empires to make itself the leading power in Europe. Charles V, though Holy Roman Emperor, was first of all king of Spain and based his immense power on that country. But Spain's greatness was to prove ephemeral. Its decline was as rapid as its rise had been. The glorious victory of Lepanto (1571) was soon followed by the disaster of the Armada sent against England in 1588.

The author of Don Quixote *was a hero of the golden age who, on his return to Spain in 1580, found himself thrust into a new, deflated generation. As this essay so effectively argues, it was because he spanned the periods of greatness and of decline that Cervantes was able to make Don Quixote so plausible and sympathetic. Professor Trevor-Roper here pays tribute to one of the world's greatest writers and to his famous masterpiece.*

THE TWO SPAINS OF DON QUIXOTE

H. R. TREVOR-ROPER

The only good book in Spanish literature, said Montesquieu, is the one which proves all the others bad. He was referring, of course, to that incomparable, irresistible, unique work, *Don Quixote*, whose first part was published in 1605, and which, it is said, killed by ridicule the "romances of chivalry" that had been the staple literary diet of Spaniards for a century. Certainly they did not survive it. The most famous, most persistent of them all, *Amadis de Gaul*, was last reissued in 1602, three years before *Don Quixote* appeared; and thereafter, in America as in Spain, the whole literary genus was practically extinct. But whether *Don Quixote* really killed them, or merely appeared as their epitaph, is a difficult question, a question to be solved, if at all, rather in the field of social than of literary history. In this essay I wish to consider the social background to Don Quixote and seek in it, if possible, the key to its unique quality and marvelous success.

Don Quixote's disastrous tilt with the windmills, as portrayed by Gustave Doré. A despairing Sancho Panza surveys the scene.

Of course no masterpiece is completely explained by circumstances. By definition, a masterpiece proceeds from the human genius of its author, not from the material which he uses. But it is undeniable that Cervantes, though his work has transcended the age which it described, was—perhaps more than any other great writer—a child of his time. No other of his works has gained immortality. Only in this did his happy spirit attain perfection. And even in this he showed himself essentially a recorder, not (like Dickens or Tolstoy) a critic or reformer of his own age. A great Hispanist, A. Morel-Fatio, has called *Don Quixote* "the great social novel of early seventeenth-century Spain"; but he has added, "No writer has been more of his time than Cervantes; he is not ahead of it by one line." Therefore, in considering its character, we are justified in looking carefully at the material out of which it was made: the personal experience of Cervantes in sixteenth-century Spain.

First of all, what is the essential quality of *Don Quixote?* The plot of the book is soon told. Don Quixote is a middle-aged Castilian hidalgo—that is, a poor but proud rustic gentleman—who for many years has lived in his decrepit manor house in La Mancha, a seedy, remote province of Spain, alone with his niece and his old housekeeper, reading "romances of chivalry." Of these romances of chivalry we shall have something to say in a moment: at present it is enough to say that the constant reading of them has, by the beginning of the story, unhinged Don Quixote's mind, and so he sets out, with his equally decrepit and equally engaging horse Rozinante, in order that he too may seek similar adventures, opposing giants, rescuing damsels from dragons and enchanters, and challenging rival knights-errant to single combat to prove the superior beauty of their respective ladies. For such a purpose Don Quixote needs a lady, and so he idealizes, as the Lady Dulcinea del Toboso, a local farmer's daughter. He also, like all knights-errant, needs a trusty squire. For this function he impresses a devoted but hard-headed, earth-bound local peasant, the perfect foil to his own high, chivalric fantasies, Sancho Panza.

Once the dramatis personae are assembled, the action seems almost automatic. Don Quixote and Sancho Panza set out: the former boldly, with all his bees buzzing in his exalted bonnet, and the latter reluctantly, awed by his master's high language, but thinking primarily of incidental cakes and ale and ultimate material reward. To Don Quixote the real world hardly exists. To him inns are castles, innkeepers their constables, windmills giants, flocks of sheep rival armies, funeral processions troops of enchanters carrying off their spellbound victims; and whenever these majestic misconceptions painfully conflict with the real world, he explains the real world away with yet more ingenious rationalizations. But to Sancho Panza, though he takes his master's theories on trust, there is ultimately only one real world, and that is the world which he has left behind in his village, exchanging it not for ideal adventures but, as he discovers, for solid bumps and bruises, the price to him of his master's chivalry.

Don Quixote and Sancho Panza are inseparable: they are the joint heroes of the book, and the book owes its character to this constant duality. But it is not a crude duality. It may begin as such, but little by little, as we read on, we find that it becomes increasingly subtle. For the contrast is not really *between* the knight and his squire, it is *in* them both. Don Quixote may be mad when conversation is of knights and ladies, dwarfs and enchanters, but in other matters he has remarkable good sense, which breaks disconcertingly through his follies. Sancho Panza may be, at bottom, a hard-headed, prosaic peasant, but periodically he too is carried away into the world of fantasy, fitting himself into his master's world and imagining himself rewarded with the government of an island. To the firm overtones there are always subtle undertones: the whole world of Cervantes is schizophrenic, and the men in his novel merely participate, in differing degrees, in both the reality and the make-believe.

Consider their attitude toward the books of chivalry, the clearly convicted source of all the make-believe. At first it seems that Don Quixote alone takes seriously what other men regard merely as foolish novelettes. But soon we realize that this is not so. Everyone may agree that these "lying histories" are pernicious works which have made the poor knight mad; but everyone, it transpires, is as deep in them as he, and perhaps just as affected by them, though in other ways. When Don Quixote has set off on his adventures, there is dismay in his home, and his housekeeper and his niece, together with the barber and the curate, as pillars of sanity, resolve to burn all the wicked books that have disordered his mind. But what is the result? As each book is identified, they all remember it, discuss its merits, argue about its fate; and half of them are ultimately saved from the burning.

Later, when the same barber and curate pursue Don Quixote to the inn in the Sierra Morena, which is the theater of his follies, they explain to the innkeeper the origin of his madness, only to discover that the innkeeper, his housekeeper, his daughter, and his maid are all passionate readers of such romances: How then, they exclaim, can such delightful reading, which keeps them alive, make anyone mad? Later still, when the curate and the barber bring Don Quixote back to his village in a cage on an oxcart—a wonderfully comic episode—they are overtaken by a canon of the Church, whom Don Quixote gravely informs that he has been bewitched and encaged by jealous enchanters. Having then heard the true story from his escort, the canon expresses indignation against those pernicious books which the Church has constantly but ineffectively condemned. But as the conversation proceeds, we soon discover that the same indignant canon has not only read as many of these pernicious books as Don Quixote but has even written one as well. And so it is with everyone: goatherds and plowmen, dukes and duchesses, all are as deeply involved as Don Quixote—whom they presume to think mad—in the same ever-expanding world of make-believe.

For as the book progresses, so does the world of make-believe. The barber and the curate, who set out to cure Don Quixote's follies, end by becoming participants in it, actors in his imaginary history. Sancho Panza starts talking his master's language. The Duke and Duchess, who receive the pair, adjust their whole dukedom to his follies, so that Don Quixote is no longer any madder than his surroundings, and Sancho, with perfect gravity, gives laws to his imaginary island. Well might a bystander cry out, on seeing our hero, "The Devil take thee for Don Quixote of La Mancha! Thou art a madman; and wert thou so in private, 'twere less evil; but thy property is to make all that converse or treat with thee madmen and coxcombs!" Finally, by an exquisite piece of fancy, Don Quixote himself becomes the champion of truth against falsehood. For in 1614, nine years after its publication, the success of Cervantes's first part had prompted a rival novelist to publish a continuation of the story. Cervantes was indignant at this plagiarism, and in his own second part, which appeared the following year, he showed Don Quixote, now made famous by the first part, continually meeting and confuting the misguided readers of "the false second part." Thus the genuine first part and the false second part of the story become additional elements in its last phase, complicating still further the delicious and now inextricable confusion of reality and make-believe.

Such, very briefly, is the character of this incomparable work. I have described it as a "schizophrenic" book because of the duality of heroism and disillusion, make-believe and reality, which so completely pervades it. It is this duality which makes the book, sustaining and animating it throughout its great length—indeed, so animating it that Dr. Johnson could describe it as the only book which one wishes were longer. And it does so because the duality is genuine. Cervantes himself, we feel, is schizophrenic; he is on both sides at once: on the side of Don Quixote and on the side of Sancho Panza. The duality, in fact, is in his own mind, and—since he is so completely "of his time"—in the society in which he lived, late sixteenth- and early seventeenth-century Spain.

In what sense was Spain, in those years, schizophrenic? If we look at it closely, I believe we can find an answer. In Cervantes's lifetime, Spain had two very different moods. They were the moods of two successive but antithetical generations. The generation of the fathers was bound together by one set of experiences which created one kind of mood, a mood of fantastic confidence, heroic tension, intoxicating romance. The generation of the sons had different experiences, and consequently a different mood. Immune from their fathers' experiences, they knew only defeat, disappointment, disillusion; and their mood was one of cynical realism, passivity, emptiness. Now the life of Cervantes straddled both these generations, and in his own person he experienced, directly, both the heroism of the fathers and the disillusion of the sons. In his book, which is in some ways an autobiography, or at least a self-portrait, he expressed—sympathetically, because he had left them both—the two mutually opposing moods, moods which met in his lifetime and, particularly, in him.

Let us look at these two generations, so close in time, so opposite in character. First, let us take the generation of the fathers, the men who grew up during the reign of Charles V, "the Emperor"; for he was Holy Roman Emperor while king of Spain. Under the Emperor, Spain found itself suddenly a world power. Not long before, it had been a poor, rural appendix at the back end of Europe; now its armies fought and conquered on the Rhine and the Danube, in Italy and Africa, against German heretics and Turkish infidels. Spanish adventurers were conquering huge empires (and huge estates for themselves) in new-found America, and the wealth of America, spent on armies, fleets, and the imperial court, sustained and inflated an archaic feudal society, with chivalric notions imported from the magnificent Burgundy of Froissart and Comines.

It was an astonishing change, astonishing in its suddenness, comparable with the great Arab conquests of the seventh and eighth centuries; and the Spaniards who witnessed or achieved it

Few works have inspired as many varied artistic interpretations as Don Quixote. Above is Daumier's sketch of the gaunt knight on his shambling horse, trailed by Sancho. On the opposite page, a woodcut by the American Antonio Frasconi depicts the Don charging a windmill under a spectacular sun and star. In a Japanese view below, the samurai-like knight braves a tigerish lion in its den.

were inspired by a sense of divine mission and superhuman power. God was behind them, they felt, and nothing beyond them. They flinched before no obstacle, accepted no authority except that of their own king. Even the Pope received scant respect from them: when he was tiresome, the imperial court, inspired by the exciting, liberal doctrines of Erasmus, did not hesitate to strike at him, and the imperial armies seized and sacked the Holy City itself. Only the Emperor himself commanded unconditional respect; and he commanded it the more because, from a foreigner, a Fleming who knew no Spanish, he had become a Spaniard: *"esta figura tan española!"* ("this truly Spanish figure!") as a great historian has called him, who refused, even to the Pope's ambassador, to speak any language but the Spanish which he had lately learned.

It was this mood of exaltation in the time of the Emperor which found its popular expression in the famous "romances of chivalry." Throughout the sixteenth century, but particularly in the Emperor's reign, they were the best sellers of Spain, the equivalent of our "science fiction"; for though absurd in content, they symbolized a boundless new confidence which found nothing impossible. The adventures of Amadis de Gaul, Policisne de Boecia, Palmerin de Oliva, and their descendants were published and republished in serial form—scholars have counted 316 editions in

15

the sixteenth century—and there is scarcely a famous Spaniard of "the golden century" who was not an avowed or secret reader of them: for the condemnation of the Church was powerless to suppress them. Wounded at Pamplona, the young Ignatius of Loyola spent his convalescence reading them, and when he became a missionary saint, his activities read like one of them: he became a knight-errant of religion. Saint Teresa of Avila confesses that in her youth she was never happy unless she was secretly reading them.

The Emperor himself, ignoring the protests of his clergy, was a constant reader and even wrote a sequel to one of them. They were the favorite reading of his soldiers in Italy. In spite of an ófficial ban they poured into the Indies. When the companions of Cortes looked for the first time on the lake of Mexico, studded with Aztec cities, "we were amazed," says one of them, "and said that it was like the enchanted things related in the book of Amadis de Gaul." The passion of the Spanish soldiers in America for these "lying histories" has left its traces today: California in the Northern Hemisphere, Patagonia in the Southern, are both named after heroines of these trashy novelettes.

Charles V abdicated the Spanish throne in 1556, retiring (with two books of chivalry in his luggage) to the monastery of Yuste, and three years later his son and successor, Philip II, came to Spain. Later historians have seen Philip II as a great ruler, but it is worth noting that this respect for the uniformly unsuccessful bureaucrat-king did not begin until the reign of his grandson, when few could remember him. To contemporaries he was a poor figure, mean, jealous, and suspicious. In his reign the old liberalism of Charles V was finally crushed, the last of the old "Erasmians" burnt; the Empire was frayed at its edges and rotted at its core. But this decline was not at first apparent. For a decade, at least, after 1560, the heirs of Charles V kept his spirit alive. Particularly it lived on in Italy, away from the stuffy bigotry and waspish intrigues of the new court. There all eyes looked south and east to the great crusade which Charles V had conducted from Italy, the defense of the Mediterranean against the Turk. In 1571 the dead Emperor seemed to live again when his bastard son, Don John of Austria, of whom his legitimate son was so jealous, won a resounding naval victory at Lepanto (for which the church bells were rung even in Protestant England) and went on to occupy Tunis, ending forever the Turkish domination of the Mediterranean.

But if Lepanto echoed the imperial age, it was the last echo. In the 1570's Don John was undermined by his royal brother and died, and meanwhile Spain itself was being slowly ruined by a gigantic, ill-conceived, desk-dictated policy of religious and political reaction in northern Europe. By 1590 the new generation had grown up: a generation with no memory of the imperial days and their buoyant mood. Instead it had experienced only disillusion and defeat. For the last twenty years it had seen Spain mobilizing massive efforts which only disintegrated in humiliating disaster and squalid recrimination. All the wealth of America had been poured out in vain. The long revolt in the Netherlands was still unquenched. The Invincible Armada had been shattered. The attempt to conquer France had failed. In the years that followed, the disasters pressed nearer home. In the 1590's there was both plague and famine in Spain. The Crown was bankrupt, the nation impoverished. The political and military scandals were great and public. In 1596 an English force, under Queen Elizabeth's Earl of Essex, actually landed in Spain and seized and sacked its greatest port, Cádiz. Two years later, after a long and terrible illness, as slow and agonizing as his reign, Philip II died, and with his son, Philip III, was enthroned the new spirit of Spain—the spirit of cynicism and disillusion, the negation of all heroism, the cult not of religious crusades but of passive, superstitious piety.

The contrast between the new spirit and the old is remarkable. Wherever we look, it is there. In politics a wooden defensiveness replaces adventure; in literature satire replaces bombast. Social values are different: the old aristocracy had been military leaders; the new give themselves up to the giddy pursuit of official status and expensive pleasure. And religion reflects the same change. In the sixteenth century the Spanish Church had been active, crusading, missionary: its heroes had been Las Casas, Loyola, Saint Teresa; in the seventeenth, it is dull and passive: its only great figure is Molinos, the founder, appropriately, of religious quietism.

Perhaps the most striking illustration of this new spirit is the sudden change which took place, early in the seventeenth century, in the patron saint of Spain. For centuries that saint had been *Santiago*—Saint James, who was reputed to have come to Spain, and who was there transformed into a fighting saint, the patron of holy war. He was known as *Santiago Matamoros*, "Santiago, the killer of Moors." All through the Middle Ages, Santiago inspired Spanish Christians fighting against the infidel. Again and again, in the critical moment of battles, he appeared to them, mounted on a white horse in the sky, to give them fresh courage and turn defeat into victory. In America, too, fighting far from home against overwhelming odds, the conquistadors often saw Santiago, sometimes alone on his white horse, sometimes at the head of an ethereal army, doing battle for them in the clouds. More than two hundred places in Latin America still commemorate his name. But then, quite suddenly, in Spain and America alike, his authenticity was challenged. The doubters—Cervantes himself among them—raised their voices; there was a brief struggle, conducted in full legal form; and in 1617, Santiago, the saint of crusade and victory, collapsed. He was replaced, in Spain, by Saint Teresa of Avila—or rather by an imaginary Saint Teresa, not the real saint, that "gadabout nun," social, energetic, practical; but a gaping *beata*, as we see her in Bernini's effigy, the personification of passive, inexhaustible female credulity. In America, having appeared at least ten times in the sixteenth century, Santiago showed himself only once in the seventeenth and then disappeared. He was replaced in Mexico by the creole San Felipe de Jesús, in Peru by another female *beata*, the half-caste Santa Rosa de Lima. This sudden change of saints symbolizes a change in the whole religious character of Spain.

I have dwelt upon this sudden shift, in one generation of Spanish life, from heroic tension to empty disillusion, because it was the essential background to Cervantes's own life, the background to *Don Quixote*. Cervantes, in a sense, fell between the two generations, sharing the moods of both. Born in 1547, in the reign of Charles V, he was brought up in Spain by an old Erasmian teacher who still breathed the confident, liberal air of imperial times; and then, as a young man, he went to Italy and was intoxicated by the ebullience, the vitality of Italian life. He read Ariosto, the poet of gaiety, chivalry, and enchanted romance. He enlisted as a soldier, fought and was wounded in Don John's great, victorious battle of Lepanto, served in the campaign against Tunis and Goletta, and in 1575 set sail, full of honor and pride, and with letters of recommendation from Don John and the Spanish governor in his pocket, for Spain, promotion, and further glory. He was a hero, a self-conscious hero, living fully and investing heavily in that (as he was to discover) last twilight of the heroic age. Nor did his heroism end there. On his way home, off the coast of France, his ship was captured by Algerian corsairs. Seeing his letters of recommendation, the pirates presumed him to be a man of mark who would command a high ransom. Cervantes was taken to Algiers and there remained for more than five years, a prisoner and a galley slave.

18   In his captivity at Algiers, Cervantes continued his heroic ex-

ploits. He never forgot them. Long afterward, in *Don Quixote*, he recalled them. There, a captive, escaped from the Moorish galleys, meets Don Quixote and tells the story of his captivity. In it he refers to a fellow captive "called something-de-Saavedra" (Cervantes's full name was Miguel de Cervantes Saavedra), who achieved such a personal ascendancy over the Moorish governor that although "we all feared that he should be broached on the stake for the least of many things he did . . . yet he never struck him nor commanded him to be stricken, nor said as much as an evil word to him." Cervantes's own account is borne out by a contemporary who, in a history of Algiers written before *Don Quixote* had made its author famous, tells us that "of the captivity and brave deeds of Miguel de Cervantes one could write a whole history. Four times he narrowly avoided death by impaling, hanging, or burning for having set fellow captives free. And if fortune had aided his courage and ingenuity, Algiers would be in Christian hands today, for he aimed at no less." And indeed, while still a captive, Cervantes wrote to King Philip's secretary urging the conquest of Algiers. If only he were ransomed, he wrote, he would throw himself at the King's feet and say, "Great monarch, you who have enslaved a thousand barbarian peoples, who receive tribute even from the blacks of India, how can you tolerate the resistance of a miserable hovel? Ah, could you but complete the work begun by your valiant father!"

"Your valiant father"—always, in his heroic dreams, Cervantes, like other Spaniards, looks back to the Emperor Charles V. Later, in the preface which he wrote for his collected short stories, he gave a brief autobiographical sketch of himself, which compresses into two sentences his cult of heroism, his pride in his own heroic life, and his veneration for the Emperor. The author of these stories, he says, "was a soldier for many years, and a captive for five and a half years, and so learned patience in adversity. He lost his left hand from an arquebus-shot at the sea fight of Lepanto: an ugly wound, which, however, he thought comely because he had received it in the greatest, most memorable event that the past has seen or the future may hope to see, fighting under the triumphant banners of [Don John of Austria] the son of that thunderbolt of war, Charles V of happy memory."

Such was the Cervantes who, in 1580, returned from captivity to the Spain of Philip II. We can recognize him perfectly: he is a true, if somewhat belated, representative of the first of our two generations, the heroic, romantic, chivalrous generation of Charles

V. But when he returned to Spain, what did he find? Already, while he had been breathing the heady air of Italy, fighting at Lepanto, braving his infidel captors in Algiers, the new generation was taking over in Spain, and now, instead of a grateful hero-king promoting him, accepting his advice, and leading an enthusiastic people into new crusades, he found only an atmosphere of growing weariness and disillusion. Year after year Cervantes struggled to make a livelihood, first by poetry, then as a government purchaser, finally as a tax collector. None of these callings prospered. Economically—though not in spirit, for he retained, in every hardship, his own inexhaustible optimism—he sank down and down: bankrupt for small sums, excommunicated for trying to tax the clergy, finally imprisoned. In 1596, the year of the sack of Cádiz, he reached his lowest ebb, and wrote a wry, sardonic poem on that national humiliation. Two years later the death of Philip II drew from him an even more sardonic epitaph. Clearly the days of heroism were over: the days of disillusion had come. It was in those years of lowest ebb that Cervantes, in prison, conceived the idea of Don Quixote, the hero, the reader of romances, the Erasmian (for *Don Quixote* has many sly "Erasmian" touches which were duly pounced on by the Inquisition), who discovered that the real world—the world of narrow, materialist common sense—thought him mad.

For of course Don Quixote is Cervantes. This is well pointed out by one of the most perceptive writers on Spanish literature, Gerald Brenan. "I think we ought to take note," he says, "that the famous knight had many features in common with his creator. We learn, for example, that Don Quixote was of the same age as Cervantes when he set out on his adventures, and that he had the same physical appearance: we read of his wits being dry and sterile and his head turned by too much reading, just as we are told in the preface that his author's were. Moreover, he was the incorrigible optimist and idealist who set out to reform the world by force of arms and instead was beaten by it. Must not this, or something like it, have been Cervantes's view of his own history? . . . I suggest therefore that one of the sources of Don Quixote's power to move us comes from his being a projection of a discarded part of Cervantes himself: that is to say, of the noble intentions and failure of his life. It is for this reason that the irony in this most ironical of books has often the deep and searching quality of self-irony."

No doubt it is self-irony, but also it is a delicate self-irony: that is why it is so attractive, why it makes so great a book. When a

man makes steppingstones of his dead selves, he is very likely (as
Samuel Butler once wrote) to jump upon them to some tune. But
Cervantes did not jump. If he is disillusioned, there is nothing
vindictive or cynical about his disillusion. How could there be,
when half of his own life had been invested in those illusions which
he now found himself, with all Spain, forced to mock? A generation
would come which had made no such investment and which could
afford to be severe against the fantasies of the past. But Cervantes
could not, for he had a foot in either world. And so he wrote essentially not for the future (though the eighteenth century would re-
discover him and set him among the immortals), but for his own
generation, the generation of the disillusioned, which could yet
regret its illusions: for they were its own.

*One reads of the greatness of the Dutch Republic only with amazement,
not to say incredulity. How this small, none-too-well endowed corner
of Europe should, for more than a century, have attained such wealth,
such eminence in almost every field of human endeavor, will forever
remain something of a mystery. The long struggle against Spanish
rule, inspired by religion, seems to have released energies that then
found expression in commerce, literature, and the arts, achievements
immortalized by the great Dutch genre painters as few other phases
of European culture have been recorded. Yet the period of Dutch
greatness was relatively short, coincident with the decline of Spain,
the religious conflicts in France, the civil strife in England, and the
Thirty Years' War in central Europe. It remains, then, as one of
the bright spots in the history of European achievement, brilliantly
reviewed by one of the leading historians of the seventeenth century.*

THE GOLDEN AGE OF THE DUTCH REPUBLIC

C. V. WEDGWOOD

On a narrow, low-lying strip of coastal country in northern
Europe, scarcely two hundred miles long—a country so water-
logged that enemies and rivals spoke of it as a mud flat—there
arose in the seventeenth century one of the great civilizations of
the world. The Golden Age of the Dutch Republic stands out as
one of the most comprehensive, most astonishing, and most admirable achievements of mankind, a monument alike to human
industry and the human spirit.

From this little country, with its windy sand dunes and its damp
pastures, ships went out to sail the farthest seas. On the mud flats
large, solid, prosperous cities came into being. Their quays received the goods of all the world, which their merchants exchanged
and distributed again to all the world. Their great banking houses
financed the sovereigns of Europe. Thanks to its geographical position and the enterprise and energy of its people, the Dutch Republic was—only two generations after its founding—the richest commercial community Europe had yet seen.

*This unknown officer, portrayed by Frans Hals, typifies the sturdy
citizen-soldiers who maintained the Dutch Republic's independence.*   23

Such a civilization, built on trade and industry, on hard work
and financial acumen, might have been wholly materialist in all its
manifestations. The Golden Age of the Dutch Republic might have
been a golden age only in the narrowest and hardest sense. It was
not so. The mercantile people, with their code of self-reliance and
hard work, of enterprise, courage, and good craftsmanship, gave
much more to the world than mere material gain. Scientists, thinkers, and poets flourished among them. The works of their great
painters, luminous, tranquil, and profound, shine out among us
still. Spiritual and material greatness were deeply, inextricably
interwoven in the great achievement of the Dutch.

No precise bounds can be set to the epoch of their glory, but the
generation from 1625 to 1648, during which Frederick Henry,
Prince of Orange, guided their affairs, is usually taken as the high
noon of the Golden Age. Rembrandt was painting, Frans Hals was
at the height of his powers, Hugo Grotius was laying down the
foundations of international law, Vondel was composing his great
poetic dramas, Abel Tasman was exploring the far Pacific, and the
great Dutch admirals Piet Heyn and Martin Tromp were sweeping
the Spaniards off the seas. But this golden summer had already
been preceded by a wonderfully promising spring and was to be
followed by a fruitful autumn. The last of the harvest was not
gathered until the end of the century.

The political story of the free and independent Dutch had begun
a hundred years earlier. The Netherlands had come by a series of
dynastic marriages to form a part of the great Hapsburg dominions, and in 1555 they were assigned to King Philip II of Spain
as his share in the family inheritance. At that time the Reformation had shaken and divided Europe, and Philip II saw it as his
mission to reunite Europe within the fold of the Roman Catholic
Church under the dominating influence of Spain. The Netherlands
were to play an important part in his design, partly because of
their strategic position at the mouth of the Rhine and opposite the
English coast, and partly because of the great wealth of the southern Netherlands with their prosperous trading cities and their
great port of Antwerp.

It was unfortunate for Philip's projects that the Protestant religion in various forms had already penetrated into the Netherlands.
His attempts to stamp it out, combined with an interfering economic policy, brought the country to the verge of revolt. At this,
in 1567, he sent the Duke of Alva to impose an iron military rule
on the recalcitrant people. But the Netherlanders found a leader

in one of their noblemen, the Prince of Orange, William of Nassau —or William the Silent as he came to be called. Organizing a rebellion with heroic tenacity and against fearful odds, he succeeded in dislodging the Spaniards from the northern half of the country. He had hoped to liberate and to hold united the whole of the Netherlands, but after his assassination in 1584 it became clear that the rich southern provinces, which were Catholic in sympathy, would remain with Spain, while the northern regions alone would form the new and independent Dutch Republic.

Gradually this small new nation was recognized by surrounding European powers. It was a federated republic governed by elected representatives, although two sons of William the Silent in turn held the highest offices in the state, both civil and military. Prince Maurice, the elder son, was a soldier of formidable intelligence who fought the Spaniards to a standstill and made a twelve years' truce with them in 1609. He died in 1625, shortly after the resumption of the war. The rule of his brother Frederick Henry, which was later to be so fruitful and so glorious, began inauspiciously with the loss of the border fortress of Breda.

The capture of Breda was the last significant Spanish victory over the Dutch. Frederick Henry, the new Dutch leader, was not a military genius like his elder brother, but he had great tenacity and great patience, and he had inherited from his famous father, William the Silent, an inspiring capacity for remaining calm in the face of disaster. As a statesman he was to show himself, at least during his first and best years, just, tolerant, and wise; in external politics he was a persuasive and often subtle diplomat. He did not cause the Golden Age of Holland, but it is impossible to imagine it without his generous and reassuring presence in the background. Under his leadership the Dutch soon re-established equilibrium in the war with Spain and pushed doggedly on to final victory at the Peace of Münster in 1648. During all these years Spain was visibly a declining power, while the young Dutch Republic went from strength to strength.

From the very outset of the war of liberation, sea power had been of the first importance to the Dutch. There were two reasons for this: first, they had to prevent the Spanish fleet from feeding the battle front in the southern Netherlands with sea-borne reinforcements of men and arms and money; secondly, they had to keep open the channels of trade into their own country. They had built their prosperity on overseas trade and in particular on the herring industry; their fisheries were the basis of a great commerce in salt fish, a universal part of diet in an age when there was no canned food.

The Dutch now extended their trading ventures with increasing boldness, fiercely competing with other nations. Thus, early in the seventeenth century, Sir Walter Raleigh warned the English that they were losing ground in the northern waters. "We had a great trade in Russia seventy years," he asserted, "and about fourteen years past we sent store of goodly ships to trade in those parts, and three years past we sent out but four and this last year two or three; but to the contrary the Hollanders about twenty years since traded thither with two ships only, yet now they are increased to about thirty or forty, and one of their ships is as great as two of ours."

Dutch expansion was not confined to northern seas. Their ships boldly entered the enclosed waters of the Mediterranean and established commercial contact with Constantinople. With splendid daring they challenged the power of Spain on remoter seas in the West Indies, and sent out expeditions to find a northeastern or a northwestern passage to the treasures of the East. The survivors of one such expedition led by Willem Barents in 1595 came back with fearful stories of an Arctic winter spent on Novaya Zemlya. Henry Hudson, the English leader of another Dutch expedition in search of a northwest passage, sailed up the unknown majestic river which now bears his name and anchored off Manhattan island where soon the Dutch settlement of New Amsterdam would arise. Dutch navigators scattered their names over the map of the world; Cape Horn was named by Willem Schouten, who rounded it in 1616, after the little Dutch town of Hoorn, where he had been born. Abel Tasman, who in 1642 established the fact that Australia was an island, is commemorated in the name of Tasmania. But the energy and ambition of Dutch traders centered on the East Indies.

In 1595 Cornelis de Houtman sailed for the East Indies, returning two and a half years later from Java, to set all the church bells in Amsterdam ringing for joy of his arrival, laden with the spices of the East. It was the beginning of the Dutch East Indian empire. In 1602 the Dutch East India Company was founded, which competed ruthlessly with its English rival. Java, with its capital at Batavia, became the center of Dutch power in the East. They drove their English rivals out of the Malay Archipelago; they thrust the Portuguese out of Ceylon; they made themselves a foothold in Formosa. In energy and daring, in single-minded enterprise, they had not their equals; and the small country far off in

Europe grew rich and confident as Dutch seamen and Dutch merchants took toll of the whole world.

The young, energetic people were proud of their mounting achievements. Books were written about them, pictures painted. The journeys of explorers were celebrated in poetry and carefully recorded in prose. The profit and glory of Dutch merchants was the perennial subject for painters, commissioned to paint portraits that were often set against the background of some Eastern scene, or showed in the distance some splendid ship unloading at the quay. The Dutch East Indiamen were the largest vessels afloat, palatial monsters of the high seas, armed against pirates and storms.

The English were rivals for the herring fisheries and competitors in the East Indian trade, but the Spaniards were still the principal enemy. Themselves a great seafaring nation and pioneers in exploration, it was long before they could bring themselves to realize that the Dutch had outdistanced them. But in 1628 Piet Heyn, veteran Dutch admiral and daring seaman, who had long harried the Spaniards in the West Indies, intercepted the Spanish treasure fleet off Cuba and destroyed it in the Bay of Matanzas. The booty that he brought home to Holland from the wrecked and captured Spanish vessels amounted in silver ore and goods to the value of eleven and a half million Dutch florins; its effect on the Netherlands' prosperity may be gathered from the fact that in that year the shareholders of the Dutch West India Company, which had financed Heyn's expedition, received a dividend of 50 per cent.

Such a loss, financial as well as naval, was crippling to Spain. Eleven years later, in 1639, the Dutch admiral Martin Tromp almost wholly destroyed, off the English coast, a Spanish fleet of seventy-seven vessels, an armada bringing troops and arms to prosecute the war in the Netherlands. From this second blow the staggering Spanish fortunes never recovered.

Dutch merchants consolidated the position prepared for them by Dutch explorers and Dutch admirals. In 1629 the burghers of Amsterdam declared with pride: "Through our economic management and exertions we have sailed all other nations off the seas, drawn almost all trade from other lands hither and served the whole of Europe with our ships." The statement was hardly an exaggeration. Besides their ancient trade in fish and their new expansion to the Indies, the Dutch had made themselves the intermediaries and the carriers for all Europe. The banks of Amsterdam now financed private and public enterprise far beyond the borders of Holland; the granaries of Amsterdam received corn brought from other countries in Dutch vessels and redistributed it through western Europe. Even the Spanish government had to turn a blind eye to the Dutch grain ships in their ports, without which people would have starved.

Once Antwerp in the Spanish Netherlands had been the financial center of the Western world and the greatest port in northern Europe. But Amsterdam took her trade and her pre-eminence from her. As early as 1619 an English traveler wrote, not without anxious envy, that Amsterdam, once a small fishing village, had "come in a short revolution of time by a monstrous increase of commerce and navigation to be one of the greatest marts in Europe."

The citizens of the young, expanding city behaved with unusual vision. Instead of leaving its growth to chance, they evolved in 1612 one of the earliest and most enlightened town-planning schemes in Europe. The expansion of Amsterdam has truly been called a "triumph of communal co-operation," for the scheme that was laid down by a highly intelligent committee was obediently put into effect by succeeding generations of citizens. The plan was in essence simple: a series of concentric canals, the three *Grachten*, were to contain the city. They were planned spaciously, like three great horseshoes one inside the other, and it was believed that allowance had been made for the utmost development of the city. In fact the plan fulfilled the needs of Amsterdam for over two hundred years, and few town planners in our own time would hope for better success.

Although Amsterdam towered in importance over all the Dutch cities, all shared in the prosperity of the age and each had its proper civic pride. With the change of religion, the ancient Gothic churches of the older towns had been strenuously cleared of "idolatrous" images, but the structures were carefully preserved. The severely whitewashed interiors of these lofty buildings have been recorded by many a painter of the seventeenth century, often with a black-gowned Calvinist preacher in the pulpit and a full congregation of burghers and their wives intently listening.

The buildings of ancient convents and monasteries were also usually preserved. Some of them were transformed into the residences of the rich, like the convent at Delft where William the Silent made his home. Others were used as civic buildings; still others were turned into orphanages or homes for the aged. The Dutch cities prided themselves on the orderly if sometimes rather authoritative benevolence that kept their streets free of beggars.

The occasional appearance of a beggar in street scenes painted by

Dutch artists suggests that they were not quite uniformly successful, but we have the contemporary evidence of travelers that it was a rare thing to see a beggar among the Dutch—and this at a time when most great cities teemed with them.

Deserted and orphan children were brought together into institutions and carefully educated to be respectable citizens. Old and disabled soldiers were regularly pensioned—a system that scarcely existed in any other country at this time. The aged poor were gathered together and decently cared for in almshouses. Frans Hals, the great painter, who fell on evil days, spent much of his time in later years in one of these at Haarlem, which today houses a museum containing the last pictures that he painted, portrait groups of the governors of the almshouse.

From energy and industry had come great wealth, and the

*Indoor scenes of gentle and quiet domesticity were a specialty with
Pieter de Hooch. He titled this canvas* The Bedroom.

Dutch merchants, both in their civic and their private lives, showed an orderly discrimination in the uses to which they put their money. Although three great noblemen, the Princes of Orange, remained for many years at the head of the state, and the small, exclusive group of Dutch nobility preserved their existence and their identity as a class, the whole tone of the young Republic was that of the mercantile middle class. It was their wealth and vigor, their aspirations and prejudices which gave force and direction to every part of the national life.

How came it that this civilization of hard-headed, hard-working merchants, adventurers, industrialists, dairy farmers, and seamen inspired great literature, great thought, and even greater painting? What made this mercantile society, in the words of the modern Dutch historian Pieter Geyl, "so abundant, so free, so receptive?" The secret lies, paradoxically almost, in the Dutch religion. The Calvinists had formed the spearhead of the revolt against Spain, and they remained dominant in the young Republic. Calvinism is not a religion that greatly encourages freedom of speculation or, for that matter, aesthetic sensibility. But these people had fought for freedom of conscience for themselves and were therefore committed to it. The Calvinist Dutch might bitterly disapprove of other religious doctrines; they might curtail the civil and political power of those who held them, but they could not deny them the right to worship and believe as they chose. Moreover, quite apart from the principle of religious liberty for which they had fought, the Dutch could not, for practical reasons, do without the industry and skill of the religious minorities. There remained always within the Republic a considerable Roman Catholic minority who had never changed their faith; there was, especially in Amsterdam, a large and growing Jewish community; and Protestant refugees of many different sects continuously flooded in from all parts of Europe. The work and co-operation of all these were needed by the young Republic, and the existence of so many different communities within a small country naturally stimulated the circulation of ideas.

Religious conflict was by no means at an end. There was constant jealousy and fear of the Roman Catholic minority, and there was from time to time harsh conflict between Protestant groups which broke out in violence. A bitter struggle during the years of truce with Spain had ended only when Prince Maurice made himself virtually—for a space—dictator. But this very friction stimulated the growth of ideas and generated new energy. Indeed the extraordinary vitality of Dutch culture at this epoch may well have been an outcome of the tension between the new and the old, the experimental and the conventional.

A mercantile community, to be successful, as the Dutch so transcendently were at this time, must encourage not only self-reliance and industry among its members but also originality and enterprise. No one can accuse the Dutch merchants of the Golden Age of being hidebound or conventional in their business operations. Here they showed courage and imagination. In politics, in religion, in the arts, they might be—and probably most of them were—extremely conventional. But in such a society, where courage, originality, and enterprise are encouraged because of their value in business, there will always be a considerable number of men and women in whom these same valuable qualities will be directed to quite different ends—to scientific enquiry, to philosophic speculation, to art or literature. Some of these may come into conflict with the community; others will find a way of being accepted. A vigorous mercantile community can thus provide the artist and the thinker with that mixture of encouragement and frustration, of opposition and of stimulation, in which many talents flower. The Renaissance culture of the Italian cities had had something of this in it; the pattern can be detected in such great and prosperous societies as England in the nineteenth century or the United States in the twentieth. It was evident in seventeenth-century Holland.

The contrast and the challenge is seen at its clearest in the world of learning. One of the first acts of William the Silent had been the foundation of the first Dutch university, at Leiden in 1575, when only a small part of the country had been liberated and the war was still in a critical stage. In the ensuing fifty years, provinces had vied with each other in the encouragement of learning, and universities had been founded at Groningen, Utrecht, and Harderwijk. These universities were seats of learning where a fine tradition of scholarship was steadily built up, but they were often the scene of violent disputes between traditional teaching and new ideas. At Utrecht the theories of Galileo were vehemently opposed, as were also those of the French scientist and philosopher Descartes. The professor of medicine was required to teach only such doctrine as had been laid down by the ancients. Doubts were felt as to whether the theory that the blood circulated in the body, as the Englishman Harvey had recently argued, could be reconciled with the Scriptures. As late as 1642 the Senate of Utrecht passed a resolution against the new scientific teaching which was making converts

31

among the younger professors. "It is contrary to the ancient philosophy which the universities of the whole world have thus far taught with wise deliberation," they said, and added a warning that "there may be deduced from it by inexperienced youth several false and preposterous notions which conflict with the other sciences and faculties and above all with the orthodox religion."

Yet the country whose academic teachers passed this resolution counted among its citizens some of the greatest pioneers of modern science. Anton van Leeuwenhoek, combining immense technical dexterity with concentrated powers of observation, first greatly improved the magnifying powers of the microscope and then used it to penetrate secrets of nature. He was the first to describe accurately blood corpuscles and to discern bacteria. His contemporary, Jan Swammerdam, who also, in a way which seems to have been peculiarly Dutch, combined great technical skill with an inquiring and patient observation, studied the anatomy of invertebrates and was the first fully to observe (and most delicately to illustrate) the transformation of insects. He watched and recorded the process by which a caterpillar becomes a butterfly and the frog emerges from the tadpole. But both these men were, in the modern sense, amateurs; they worked outside the universities, discussing their ideas with like-minded friends and exchanging discoveries and information with other interested experimenters in different walks of life.

In spite of some academic opposition, the atmosphere of educated Dutch society was sympathetic and stimulating to men with new ideas. Whatever the pundits of Utrecht might say, it was in the congenial atmosphere of Holland that the greatest of all the new philosophers, the Frenchman René Descartes, lived his happiest years and wrote his *Discours de la Methode*, long to be regarded as the foundation of modern philosophy.

In the field of political philosophy the Dutch themselves can claim Hugo Grotius as one of the greatest pioneers of modern thought. His epoch-making book *De Jure Belli et Pacis* laid the foundations of international law. But he wrote it in exile, in France. Here was an odd paradox, that the Dutch Republic, which gave asylum to religious refugees and men of learning from all over Europe, forced one of its greatest thinkers to seek safety outside its borders. It was not, however, on account of his opinions that Grotius fled the country, but because he was one of the victims involved in the political crisis at the end of Prince Maurice's rule.

Dutch literature of the seventeenth century reflects the same conflicting tendencies. This young independent people had a language and a way of thought very much their own. But their past history had made them also conscious of a position in western Europe; they could not sever the links that still bound them to the southern Spanish Netherlands from which they had so recently separated themselves. The culture of the south was the international culture of late Renaissance Europe: its greatest painter was Peter Paul Rubens, its poets and writers belonged to the wide and rich tradition common to such princely and aristocratic lands as France, Spain, and contemporary Italy. But in the Dutch Republic—geographically so near, politically so different—international influences and the strong individual flavor of the new mercantile republic was strangely and often attractively mingled.

The most famous poets of the time present a study in contrasts. There was Constantijn Huygens, a man of wide culture and learning, a diplomat well versed in European society, whose poems have all the mannered subtlety of the cultivated poets of the earlier seventeenth century in England, in France, in Germany, or in Spain. He admired and translated John Donne with a rare skill. A younger man, Joost van den Vondel, has often been compared to Milton, not merely because one of his greatest works was the poetic drama *Lucifer*. He managed, with a ravishing fluency, to capture in Dutch (which is not the easiest of languages for poetry) the subtlety and ripeness of baroque culture.

In sharp contrast is the work of Jacob Cats, who celebrated in anecdotal, didactic verse the domestic joys and duties, the morality and prejudices of contemporary Dutch civilization. His popular fame was, and remained, enormous; his works were, next to the Bible, the literature best known to the Dutch people for centuries. He was the people's poet par excellence and was familiarly thought of as "Father Cats." But he owed his permanent position in literature to more remarkable qualities. He illuminated his conventional opinions with much genuine wisdom and with an understanding of men and women, in the daily problems of life, which is both humorous and humane.

The most famous center of Dutch literary life during the Golden Age was the castle of Muiden on the Zuider Zee where Pieter Corneliszoon Hooft gathered about him a remarkable group of friends who, in the pleasant atmosphere of his country house, exchanged ideas, discussed each other's writings, made music, and followed the new theories and the new discoveries that seemed to flower almost daily in the brave new world. Hooft himself wrote a famous history of the recent wars with Spain, a work conceived in the classical manner and based on the style of Tacitus. The circle included also Constantijn Huygens; occasionally Joost van den Vondel; the famous scholar Gerard Vossius; Laurens Reaal, soldier, seaman, and poet; Samuel Coster, who was both a physician and a dramatist; and the two sister poetesses, both women of exceptional charm, Anna and Maria Visscher.

Women were not excluded from the culture of the Dutch Golden Age. Indeed they could hardly have been, for it is one of the characteristics of a hard-working mercantile society that the woman is expected to show energy, industry, and intelligence in the management of her household, and sometimes to take a part in her husband's business. Moreover, a seafaring people, whose menfolk are often absent for long periods, will naturally delegate responsibility to their women. There was, of course, no question of equality; it is clear from the poems of Cats (and indeed from the whole domestic morality of Calvinism) that the woman's place was one of obedience to the man, but it was none the less a recognized and valuable place. The Dutch woman was not brought up to be a voiceless drudge nor, in a higher class of society, to be merely decorative. She was brought up to be an intelligent and valued, if junior, partner in a man's world.

It was natural therefore that a few women at least should make their mark in the world of learning and the arts. The most famous of them was Anna Maria van Schuurman, who was famous rather for the multiplicity of her talents than for her supreme excellence in any one field. She was an artist of distinction, a linguist, scholar, and theologian, who corresponded with some of the most learned men of her time. Among the painters, the most famous was Judith Leyster, one of whose most striking pictures, *The Lute Player*, was for a long time thought to be the work of Frans Hals.

When we think of the Golden Age of the Dutch Republic we think above all of the great painters. A wonderful series of canvases from many different hands have recorded both the outward face and the inward spirit of that great epoch. Such landscape painters as Philips de Koninck, Jacob van Ruisdael, Jan van Goyen, and Aart van der Neer have recorded the physical appearance of their country at this time. We can see, in every detail, the farmsteads with their red-tiled roofs, the water mills and the windmills, the wide flat fields over which the windy clouds make moving patterns of sun and shade, the winding canals, the neat little towns with their towers and spires seen across pastures where cattle graze. We can see the people who inhabited these fields and towns about their everyday work and their holiday amusements. In the foreground of Ruisdael's *View of Haarlem* they are bleaching great strips of linen cloth in the sunny fields; Aelbert Cuyp and Paul Potter preferred to show them pasturing their fine dairy cattle Jan van Goyen shows them sailing their canals or putting their ships out to sea; Wouwerman, when he is not painting battle scenes, has caught the atmosphere of salt and sand and wind on the dunes as the fishermen bring in their catch; Avercamp, Adriaen van der Venne, and Aart van der Neer liked to show them during the winter, skating and sleighing on their frozen canals.

Other painters preferred indoor scenes. Thanks to them we know more of the Dutch middle classes in their everyday setting than of any other people at this period. Gerard Terborch captures the

The pleasures of an inn, by Jan Steen. Steen, himself an innkeeper, was unexcelled at recording the lusty exuberance of the Dutch.

moment of concentration as young people make music in a comfortable, well-appointed room; Pieter de Hooch has shown them in the small gardens of their town houses, playing at skittles or taking a glass of wine in the quiet mellow afternoon; or, moving within doors, he catches the vista from some shadowed, tile-floored room where two young people sedately sit along the sun-streaked corridor with a distant glimpse of a serving maid or some gay, peeping child. Jan Steen, equally at home in the fresh air or the congested interior, has shown roistering parties of country folk dancing in the courtyard of an inn, or enjoying the fun of the fair, or family parties celebrating a christening or perhaps the feast of Saint Nicholas in some four-square, cheerfully overcrowded room. Certain characters in his pictures come in again and again—the kindly Granny, the funny, ugly little girl, the naughty grimacing boy. These are surely his own family, seen with love and humor, and the rooms must be those of his own home, for when he was not a painter he was a jolly innkeeper.

These painters of popular scenes flourished in response to a demand for a new kind of picture. In earlier times and in other countries painters had worked for the Church, for princes, or for wealthy private patrons. They had painted great religious subjects for altarpieces or had decorated the walls of palaces. But, apart from portraits and occasional traveling altarpieces painted for diplomats and princes, the demand for smaller paintings, for easel paintings, had been light. But the new Dutch middle class wanted homely paintings to decorate the walls of their comfortable rooms. They wanted secular paintings because they were predominantly Protestant, and they valued above all lifelike representations of their countryside, their domestic life, and the objects that gave them pleasure—great baskets of fruit and flowers or an arrangement of crystal goblets on a precious piece of oriental carpet. The demand for them made these paintings into an investment; especially good examples changed hands for high prices, and even quite humble Dutch burghers and Dutch farmers thought it not only a pleasant thing in itself to buy paintings, but a good speculation. John Evelyn, the English diarist, thus describes a Dutch picture market at Rotterdam in 1641:

"We arrived late at Rotterdam where was their annual mart or fair, so furnished with pictures (especially landscapes and drolleries) that I was amazed. Some I bought and sent into England. The reason for this store of pictures and their cheapness proceeds from their want of land to employ their stock, so that it is an ordinary thing to find a common farmer lay out two or three thousand pounds in this commodity. Their houses are full of them, and they vend them at the fairs to very great gain."

There was a rising demand for portraits too, as the Dutch burghers gained in wealth and confidence and liked to hang on their walls paintings of themselves, their wives and children that captured not only a likeness but also fitly represented the social standing, the prosperity, and distinction of the sitter. The clothes are usually somber, but the quality of the stuff is carefully shown; black silk facings shine against the deeper richness of black velvet—no easy trick for a painter to catch the precise texture of the different materials. A gleaming jewel, a gold chain, the snowy contrast of a fine muslin ruff or a lace collar—these are the principal ornaments, and for the artist often the only points of color and excitement that he can use to emphasize his composition. Dutch portrait painters acquired an extraordinary forcefulness in the treatment of the human face and hands, and an extraordinary skill in working out a striking design with small points of color and relief.

An easier task confronted the artist who was required to paint one of the group paintings, which were also immensely in demand. Companies of merchants, learned societies, and above all—for this was a country still at war—the officers of the local volunteers wished to be painted in groups. So there came into being the innumerable group portraits of citizen-officers, wearing the broad, gold-fringed, many-colored sashes which at that time were the designating marks of military men. The only essential was that the face of each man should be clearly shown.

Rembrandt gave offense by breaking this rule. Carried away by his own more profound and subtle vision of the play of light and shade, he painted in *The Sortie of the Banning Cocq Company* (familiarly and quite incorrectly known as *The Night Watch*) one of the greatest of his pictures, and certainly the most memorable of all the group portraits of this epoch. But it is easy to understand why some of the sitters, whose forms and faces are lost in shadow, were far from pleased with the result.

Rembrandt was for a time a fashionable and successful portrait painter, but he stands apart from the portrait painters and genre painters who supplied the new and eager demands of the Dutch. He has the quality of genius which (like that of Shakespeare in another sphere) is outside historic time and place. But this can and should be said: Rembrandt could have achieved the fulfillment of his genius probably nowhere else so well as in seventeenth-century

In paintings like A Woman Weighing Gold, *Jan Vermeer raised the seventeenth-century Dutch genius for genre art to new heights.*

Holland. Amsterdam with its world-wide trade provided him with exciting and infinite visual material; his book was life, and he read men and learned in the end to set down what he had read with a sad and silent wisdom that has never been equaled. In Amsterdam his penetrating talent could draw on a multitude of different kinds of men and women—the philosopher, the merchant, the soldier, the rich young girl, the grizzled seaman, the kitchen maid, or the withdrawn faces of rabbis.

For a time he was successful, but genius so individual and so strong can rarely retain popular favor. He went beyond his public and fell into disfavor. But he was never utterly neglected. He always retained a small group of discriminating admirers and of patrons who valued and bought his pictures. It is the great merit of a society like that of seventeenth-century Holland—so competitive and so various—that it has room for small groups, literary and artistic cliques, which can sustain and encourage work outside the grasp of the general public.

It would not be strictly true to say that Rembrandt reveals the inner spirit of the Dutch at this time. He is a painter of the spirit, but his message is at the same time so individual and so universal that it would be a belittlement to attach it merely to the Dutch Golden Age. But no epoch, however fruitful, can be held to be truly great unless it has produced one giant of universal stature, one genius who transcends time and place. For the Golden Age of the Dutch Republic that giant is Rembrandt.

One other painter of this time has a claim to rank among the greatest—a painter whose achievement, unlike that of Rembrandt, belongs in time and space and by every outward convention to Holland in the seventeenth century and to no other epoch or place in the world. That painter is Jan Vermeer of Delft. He depicted with absolute faithfulness the domestic scenes and simple views that were so dear to Dutch collectors. A girl offers a glass of wine to a visitor; a housewife sits sewing in her doorway; a youthful party make music at the virginals; a young woman is discovered reading a love letter. The broom is propped against the wall, the paved floor has been mopped clean, the sun throws onto the dazzlingly white wall the harsh shadows of the heavy picture frames, picks up the sheen of a satin skirt, lingers in the soft glow of a pearl earring. It is the world of Gerard Terborch, of Jan Steen, and Pieter de Hooch. But it is also—and who can say why?—a moment stopped out of time. Here is an incident of no importance, a fragment from the lives of unknown people held forever, not just as a picture but as a reality. With the other Dutch genre painters we know we are looking at a picture; with Jan Vermeer we are experiencing a living moment.

With him, therefore, we come nearest to the inner essence of the Dutch seventeenth century. The zest for liberation, the adventurousness, the energy, and the wealth of this remarkable people do not explain all. Politically they achieved freedom; materially they achieved wealth; their Golden Age was built on these things, but they are not the spirit and the secret of its greatness. What else must there have been? Does the secret lie in this intensity of *living*, this concentration of the spirit, which Vermeer has so perfectly and so indefinably captured within the narrow limits of his few surviving paintings?

D. ISAACVS NEWTON EQVES
REG. SOCIETATIS PRÆSES. AN°. 1703.

Now that scientific thought has gone beyond the Newtonian "philosophy," it is perhaps easier to see the magnitude of the achievement of that gigantic figure in perspective. It is bold of a layman to encroach on the difficult field of modern science, but Mr. Karp, the author of the present essay as well as of a biographical study of Darwin, is quite competent to do so. At the very least he has succeeded in making understandable to the "man in the street" the relationship of Newton to contemporary and near-contemporary theorists such as Kepler, Galileo, and Descartes, and to convey some notion of the problems of light and color, and particularly of universal gravitation, with which Newton wrestled so successfully for many years. The current definitive edition of Newton's writings and correspondence serves to highlight even more the character of this strange, austere, self-assured, and rather intolerant man, and to stress once again his almost unique contribution to the development of the modern world.

SIR ISAAC NEWTON

WALTER KARP

He voyaged, wrote Wordsworth, "through strange seas of Thought, alone." Such, to the poet, was "Newton with his prism and silent face." In life the eyes of that silent face were protuberant, and often they appeared glazed, which made Newton look somewhat less than intelligent. He had the dim expression of a man whose thoughts turn inward, incessantly. This was not from love of solitude or contempt for the world, for Newton looked upon the world of men and affairs with admiration, and expressed, in moments of irritation, a corresponding dislike of "mathematical trifles." He was often irritable and almost invariably somber. It was said of him by an intimate that he only laughed "but once." The event was occasioned by someone asking him what use in life Euclid's geometry was. Whereupon Newton laughed.

The incident illustrates a profound characteristic of Newton's: he always gave the briefest possible answers to questions—even at the risk of being misunderstood. In doing so he was faithful to an austere ideal: that of mathematical elegance, the aesthetic quality that mathematicians find in the most concise of demonstrations. This formal austerity Newton elevated into a personal style and

In 1703, with his genius finally acknowledged by all, Newton agreed to head the Royal Society; this portrait commemorated the event.

the mode of his thought. In the prime of his scientific career he compressed all of mechanics into three concise laws of motion. At the end of a long life he labored to reduce all Christian doctrine to what he took to be its minimal number of essential propositions. At all times he spoke laconically, as if an excess number of words was as inelegant as an excess number of steps in a proof. Once someone asked Newton how he had made all his discoveries, and Newton replied with perfect Newtonian concision: "By always thinking unto the problem." The answer is indisputable. He would concentrate his awesome mental powers on a problem for days, until, as he said, "gradually the light would dawn." The light that dawned was the most monumental achievement in the entire history of science, and Newton is, beyond dispute, the greatest scientist who ever lived, the only one of whom it can be said: had he not lived, the course of science might have been radically altered.

The nature of Isaac Newton's vast achievement is easier to state than to grasp, but a singular lexical fact may suggest its magnitude. During Newton's lifetime, what we know as modern science was known to many simply as "the Newtonian Philosophy." It seemed to be his own personal doctrine, and to a remarkable extent it was. He did not himself "discover" science. No one man could have done that. Science was not some compact instrument simply waiting to be used. It was rather a complex invention that men had painstakingly to put together out of quite disparate elements. Physical science is an abstruse meld. It unites, for one thing, the abstractions of mathematics, which have no physical meaning, with concrete physical phenomena, which have no inherent mathematical form. It employs a skeptical and exacting experimental method but combines that method with the most sweeping assumptions about the mechanical nature of reality. Being empirical, it assumes that truth will emerge from the investigation of things as they are; being mathematical and mechanical, it also assumes that things as they are, are never what they seem to be. How these elements might be combined is not readily apparent, but their combination and synthesis was Newton's. If modern science and its methods can be likened to a machine, then it was Newton who assembled its parts and demonstrated its awesome power.

He was a great genius, and he was born, as Einstein once wistfully remarked, at exactly the right time.

Around 1642, the year Newton was born, science was most markedly in pieces, although four of the greatest figures in the scientific revolution had already completed their work. The monk

Copernicus, who began the vast enterprise by reconstructing the heavens with the sun at the center, had been dead for a century. Francis Bacon had died in 1626, Johannes Kepler in 1630, Galileo in the very year of Newton's birth. A fifth great figure, René Descartes, had already published his *Discourse on Method* and was within two years to publish his monumental treatise on the mechanical principles of philosophy. Still, it can be said that science did not yet exist; its methods and its goals had not yet been agreed upon. What the great pioneers shared (the long-dead Copernicus excepted) was not science but a deep disdain for the Aristotelian philosophy and an overriding desire to replace it with something better. In the parlance of the day, they were "new philosophers," united in rebellion against the "old philosophy" of Aristotle.

Within this broad unity, however, the disunity among these pioneers was sharp and deep. For example, Galileo, Kepler's peer and acquaintance, looked with utter scorn upon Kepler's most fundamental conceptions. With characteristic audacity Kepler had supposed that an invisible "moving force," emanating like spokes from the sun, drags the planets around in their orbits and that a "mutual gravitation" between the earth and its companion the moon—like moving toward like—causes the tides. This radical conception, that even the unchanging heavens require some natural force to keep them in motion, was the foundation of all Kepler's work in astronomy, yet Galileo professed to be "astonished" that so acute a man as Kepler "has nevertheless lent his ear and given his assent to the moon's dominion over the waters, to occult properties and to such puerilities." This was not mere backbiting; Galileo's disdain flowed directly from his deepest conception of what the new philosophy must be. That philosophy, first and foremost to Galileo, had to bid a good riddance to solar emanations, occult forces, and all such quasi-magical explanations of why things are as they are. It was not, in Galileo's view, the task of philosophers to fabricate fanciful hidden causes of things. It was their object to demonstrate *how* phenomena occur and to express this "how" in the simple, precise terms of mathematics. So Galileo himself had studied falling bodies and demonstrated that, in falling, a body will cover a distance proportional to the square of the time it spends falling that distance. But *why* bodies gravitate toward the earth's center in the first place he did not choose to say.

Descartes, arriving later, disagreed with both thinkers. That invisible forces and similar occult causes must be eliminated from philosophy was indeed one of Descartes's fundamental beliefs, as it

43

was Galileo's. Apart from "mind," the world consists only of corporeal substance, and this matter has but one real property: extension—its size, shape, and volume. No body, for example, possesses color. It merely arouses in us, due to its particular physical structure, a certain subjective sensation that we deem its color to be. The only real differences between any two things are the differences in size, shape, arrangement, and motions of the tiny corporeal particles comprising them. Bald matter and its motion must—and will—explain everything. In this stark mechanical world of Descartes's no forces, powers, spirits, or attractions exist. If a body begins to move, that motion can have but one cause: the impact upon that body of another moving body. So, according to Descartes, bodies fall to the earth because they are pushed downward by extremely fine particles that swirl around our planet, while other vast whirlpools of these same fine particles keep the planets moving in circles. There was clearly no place for Kepler's ideas in this new universe.

The Cartesian philosophy was lucid, comprehensive, and enormously persuasive; yet not even Descartes was taken to represent all that was valued in the new philosophy. Contemporary students of nature had also to reckon with Francis Bacon, whose new program for "the advancement of learning" was diametrically opposed in spirit to the philosophy of Descartes.

Between these two new philosophers the disparities were glaring. Descartes bade men to start with first principles and then, by deduction, to explain the phenomena of the world. Bacon bade men to begin by examining phenomena and then, by induction, to work up gradually to the most general principles. Bacon called upon men to open their eyes wide to the subtle powers of nature, and he recommended experimentation as the prime means to force nature to reveal yet more of her hidden powers. Descartes, on the other hand, asked men to shut their eyes and meditate on the "clear and distinct ideas" they found within themselves. Where Bacon and the Baconians thought that all was profoundly subtle, Descartes and the Cartesians thought all was essentially plain.

Thus there existed, in no clear interrelationships, the mathematical approach of Galileo, the mechanical philosophy of Descartes, the experimentalism of Bacon, and, more obscurely, the abstruse astronomy of Kepler. Such were the leading elements of the "new philosophy" when Newton was growing up in Lincolnshire.

The Newtons were yeoman farmers who lived for some time in a meager hamlet known as Woolsthorpe. As a child, Newton was virtually an orphan and a somewhat neglected one. His father had died some months before he was born, and his mother, upon remarrying a neighboring rector, left him for several years with his grandmother. In and around Woolsthorpe he was remembered as "always a sober, silent, thinking lad, and was never known scarce to play with the boys abroad." He amused his elders by devising ingenious instruments such as sundials and water clocks. He also collected magic tricks and formulas for compounding colored inks, which he duly recorded in a notebook. Even at that age Newton was communing chiefly with himself; whittling was one of his main occupations. Altogether he was the kind of solitary, self-sufficient youth we would instantly describe today as "mechanically inclined."

A slight scholarly superiority to the other local farm boys saved him from his preordained fate of plowing furrows in Lincolnshire. At eighteen, thanks to his uncle's intercession with his mother, he was sent off to Trinity College, Cambridge, which was to be his home for the next thirty-five years.

As an undergraduate Newton was particularly interested in mathematics, astronomy, and optics, but he was mainly learning what there was to learn, and he won no special honors beyond being accepted for graduate studies. Awarded his bachelor's degree in January, 1665, he probably seemed merely another future don destined to teach mathematics to an endless line of indifferent Trinity students.

This lack of distinction, however, was not due to the fact that Newton's genius was ripening slowly. His genius did not ripen. It simply burst forth. Two years after Newton completed his undergraduate studies, it could be said that of all the achievements of seventeenth-century science the better half were located, then and there, inside Newton's head—and there they stayed for some time, unknown to anybody. By the end of 1666 he had invented calculus, one of the supreme accomplishments in mathematics. He had discovered a profound truth about the nature of light and color, one of the foremost achievements of experimental investigation. He had, while espying an apple fall at Woolsthorpe, conceived the moon as a body "falling" perpetually toward the earth, like the apple, and had devised a mathematical way to express the power producing these falls. He was on the way, that is, to arriving at his theory of universal gravitation, the greatest single discovery in physical science.

The gifts of mind Newton was bringing to bear on these topics were, of course, extraordinary, but the most extraordinary thing about them was their presence in one and the same person. The gifts were such that the possession of any one of them seems to preclude possession of the others. In the history of science the most brilliant experimental investigators have rarely been notable theoreticians; the finest theoreticians—Einstein, for example—have rarely been superior, or even adequate, experimental scientists. Yet Newton was a supreme experimental scientist and a supreme theoretical scientist as well. What is more, he alone among the very great scientists was one of the supreme figures in the realm of pure mathematics. He was to achieve in three distinct modes of thought what only a few scientists have been able to achieve in one. Such were the gifts that Newton, in his twenty-fourth year, was applying to certain comprehensive topics that took his silent fancy.

Newton's optical work—his favorite study and his first published effort—took its departure from the phenomenon of color and from the new mechanical philosophy of Descartes. Light, according to the leading men of science, consisted of wavelike motions in Descartes's whirling subtle matter, or ether. These waves radiated evenly from a light source, like ripples in a pond when a pebble is dropped into it. Light from the sun was pure, homogeneous, and, of course, colorless. Color, then, was the effect produced when this uniform sunlight became disturbed or modified in some mechanical way or other. Light modified in one way produced one sort of color sensation. The same colorless light striking a body with a different sort of surface structure would be modified in a different way and so produce a different sort of color sensation. Since light when it passes through a prism will appear as a spectrum of colors on a wall, it was held that the prism, in refracting (i.e., bending) the light passing through it, also disturbed white light and so produced the spectrum. Such was the prevailing view when young Newton bought some prisms and pushed the experimental method farther than it had probably ever been pushed.

What Newton did was grasp a certain discrepant fact that he refused to explain away until it yielded the basis of an extraordinary discovery. This discrepancy arose in a precise experiment he made with a prism after many months of trial. He cut a circular hole, one-quarter inch in diameter, in the closed shutter of his room at Trinity College. Through this hole a narrow beam of sunlight entered his darkened chamber. Placing a prism near the hole, he cast the well-known spectrum of colors against the opposite wall. What he now saw, with the eye of a mathematician, others had seen but overlooked: the spectrum of colors, instead of being circular—because the hole in the shutter was circular—was an oblong. This curious elongation of the circle seized his attention.

As Newton well knew, there existed a mathematical law, discovered by Descartes, for determining how much a ray of light will be bent when it passes through a prism at any given angle. According to that law the beam, in passing through Newton's prism, ought to have cast upon the opposite wall a circle of colors $2\frac{5}{8}$ inches in diameter. The oblong image, he found, was indeed $2\frac{5}{8}$ inches *wide*, but it was $13\frac{1}{4}$ inches *high*—five times longer than it should have been. The top part of the beam had been bent more than it ought to have been according to the law of refraction; the bottom part of the beam less, which was why the beam's height was elongated. Something was radically wrong with the beautifully precise law of refraction.

He set aside for the moment the whole question of colors and focussed his attention solely on the apparent flaw in the regularity of refraction. Taking a second prism, he placed it between the first prism and the wall and intercepted different parts of the refracted beam. This was the "crucial experiment." In making it Newton discovered that the part of the beam that was bent too much the first time was also bent too much when refracted a second time— exactly the same amount too much. The part of the beam that was bent too little was, when refracted again, again bent too little— exactly the same amount too little. Any time a given part of the beam was refracted by the prism, it always exhibited the same fixed degree of bending, or refrangibility. Refraction, in other words, was lawful and regular for the several parts of the light beam, though not for the beam as a whole. "And so," Newton concluded, "the true cause of the length of that Image was detected to be no other, than that *Light* consists of Rays *differently refrangible*, which . . . were, according to their degrees of refrangibility, transmitted towards divers parts of the wall."

Now it was not lost upon Newton that rays "differently refrangible" were also differently colored. When his second prism intercepted the blue part of the refracted beam, not only did that part bend to the same degree, it also remained blue. No amount of further refraction could change the color, just as no amount of further refraction could change that ray's degree of refrangibility. "To the same degree of Refrangibility," he then concluded, "ever belongs the same color, and to the same color ever belongs the same degree of Refrangibility."

As Newton now saw, something was wrong with the prevailing theory of colors. The doctrine that colors are produced when pure colorless light is disturbed could not be sustained. According to that theory, the prism causes a change in homogeneous light that results in the production of a color. A second refraction of this changed light ought, therefore, to change it more, producing yet another color. This was not the case. Blue remained blue, red stayed red. These and five other "primary colors" could not be changed no matter how many times they were refracted. The prism, therefore, did not modify pure white light, it merely *separated* different parts of white light according to their fixed and distinctive degrees

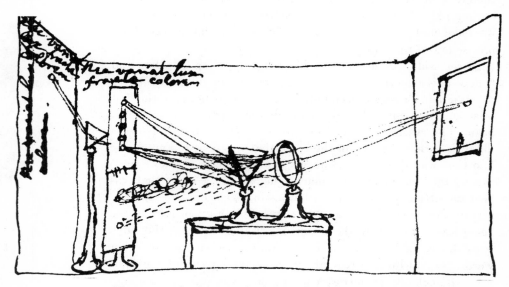

Newton made this rough sketch of the "crucial experiment" in his study of light: the refraction of a light beam through two prisms.

of bending. So Newton concluded: "Colors are not *Qualifications* [i.e., modifications] of *Light*, derived from Refractions, or Reflections of natural Bodies (as tis generally believed), but *Original* and *connate properties*, which in divers Rays are divers. Some Rays are disposed to exhibit a red color and no other; some a yellow and no other . . ." White light, pure homogeneous light from the sun, was not, as everyone believed, pure and homogeneous at all. It was, said Newton, "a confused aggregate of Rays" endowed with different degrees of refrangibility and different dispositions to cause a color sensation within us. Against all reason, so it seemed, colors were inherent in ordinary colorless light.

In an essay of thirteen mercilessly concise pages Newton set forth his discovery. Then in 1672, six years after making it, he presented it to the world of science, or rather to its illustrious new epitome, the Royal Society of London. With no false modesty whatever he described it to the membership as "the oddest if not the most considerable detection wch hath hitherto beene made in the operations of Nature." With that, Newton sat back to await acclaim. Instead, to his dismay, he found himself in the most exasperating of disputes.

The two great students of light, Robert Hooke at the Royal Society and Christian Huygens of the French Académie des Sciences, had their own theory of colors—the prevailing one. More decisively, they had their own ingrained conception of what the new mechanical philosophy was supposed to be. To them it meant devising mechanical hypotheses to explain given sets of facts. This unknown Isaac Newton, as far as they could see, had merely offered an alternative "hypothesis"—and how Newton hated the term! He had, as they saw it, explained colors by *supposing* that seven primary colors somehow pre-existed in white light, a hypothesis hard to believe. Then, to explain how a prism produces the colored spectrum, Newton, in their view, had further supposed that these differently colored rays were differently refrangible. It was, they conceded, an "ingenious" hypothesis, though distinctly inferior to their own.

With increasing vexation Newton tried to explain to his critics that they had turned his discovery upside down. He had not invented a hypothesis about color and then fitted it to the facts. The very reverse was true. He had found directly from experiment "certain properties of light . . . which if I did not know to be true, I should prefer to reject as vain and empty speculation, than acknowledge even as hypothesis." He had not supposed that white light was a confused bundle of rays differently refrangible; he was driven to that conclusion by his experimental findings. These findings could not be explained by the prevailing theory, as he pointed out to Hooke with biting scorn. His critics remained unconvinced.

For Newton it was a bitter experience. He felt cheated and victimized. He had offered the world a great new discovery, but the grandees of science had robbed him of his credit because his discovery did not square with their own mechanical preconceptions. To Newton, who had not the smallest doubt about his own immense superiority, there was only one recourse: the grandees must be taught like children what the true method of philosophy is. He told them: "First, to inquire directly into the properties of things, and establish them by experiment; and then to proceed more slowly to hypotheses for explaining them. For hypotheses should be subservient only in explaining the properties of things, but not assumed in determining them." To call an experimentally discovered property false because it contradicts a plausible hypothesis is to reverse the order of inquiry. Such was Newton's advice to his elders, and its implications are profound. Natural philosophy, he was arguing, must rid itself of the shackles of mere rationality. The properties of things, experimentally established, may *seem* unintelligible and inexplicable according to prevailing principles of reason and philosophy. Yet properties they are, and they must not be rejected a priori according to the principles of any philosophical scheme, including the one of mechanical philosophy. But Newton was only a young and obscure mathematics professor, and it would take more than a few irate letters to imprint his conception of science on the minds of men.

After this, his first public encounter with other men, Newton was bitter in the way that a haughty and capricious child is bitter. He fumed and sulked and withdrew into the thick shell of his temperament. From Cambridge he was heard to mutter peevishly that natural philosophy was "litigious" and filled with "no end of fancying." When men approached him with scientific questions, he could reply loftily that he had "laid aside philosophical speculations"; and in fact he often did. For long periods of time he preferred investigating the doctrine of the Trinity (which he secretly doubted), the legal authority of the Nicene Council (which he wished to undermine), and the prophecies in the Book of Daniel (which he hoped to decipher).

Rule or sulk was the principle of Newton's life, until the day would come when he would rule like a monarch. In the meantime he led a monkish life at Cambridge as a fellow of Trinity College and Lucasian Professor of Mathematics who gave abstruse public lectures that few students attended and nobody understood. He did not have many friends at the university, which he looked on as a backwater not quite fit for a gentleman. There was little warmth in his character, and what there was seemed reserved for his widowed mother, whom he duly visited each year at Woolsthorpe.

For a man who hated to be wrong—who dreaded even appearing to be wrong—the theory of universal gravitation presented a vexatious quandary, and one that Newton lived with for a long time. Unless that theory could be proved true beyond a doubt, it would be rejected by every rational thinker as false, pernicious, and even laughable. This is the most important historical fact about the theory of gravitation. Newton's resolution of the quandary was characteristic. From the autumn day at Woolsthorpe when the idea first entered his mind until the day eighteen years later when he sat down to write about it, the notion of universal gravitation took its place alongside Newton's doubts about the Trinity in his library of secret beliefs. Then, when he published the theory, he produced the greatest single work in the history of science: the mighty *Philosophiae Naturalis Principia Mathematica*— the mathematical principles of natural philosophy.

As its prime challenge to credibility the gravity doctrine proposes that the center of a material body can, in some utterly mysterious fashion, draw, or "attract," another body across millions of miles of space without being in any way in contact with it. This inexplicable "action-at-a-distance" is further held to act instantaneously, regardless of how far apart the two bodies are. It is, moreover, a power that is miraculously inexhaustible, for it never seems to weaken. It is a power, too, that nothing whatever can balk or diminish, since it penetrates every known substance. It is everywhere and nowhere, a paradoxical principle that cannot, on the face of it, be accepted.

The fundamental discovery that points the way to universal gravitation was made independently by both Newton and Huygens. With this discovery—great in itself—Huygens did nothing, Newton everything. The discovery is known as the law of centrifugal force. As a problem to be solved it arose from the inertia principle laid down in 1644 by Descartes: a material body, unless impeded by another body, will naturally move in a straight-line course at constant speed forever. When a body travels in a circle, therefore, it must be constantly "endeavoring" to move in its natural rectilinear course along a tangent to the circle. A body twirling on a string is pulled back by the string, but the endeavor, as Huygens observed, is felt as a "tension" on the taut string. Both Newton and Huygens found a means to express mathematically this endeavor to fly from the center of rotation. Gifted with hindsight, we see its immediate application to the heavens, where the planets, too, move in orbits. Plainly they must be endeavoring to fly from their centers of rotation. Some power, therefore, equal to this centrifugal tendency must be exerted in the opposite direction, because the planets do not, obviously, fly away. Great scientist though Huygens was, it never occurred to him to conceive of this counterpower as a pull, or attraction. Indeed, why should it have? Planets are not attached to the sun by strings, and imagining invisible strings or immaterial pulls would be puerile. Huygens supposed, as Descartes had, that ethereal whirlpools continuously *push* each planet back into its orbit, just as a whirlpool surrounding the earth causes a piece of fruit to be pushed toward the earth's center. Apples could have fallen at Huygens's feet through eternity, and he would never have supposed otherwise. Being a rational philosopher, he was a prisoner of the "true and sane philosophy" all his life. Newton was not, for he was never merely a rational philosopher.

Once again, a perfect mixture of credulity and skepticism lay behind the intuitions of genius. A conviction more powerful than the "true and sane philosophy" colored Newton's thoughts, and in doing so, liberated them. The conviction was a religious one. Consistent with his doubts about Christ's divinity, Newton believed as fervently as any Lincolnshire Puritan in the fierce, absolute God of the Old Testament, the Hebraic God of arbitrary power and mysterious ways. Newton believed, and longed to find reason for his belief, that the providential God had not only created the world but ruled it and sustained it every moment by his will. A Supreme Being who merely created a world that ran by itself was, to Newton, the god of disguised infidels like M. Descartes, whom he detested as vehemently as any rustic clergyman. To prove that God truly governed and sustained his creation was the deepest purpose of Newton's life. This purpose and conviction gave Newton the liberty to doubt that the impact of bodies was the ultimate cause of all natural phenomena. He was willing, indeed eager, to imagine that the ultimate principle was not matter at all but immaterial powers: "active principles," he called them, directly propagated by the lawful will of God. If such immaterial powers demonstrably existed, then the world could not survive for a moment without the direct action of the Creator, and the providence of God would be upheld against the disguised infidelity of the mechanical philosophy.

So it was not inconceivable to Newton, for example, that bodies should fall toward the earth's center by means of an immaterial attractive power exerted toward the earth's center. Thus, when the famed apple fell, he was free to conceive that the very same power extended far beyond the earth's surface and caused the moon, too, to "fall" toward the earth. Never mind that such a power would make no sense to the new philosophers; it could be investigated nonetheless. Clearly this "fall," which was directed toward the

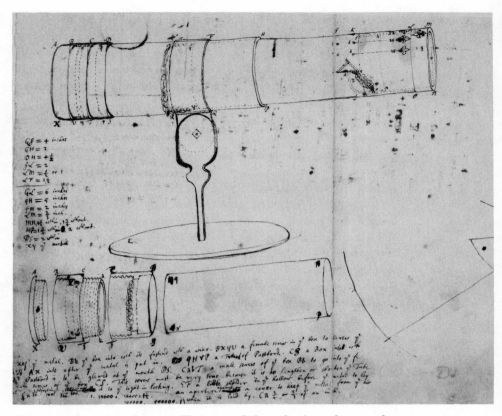

Newton's plan of a telescope. He invented the reflecting telescope that used a curved mirror rather than a lens to focus starlight.

earth's center, was equal to the moon's tendency to fly from that center, since the moon remained in its path. Because he now knew how to measure the centrifugal force, Newton could also calculate this balancing tendency. Specifically, he could calculate how far in any one second the moon was being pulled toward the earth. Also he knew how far gravity would draw a falling apple in one second's time: 16.1 feet. Were the force pulling the moon and the force pulling the apple the same force? By comparing the two one-second falls Newton reached an interesting result. The power, if indeed it was the same power, grew weaker the farther away from the earth it had to act. What was more tantalizing, it grew weaker almost but not quite according to a simple mathematical rule: the gravitational force diminished in proportion to the square of the distance; at three times the distance, it was one-ninth its strength, and so forth. Almost but not quite, since Newton's first calculations were

53

somewhat crude. This was the point he had reached as far back as 1666 at Woolsthorpe, before anybody but his professors knew his name. For thirteen more years Newton kept his gravitational work at the back of his mind, while he turned to more immediately fruitful tasks: his optics, calculus, and his diligent inquiries into esoteric branches of divinity.

The next great move came in 1679, when Newton discovered to his dismay that there was one other man entertaining the idea of a gravitational attraction varying inversely with the square of the distance. He was none other than the man Newton hated most: Robert Hooke. Using calculus, the mighty mathematical tool that he himself had invented (and so far kept to himself), Newton brought the gravity law one giant step closer to reality. He demonstrated mathematically that such a force, varying inversely with the square of the distance, would "bend" a moving body into an exactly elliptical orbit. This was a fundamental confirmation of the theory, for by Kepler's law the ellipse is the actual path of the planets. Since such a proof was beyond the powers of anybody, including Hooke, Newton was satisfied to drop the subject again. He had gained a private triumph, so private, indeed, that he set aside the papers containing his proofs and lost them.

Yet the forces pushing and pulling at him must have been very nearly in balance, because four years after triumphing over Hooke the mere coaxing of a tactful stranger convinced Newton to declare all that he knew about universal gravitation. The stranger, a brilliant young astronomer named Edmund Halley, simply approached Newton as he liked to be approached: as a supplicant begging help from the master. Halley pleaded with the strange man before him to set it all down. This Newton promptly did. In twenty months of incredibly concentrated effort Newton completed the *Principia Mathematica*. Published at Halley's expense, it appeared in the summer of 1687 and sold for seven shillings.

Simply to look at, the *Principia* is dazzling. It appears to be some kind of awesome geometry book, packed with propositions and theorems that are rigidly demonstrated by geometrical proofs accompanied by intricate diagrams. It looks, moreover, like a geometry raised to some higher power, for its subject is not static lines and areas, but "forces" that vary and "bodies" that move and accelerate; a geometry that is to the old geometry of Euclid as a motion picture is to a still photograph. Like a geometry book, too, the *Principia* is set forth in the grand deductive manner of ancient Greek mathematics. Beginning with a brief set of definitions and axioms—the three laws of motion—Newton proceeds step by step to deduce a vast array of propositions of ever-increasing complexity; some of them, indeed, deduced solely for the sake of deducing them. Having at last unburdened his mind, Newton, it seems, was determined to empty it. The relentless march of the proofs reaches its grand climax in Book Three with Newton's demonstration of the truly astounding proposition that between *any* two bodies in the universe there exists a mutual attraction that varies inversely with the square of the distance between them and directly with the product of their masses. This is the law of "universal gravitation." *Quod erat demonstrandum* Newton could justly write. Nonetheless it is certainly action-at-a-distance with a vengeance, for gravity, according to Newton, acts not only between the vast heavenly bodies but between any two particles of matter whatever. How two flecks of dust can attract each other according to Newton's law is something that no mechanism of hypothetical pushes would ever be likely to explain.

Nor does the *Principia* end here. With his law firmly established, Newton now "returns to the phenomena," as he says, in order to unravel mysteries that had baffled thinkers for millenniums. With his law he will explain mathematically why the twice-daily tides occur and why there are spring tides and neap tides. He will even calculate how high the tide reaches in mid-ocean. He will explain, at last, the mysterious path of the comets, demonstrate that the globular earth is flattened at the poles and calculate by how much. He will estimate the mass of the sun and planets and explain why the axis of the earth makes its own revolution once every twenty-five thousand years, a problem that even Kepler had pronounced to be insoluble. He will explain the general motions of the moon and account mathematically for a variety of subtle perturbations in the moon's motions that had long puzzled astronomers. By his law of gravitation he will not only explain a vast array of phenomena, he will explain them in terms more precise than anyone had dreamed possible. From only a few laws of motion, themselves derived from phenomena, he has locked the universe into one lawful system, as comprehensive as the most daring speculations of ancient Greek philosophy and as precise in its operation as a railway timetable. The achievement was a titanic one, as readers saw at once.

Yet the fundamental problem remained: what, after all, is this impalpable attractive force that acts at a distance, against all reason, all philosophy, and all sound sense? The question haunts the pages of the *Principia*, as it must have haunted Newton himself. Time and again he anxiously warns his readers not to misunderstand him. He does *not* believe that a material body can literally "attract" another body from a distance. The attractive force of which he speaks is not a physical pull at all. He is, he explains, "considering those forces not physically, but mathematically: wherefore the reader is not to imagine that by those words I anywhere take upon me to define the kind, or the manner of any action, the causes or the physical reason thereof, or that I attribute forces, in a true and physical sense, to certain centres (which are only mathematical points); when at any time I happen to speak of centres as attracting, or as endued with attractive powers." And again, "I here design only to give a mathematical notion of those forces, without considering their physical causes and seats."

What, then, is "force" if it is not a physical cause? To this question Newton's revolutionary answer is this: force is the "efficacy" of a cause unspecified and unknown. It is the mathematical measure of the strength of whatever unknown cause it is "that propagates it." The gravitational force does not cause a planet to move toward the sun. It is the *measure* of the strength of whatever it is that causes this motion. Though the cause of this force (and other forces) is unknown, forces themselves can be determined exactly, and this is all that philosophy requires. The force of a cause can be determined, in fact, by the three laws of motion. As the first law states, a body moves naturally in a straight line at uniform speed. Therefore, by this law, when the uniform motion is changed in any way, we know that some cause is operating on that body. The strength, or force, of that cause is measured by the *amount* of change the cause induces, or more strictly, by the amount of acceleration the cause induces in a body of a given mass. As to the explanation of the gravitational force, says Newton, he has not been able to discover it empirically "and I frame no hypotheses. . . . To use it is enough that gravity does really exist, and act according to the laws which we have explained, and abundantly serves to account for all the motions of the celestial bodies, and of our sea."

"To us it is enough." With that regal pronouncement Newton summed up the meaning of his revolution in natural philosophy. Just as he had expected, philosophers like Huygens declared that the *Principia* was incomplete. For all the book's grandeur, they said, its author had failed to give a mechanical explanation of his gravitational force. It may be true, they argued, that planets move

toward the sun in accordance with Newton's law, but surely natural philosophy must explain why they do so in terms of the material push that must propel them. Newton had said that forces measure causes unknown, but why should philosophers leave these causes unknown? Such a question is not really answerable, and Newton's reply—it cannot be called an argument—was simply: "To us it is enough." He, Newton, was satisfied. Beyond such concepts as he had laid down—beyond force, mass, and acceleration—philosophy could not go without dribbling away into vain speculation no whit superior to the old philosophy.

"The whole burden of philosophy seems to consist in this—from the phenomena of motions to investigate the forces of nature, and then from these forces to demonstrate the other phenomena." Indeed, he suggested with truly prophetic intuition, there are probably other forces like gravity that operate in nature. "Have not small particles of Bodies certain Powers, Virtues, or Forces by which they act at a distance . . . for producing a great part of the Phenomena of Nature?" If so, philosophers must investigate them and find the laws governing their operation, just as he, Newton, had investigated the force of gravitation by way of example of his mathematical method.

There was no way for Newton to prove that the "whole burden of philosophy" was one thing and not another. In brief time, however, men came to agree with him. He conquered, not by force of argument, but by the overwhelming power of his peerless example: the *Principia Mathematica* itself. If, as Newton said, the law of gravitation is but a sample of his "mathematical way," then men agreed that science need go no farther than Newton had already gone. Forces may measure causes unknown, but Newton's new mathematical science of forces was more comprehensive, more precise, and more rigorous than anything natural philosophy had ever seen before. It was also freer; for Newton's belief was not a shackle but a liberation, and that liberation is what distinguishes modern science from all previous philosophies.

The modern scientist, disciple of Newton, does not ask what causes a force, or what energy is, or how charged particles can attract each other. It is enough for scientists that concepts like force or energy be mathematically precise, derivable from experiment, and capable of explanation according to Newtonian standards of precision. What metaphysicians might say—what "reason" might demand—is of little concern to scientists; they have been freed by Newton's *Principia* to comprehend nature without deciding once and for all what nature ultimately is.

This was exactly how Newton wanted it to turn out, though his reasons were only partly scientific and only partly revealed. The truth was that he himself had no doubt about the mysterious unknown cause that propagated the force of his system. It was God himself, "incorporeal, living, intelligent, omnipresent," though Newton never dared say so outright. He could only hope that men might follow his example and cease to arrogate to matter what properly belonged to God. Ironically, the mathematical method, through which science won its freedom, was the means by which Newton hoped to preserve God's place as ruler and sustainer of his creation. Like Janus, he faced two ways—toward the science of the future and the faith of the past.

Newton was forty-four when the *Principia* appeared. He had forty more years to live and to enjoy his fame, which grew more immense with each passing year until in time he found himself being looked upon as a kind of semi-deity. Honors and emoluments came one by one, but too slowly in the first few years to prevent Newton's suffering a nervous breakdown, during which he wildly accused John Locke of "embroiling" him with women. Shortly afterward he begged Locke, like a child, to forgive him. Then his iron pose of aloofness cloaked him once more and did so until the end of his life.

Doubtless Newton's heart was not in the age in which he now lived and which looked upon him as its special hero. Infidelity and skepticism seemed to be rising. There were signs that his own grand vindication of God's providence might prove futile in the end. Eager Newtonians were coming to conceive of gravity as an inherent property of matter and so were resuscitating materialism in a new, Newtonian form. He was an old man by now, and he felt urgently the need to set his faith upon lasting foundations. He sat down to write what he called "A Short Scheme of the True Religion," a set of propositions that would both contain the essence of religion and yet withstand skeptical assault. He wrote it once, then a second time; then again, and then twice more. He could not get it right. The true religion evaded him.

In the year 1727, at the age of eighty-four, Newton died, and six peers of the realm carried his coffin to Westminster Abbey. With his quaint Biblical prophecies and his Hebraic God he was by then something of a relic; for a skeptical, experimental generation was rising, and it was out of spirit with his deepest concerns. By a curious irony, historians have sometimes called this dawning era the Newtonian Age.

*In Russia social and economic progress was achieved not through
pressure on feudal and monarchical institutions by a rising middle
class, but through the ruthless efforts of out-and-out autocrats. Peter
the Great, whose picturesque tour of the West is so vividly recounted
here by a well-known writer on Russian history, was only the first of
such rulers. In the nineteenth century Nicholas I, the "gendarme of
Europe" and the very incarnation of autocracy, took Peter as his
model and tried to make Russia keep pace with the West. And at the
very end of that century it was another autocrat, Alexander III, less
intelligent than either Peter or Nicholas, who set Russia on the path to
industrialization. All the while the landholding nobility opposed
reform and insisted on the uniqueness of Russian institutions and
culture. This class has indeed disappeared since the revolution of 1917,
yet in the Soviet Union of today, despite all its achievements in science
and technology, there persists a tendency to suspect Western culture
and aspirations, a distrust that lies at the root of many international
tensions.*

PETER AND THE WEST

CONSTANTIN DE GRUNWALD

Russia has always been a disturbing problem to the nations of
western Europe. For centuries they consigned it to Asia and
therefore, they hoped, to oblivion. But Russia was not so easily
dismissed. Immense, spectral, shadowy, full of unknown terrors, it
continued to haunt the Western mind. In the sixteenth century,
four hundred years before the Cold War began, we find the merchants of Reval (now Tallinn) rousing Lübeck and the other Han-
seatic cities to stop a handful of local artisans from going to Moscow; they feared "the evils that will fall upon Livonia and the
entire German nation if the Russians should acquire the techniques
and the military art of the West." In 1571 the Duke of Alba, the
celebrated lieutenant of Spain's Philip II, sent a message to the
Diet of Frankfurt insisting—exactly as is done today—on the necessity for prohibiting the exportation of guns, cannon, and other
military equipment to Russia. And the Polish King Sigismund was
even more peremptory: writing to Elizabeth I of England, he proposed that no ships be allowed to sail to Russia "for the most im-
perious reasons, common to the entire Christian world." In the
next century, Gustavus Adolphus of Sweden was calling the Russians "dangerous neighbors."

Thus, deliberately, Western Christendom saw fit to banish the 59

Muscovites from universal history. Sully, minister to Henry IV of France, refused to accept the "Scythian prince," as he called the czar, among the fifteen sovereigns included in his scheme for a "universal Christian republic," and insisted that admitting him into a "European confederation" would do more harm than good. The Treaty of Westphalia, the most important diplomatic document of the period, wrote off Russia, without the slightest justification in fact, as one of the "allies and adherents of Sweden" (!) and ranked its grand duke after all the other European monarchs except the prince of Transylvania. Only William Penn was broadminded enough to accord Russia ten seats out of ninety in his project for a congress of arbitration to ensure the peace of the world.

But if the leaders of the Western states felt only scorn and suspicion for Russia, the cause was first of all the Russians themselves, with their boastfulness and their intolerant and narrowminded attitude. The Iron Curtain is not an invention of our day. It cut off Russia from the outside world all through the centuries that preceded the accession of Peter the Great. Knowing nothing about conditions of life beyond their own frontiers, the Russian people, from the czar and his boyars to the lowest peasant, felt an immeasurable superiority to the outside world. The Moscow government granted admission to foreigners only upon special authorization by the sovereign himself and forbade its own subjects to travel beyond the boundaries of Russia. Even in the middle of the seventeenth century, foreigners not of the Orthodox faith were relegated to a suburb of Moscow called the "German Quarter," a sort of ghetto set apart for immigrants, though a very comfortable and prosperous one.

This whole situation was the result of a gigantic historical misunderstanding. Despite all that has been said by proponents of the contrary thesis, Russia from her beginnings enters the stage of history as a European power. Unlike the genuinely Asiatic civilizations, the whole Russian civilization is based on the teachings of Christianity. The Grand Duchy of Kiev was the cradle of the Russian empire. It was founded by Normans and Slavs, men of European descent, along the river route that leads from the Baltic to the Black Sea. That route and nothing else is the destiny of Russia. Around it arose the great cluster of principalities that were united under the House of Rurik, a powerful dynasty that married its

Resplendent in armor and sash, Peter the Great strikes the pose of the warrior-czar in a portrait painted by a Dutch artist.

daughters to the kings of France, Hungary, and Norway, to the emperors of Germany, and contracted family alliances with the emperor of Byzantium and the king of England. The bulwark of Christendom against the nomads of the steppes, in the tenth and eleventh centuries the Kievian state—connected with the great Western centers by a flourishing commerce—represented the "most active and civilized center on the Continent."

The Mongol invasion at the beginning of the thirteenth century put an end to this promising development. For two hundred years the Russian nation was to be dominated by Asiatics. After the devastation of Kiev and the banks of the Dnieper, a large part of the population scattered into regions farther north and east, where the virgin forest remained impenetrable to the enemy. The grand dukes, survivors of Rurik's dynasty, transferred their capital to the same region. It is here, around Moscow—an obscure settlement first mentioned in 1147—that the Great Russian race developed in the struggle against a rigorous climate.

But during the period of Asiatic domination there had been a break between Russian civilization and the civilization of the West. Direct and permanent contact with the other Christian nations was interrupted. Later, at the end of a long period of troubles, the Muscovy of the seventeenth century was finally deprived of all access to the sea and to the Germanic-Latin world. In the seventeenth century it was in a sense "driven back upon Asia."

At that period Russia was an "underdeveloped country," as we say today, populated by some ten million pious but ignorant peasants under a feudal regime dominated by an autocratic monarch who regarded himself as the representative of God on earth, defender of the true faith, and heir to the Byzantine emperors. Confined to the Kremlin, the first rulers of the Romanov dynasty (which came to power in 1613) led an almost monastic existence in its hallowed precincts. Every day they got up at 4 A.M. and proceeded immediately, even before greeting their wives, to the chapel. Every morning they went to Mass and every evening to Vespers. Throughout Lent they attended services lasting five or six hours at a time, during which they made more than a thousand genuflections. They appeared but rarely in the streets of Moscow; when they did they were clad in magnificent brocades, and the people flung themselves to the ground as they passed. In affairs of state they found only feeble support in a fanatical clergy and in a class of indolent and avaricious noblemen, the boyars. Occasionally they would receive in solemn audience ambassadors from European powers on special missions. Except for this, the West remained as much a closed book to them as it did to their subjects.

Nevertheless, the needs of national defense and even more urgent considerations of a commercial nature dictated a closer connection with the feared and despised West. The idea of the sea began to haunt the best minds of a nation that until then had kept its eyes fixed on the steppe and the colonization of undeveloped land.

We may suppose that even without the impulse given by Peter the Great, Russia would have been compelled to break the circle of isolation in which she was enclosed. But it was the Reformer-Czar who provided the necessary impulse for the movement, who by his savage energy succeeded in shaking his compatriots out of their inertia, and who left his stamp on all the subsequent development of his empire.

Certainly he was no ordinary figure, this man of giant stature (six feet eight inches) and a physical strength that enabled him to break horseshoes in his bare hands. Russian to the core in his pleasures and his rages no less than in his tenacity, endurance, and scorn for comfort, Peter mirrored the character of his people with their constant tendency to excess. Yet nothing could be more erroneous than to set him down, because of all that, as a "barbarian." There is a certain element of savagery in him, and it must be admitted that his rather primitive sense of humor smacks strongly of the barracks or the village carouse. But we must not forget that the extent of his knowledge and the depth of his convictions set him among the most remarkable personalities of his period.

Peter was born in Moscow in 1672 and had a stormy childhood, troubled by dynastic quarrels, clan rivalries, and popular uprisings. His father, the pious and easygoing Czar Alexis, had two unpromising sons by an earlier marriage: the sickly Fedor and the partially blind and feeble-minded Ivan. When Alexis died in 1676, Fedor inherited the throne. He lasted only six years, and upon his death the incompetent Ivan and the healthy ten-year-old Peter were proclaimed joint sovereigns of all the Russias—under the regency of their elder sister Sophia, an intelligent and ambitious virago of fifty. Although she has been compared to Semiramis and Elizabeth I of England and consciously modeled herself on the Empress Pulcheria of Byzantium, she was unable to maintain order in her own country. Relegated to the background, the adolescent Peter witnessed scenes of bloodshed that gave him a horror for the atmosphere of the Kremlin and for the traditional mores of the old Muscovy. He was brought up by his mother, Natalia Naryshkin, on the outskirts of Moscow, in a country setting where he supplemented an inadequate education by constant contacts with humble foreign artisans who lived in the nearby German Quarter. It is as though destiny itself had set him at the frontier between the two civilizations. He had always had a passion for soldiering (a list of his early toys, which still exists, shows nothing but pistols, carbines, bows and arrows, drums, and cannon). Now he organized a band of the gentlemen's sons, stableboys, and street ragamuffins who were his companions, drilled them, and learned with them how to handle arms. Other boys came to swell the ranks and the games grew more ambitious. Using boats, they mounted a full-scale assault on a small fortress that Peter had had built on a little island not far from his home. At the end of a few years he had two well-trained battalions of several hundred men each. With this first nucleus of what was to become a famous army he executed a *coup d'état* in 1689 to free himself from the hampering tutelage of his half sister, the Princess Sophia, to put an end to her dangerous intrigues, and to take over actual power.

He had become his own master. His first action was to escape from the palace into the streets. Fleeing the Kremlin with its monks and its courtiers, its atmosphere of sacred and hieratic grandeur, he sought the pure air of the city and the country; he became an assiduous visitor to the German Quarter. By this time there was little German left about it but the name, which recalled its earliest inhabitants. Since the middle of the seventeenth century all Protestants and Catholics had been required to live there. They had made it into a clean and comfortable quarter that was the envy of the native Muscovites, a place of comfortable brick houses, beds of flowers, neat tree-planted avenues, and squares filled with splashing fountains. The distractions and entertainments of the foreigners who lived there were, naturally, Western in taste and a violent contrast to the Russian way of life. Shaking off governmental routine, Peter found his way there at any and all hours. He made friends with the most prominent members of the foreign colony, attended their festivals and banquets. In their company he perfected his knowledge of Dutch; his conversations with all these "adventurers" who had traveled widely and lived intensely were a constant stimulus to him, opening new horizons almost daily.

Two really remarkable men—the old professional soldier Patrick Gordon, scion of an illustrious Scottish family, and young

François Lefort, another soldier of fortune and a native of Geneva
—became his masters in the military profession and, more simply,
in the art of living in the Western fashion. Guided by their advice,
he turned his efforts to enlarging the little troop that had enabled
him to overthrow the regime of his sister Sophia. Still under the
influence of the same two friends, he revived the old dream of giving Russia access to the sea. In 1695 he flung himself into a war
against Turkey and captured Azov at the mouth of the Don. But
even in the moment of victory he realized that his land and naval
forces were inadequate to gain him mastery of the Black Sea. He
decided to send a "Grand Embassy" to various Western countries,
not only to secure the help necessary to continue the war or to
conclude an advantageous peace, but also to build up a corps of
specialists by initiating the young representatives of his nobility
into European science.

To everyone's astonishment, Peter himself decided to join the
embassy incognito. Not only in Moscow but all over the world the
departure of the Grand Embassy aroused extraordinary curiosity.
"To the polished nations of Western Europe," Macaulay writes,
"the empire which Peter governed had till then been what Bo-
khara or Siam is to us. . . . In the estimation of statesmen that
boundless expanse of larch forest and morass . . . was of less account than the two or three square miles into which were crowded
the counting houses, the warehouses, and the innumerable masts
of Amsterdam. . . . Our ancestors therefore were not a little surprised to learn that a young barbarian, autocrat of the immense
region stretching from the confines of Sweden to those of China
. . . had determined to travel as a private man, and to discover,
by personal observation, the secret of the immense prosperity and
power enjoyed by some communities whose whole territory was far
less than the hundredth part of his dominions."

For eighteen months the czar of all the Russias traveled among
the ranks of his apprentices through the Baltic countries, the German states, Holland, and England, vainly attempting to escape
notice under the borrowed name of "Bombardier Peter Mikhailov."
Officially, the embassy was led by François Lefort, seconded by
two Russian dignitaries. But naturally all eyes were turned on the
young sovereign, taller by a head than any of his companions, who
distributed lavish gifts and was received at every court.

At Königsberg he immediately met the prince-elector of Brandenburg; then, at Koppenbrügge, the princesses of Hanover. In
Holland he had his first interview with William of Orange, king of

England, whom he was to meet again in London. In Vienna he was on intimate terms with Emperor Leopold of Austria. And on his way back to Russia, at Rawa Ruska, he made friends with Augustus of Saxony who had just been elected king of Poland.

Certain writers of the period, whether malicious or ill-informed, have left lurid reports of Peter's behavior at these courts. According to one libelous account, published in Paris in 1703, he appeared at the court of Brandenburg dressed in shaggy animal skins and flung himself on his host's daughter with the intention of raping her. But eyewitnesses portray for us rather a man who, though perhaps somewhat uncouth and unfamiliar with Western manners, was eager to learn, willing to comply with local customs, and extraordinarily talented.

At first glance the result of all these meetings may seem slight. On the purely diplomatic terrain the efforts of the Grand Embassy met with complete failure. Not one of the European cabinets would lend support to Moscow's plan for a crusade against the Turks. However, the royal traveler's immediate interest was in the entirely different direction of technique. His goals included developing his naval building program, organizing a powerful artillery, inviting selected specialists from among captains, seamen, and engineers to Russia, and building up a corps of Russians instructed in the most recent methods. He wanted to superintend the apprenticeship of the young noblemen he had brought with him, and cherished the ambition of serving as their model. His biographers never fail to point out that he ended by mastering fourteen skills, not counting that of statesman; at various times he functioned as engineer, cannoneer, artificer, carpenter, boatman, armorer, drummer, blacksmith, joiner, and even tooth-puller.

In Amsterdam, where he was to spend more than four months, the Czar concentrated on increasing his knowledge of shipbuilding. If he slighted neither the museums nor the libraries nor the laboratories nor the dissecting rooms, he spent the greater part of his time in the East India Company shipyards, and it was only after finding that the teaching there was too much mere rule of thumb that he decided to leave.

It was in England, in the yards of Deptford and the arsenals of Woolwich, that he finally completed an apprenticeship that made him an accomplished master of the art of shipbuilding. "If I had not come here," he was to say later, "I should never have been more than a plain carpenter." He also perfected himself in the technique of navigation, spent hours rowing and sailing, attended the maneuvers at Spithead, and revived the courage of British sailors during a storm by asking them: "Have you ever heard of a czar being drowned?" Later, remembering this period of his life, he often said to his courtiers, "The life of an English admiral is infinitely happier than that of a czar of Russia."

When he was not on the water, he inspected the collection of weapons at the Tower of London; visited the Mint and the Greenwich Royal Observatory; went to a masked ball, the theater, a bearfight and a cockfight; paid court to an actress; and incidentally wrecked the elegant house that he and his party were living in. He even found a moment to watch, through an attic window, the solemn opening of Parliament (thus giving a wit the chance to remark: "Today I saw something unique in the world—one sovereign on the throne and another on the roof").

The Great Embassy came to an abrupt end when Peter was summoned to Moscow by an uprising of the undisciplined and turbulent *streltsy*, or militia guards. He returned the possessor of an intellectual and technical equipment such as no Russian before him had commanded. He at once took advantage of his superiority to lead his country into a gigantic military and reforming enterprise which he was to pursue for twenty-five years, until his last breath.

Long before Peter came to the throne certain farseeing political thinkers had declared that Russia would forever remain bogged in the steppe if, without modern equipment, she persisted in seeking an access to the Black Sea, and that she would exhaust her forces in vain if she directed her attacks against Poland. Like the road to Azov, they maintained, the road to Warsaw led nowhere. Only conquest of the Baltic littoral would enable Russia to open a broad road to the West. And so, on August 8, 1700, Peter the Great made his historic decision to declare war on Sweden.

He had secured the collaboration of Poland and Denmark, but his alliance with these two rivals of Sweden was to prove unreliable and ineffectual. With nothing to rely on but his own forces, Peter was defeated at Narva by the valiant Swedish king, Charles XII. Refusing to be discouraged by this defeat, he raised and equipped new armies; he put immense effort into creating a good artillery; he worked with his own hands on the construction of the frigates that were to give him mastery of the Baltic. Then his disciplined and well-trained regiments seized the mouth of the Neva and entrenched themselves along the coveted littoral. On June 27, 1709, in a battle at Poltava, he put to flight his great adversary, Charles XII.

To achieve this brilliant success, Peter had been obliged to subject the entire structure of his country to a basic transformation. In a certain sense it emerged completely "Europeanized" and "Westernized." Even before venturing into war, Peter had undertaken to change the outward aspect of his fellow countrymen or, more precisely, of his own entourage. During his journeys in western Europe he had observed how ridiculous the long gowns and long beards of the Muscovites looked to the outside world. The day after his return from abroad, Peter received the boyars who came to greet him with a large pair of scissors in his hand and chopped off the beards of the most eminent among them. At a banquet later in the same week, the Czar's jester (an ancestor, by the way, of the novelist Turgenev) circled the table and cut off the beards of all the guests who had not yet adopted the new fashion. Three days later nearly all beards had disappeared from the court. Clothes were next. Within a few months Peter was wielding the scissors on the exaggeratedly long sleeves of his attendants. "With these full sleeves," he said, "accidents are always happening: sometimes they get dipped in the soup, sometimes they break windows."

Resistance, of course, was greater in the case of more serious reforms. Peter managed to overcome every obstacle put in his way by tradition, obscurantism, and attachment to old abuses. He established conscription as a means of recruiting a permanent and regular army with an adequate number of specialists; he did the same for the fleet. He subjected a recalcitrant church to his authority by replacing the all-powerful patriarch with an ecclesiastical body, the Holy Synod, which was given strictly limited functions. He replaced the hereditary aristocracy by a "nobility of service," entrance into which was to be open to all deserving officers and functionaries. And to put an end once and for all to the old customs and habits, he left Moscow and the Kremlin and transplanted his residence to a swampy, deserted region at the mouth of the Neva, newly conquered from Sweden. There he built his new capital, St. Petersburg (rebaptized Petrograd in World War I and now Leningrad), "a window on Europe," as he put it.

Peter himself directed the preliminary work—striding through the mud, issuing decrees, designing the fortress wall, and ordering great numbers of peasants from all over Russia to be shipped to the unpromising site and put to work. There was neither adequate food nor shelter for so many people. No one had bothered to provide the necessary tools, like picks and shovels. Wheelbarrows were still unknown in Russia, and the poor workmen had to carry earth in the skirts of their coats or in wretched sacks made of rags. Thou-

sands died, but thousands more took their place. Palaces and
churches rose out of the swamps, and ten years after it was begun a
foreign visitor was able to call the city "one of the marvels of the
world."

Permanent connection with the West—the final goal of all his
efforts—was not established without difficulty. For long years the
cabinets of Europe turned a cold shoulder to the spoilsport Czar
who took no interest in the great Spanish problem then in the lime-
light, and persisted in fighting the "invincible" king of Sweden in
what was considered a perfectly "useless" war. Russia's prestige
was very low at Versailles, Vienna, and The Hague. It was only
after the victory of Poltava that all Europe turned its eyes to the
rising star and discovered Russia, the great Russia that it was to

*A contemporary engraving pictures the czar examining the plan of his
new capital, St. Petersburg, a project he closely supervised.*

"discover" so often later, after intervals of forgetting it.

Proceeding to carry the war into Germanic territory, to the very frontiers of central Europe, the Russians extended their action to the banks of the Elbe. They camped there then as they are camped there today, making their pressure felt on the occupied countries; they held Mecklenburg, took the fortress of Friederichstadt in Norway, made themselves at home in Danzig, and advanced as far as Altona, close to Hamburg. After Poltava, the French cabinet manifested a desire for a *rapprochement* with Russia and to act as mediator in re-establishing peace with Sweden. Peter instantly set off for Paris and entered into a friendship with the French regent.

This second appearance of the Czar in the countries of the West was as pregnant with consequences as the first had been. By directing his ministers to sign the Amsterdam Agreement with France and Prussia in 1717, Peter inaugurated a system of interchangeable alliances that was to be employed by his successors on a great scale. By submitting to the admiration of the Parisian populace, by showing a charming affection for the boy king, Louis XV, by visiting Madame de Maintenon (Louis XIV's durable mistress), Peter laid the foundation for his fame throughout the entire world.

In Russia that fame was marred by Peter's treatment of his son and heir, the Czarevich Alexis. The two men could hardly have been more different: Peter was creating a new Russia; Alexis, who might have made a fairly good priest if he had not been inclined to debauchery, preferred the old Russia with its indolent quietism and its horror of innovation. Incapable of leading a revolt himself, he became—quite without premeditation—a symbol around whom all the malcontents in Russia rallied. The contest between them came to a climax in 1718, when Peter imprisoned Alexis and appointed a supreme court to judge him. He let the son of his own flesh be tortured, even in his presence. All the details are in the official reports, which conclude: "The rack was applied at eleven o'clock. . . . That same day, at six o'clock in the afternoon, the Czarevich gave up his soul." Peter had presided at the murder of his own son, and it was one of his few—but lasting—defeats.

As the years wore on, he had many victories. The surrender of the Swedish fleet after the naval battle of Hangö-Udde in 1714, the military occupation of Finland, and two raids into Skåne in southern Sweden, finally led—on August 30, 1721—to the signing of the Treaty of Nystadt. It gave Russia full possession of Estonia, Livonia, Ingria, Karelia, and a part of Finland with the fortress of Viborg.

Peter's triumph was complete. He had conquered the Baltic littoral, his coveted objective. He had further succeeded in establishing a sort of veiled protectorate over Poland and in setting up a series of duchies along the western Baltic (Courland and Mecklenburg, soon followed by Holstein). On October 22, 1721, in the cathedral in St. Petersburg, he was proclaimed "Emperor of all the Russias," and the Senate bestowed on him the title of "the Great."

Like a warship launched from the ways, Russia had made her entrance into Europe to the clang of hammers and the thunder of guns. Thenceforth nothing would be done on the European continent without her. In all the splendor of embroidery, wigs, silk stockings, and dress swords, the Russian ambassadors, once the laughingstock of the common people, would take part in conferences and congresses on an equal footing and compete in elegance with their most munificent colleagues. The armed forces were to follow in the footsteps of the diplomats. Ten years after Peter's death, 20,000 Russian grenadiers for the first time occupied the banks of a tributary of the Rhine as allies of the German emperor, and at Versailles the fear was already expressed that "the whole of Germany would be overrun by barbarian hordes." Under the rule of Elizabeth, Peter's daughter, Russia took part in the Seven Years' War, occupied Berlin in 1760, and proposed that eastern Prussia be ceded to Poland (thus creating a precedent that should not be forgotten). Later, in the course of the nineteenth century, victorious Russian regiments camped in the Champs Elysées of Paris, at the gates of Naples and Constantinople, in the streets of Warsaw and Budapest and Bucharest, each time—it must be admitted—withdrawing once their task was accomplished.

As for the country's cultural connections with the West, they never ceased to grow, despite passing eclipses. The same is true of commercial relations. Even in Peter's lifetime the value of Russian exports had doubled. Several hundred ships entered the new port of St. Petersburg every year, and local shipowners were already sending their first vessels abroad. Under Peter's successors a naval expedition was dispatched to the distant Pacific, where its Danish leader, the famous Captain Bering, discovered the strait that today bears his name. Russian merchants and consuls took up residence in Amsterdam, Bordeaux, and Cádiz, to organize deliveries of hemp, flax, wood, wheat, and even of cannon and munitions. Scientific knowledge, drawn from Western sources, spread with extraordinary rapidity. By hundreds at first, but soon by thousands, young Russians of every condition were sent to the Western countries to learn shipbuilding and the art of navigation, to study medicine and administrative law, but also architecture and painting. In Russia itself the educational system was reorganized from top to bottom and acquired a technical nature that had no connection with the old medieval methods. The founding of a naval academy was followed by that of an Academy of Sciences; fifteen eminent foreign scholars were engaged to teach in it, including two men of world-wide fame, Leonhard Euler and Daniel Bernoulli, the Swiss mathematicians. Thenceforth no one could seriously class Russia among the so-called barbarian countries.

Admired by the West, the work of Peter the Great has been severely criticized by some of his compatriots. He has never been reproached for his inclinations toward conquest: for the last two hundred and fifty years all Russians have regarded the shores of the Baltic as an integral part of the national patrimony.

The Russians have forgiven the great reformer his brutalities, inevitable in a period of transition. But in the course of succeeding generations they have accused him of having "torn Russia from its roots." "We have become citizens of the world," the historian Karamzin wrote, "but in certain respects we have ceased to be citizens of Russia."

And in fact there is no denying that a somewhat hurried Europeanization resulted in a dangerous breach in the structure of Russian society. Peter neglected the interests of millions of his subjects, peasants who bore the yoke of serfdom; he ruined them by his conscriptions and his taxes; he left them to stagnate in want and ignorance. The upper strata of the nation alone benefited from his reforms. But by becoming completely "unlike the muzhik of the fields," the newly educated officers, officials, and landed proprietors no longer had what their ancestors had always possessed—a common language with the laboring classes. Henceforth there was an absolute difference not only in outward appearance but also in ways of life and beliefs. The peasants remained true to their beards, their boots, their belted shirts worn over their trousers, their local customs, their ancestral faith; the upper classes dressed in the style of Versailles, spoke and wrote almost exclusively in French, and become successively devotees of Voltaire, of a mystical Freemasonry, and, much later, of Schelling, Hegel, and Western socialism. The dynasty itself partly lost its national character. Allied with the petty reigning houses of Germany, the successors of Peter the Great sometimes found themselves at odds with their councilors, defenders of the true interests of Russia; in addition they permitted the training of their armies to be infiltrated by the implacable automatism of the Prussian spirit.

This mutual lack of comprehension between the two parts of the Russian nation, this abyss that opened between them in the reign of Peter the Great, was certainly one of the determining causes of the Revolution of 1917. Only in the universal greyness of the "classless" society established by the Soviet regime has the gap been closed. Since then, Russia's policy has taken a new course. With the massive colonization of Siberia and intensive exploitation of its rich natural resources, with its attention increasingly focused eastward, the U.S.S.R. is in a certain sense in the process of becoming an Asiatic power before our eyes. But history knows no turning back. The destinies of Russia, Westernized by Peter the Great, remain indissolubly linked with those of all Europe.

Among the figures of the Enlightenment, Voltaire stands pre-eminent; it was he who made "enlightenment" the common attitude of the educated of his day.

Members of the older generation find it strange that the youth of today should be so negative, not to say hostile, in their attitude toward the Enlightenment of the eighteenth century, and that it should be necessary to defend it, as Peter Gay, one of the foremost students of the period, does in this essay. For the Enlightenment has always been thought of as one of the brighter periods of history, when reason was applied to social institutions and problems and there was hope of a happier and more just social order. It is true, of course, that despite the brilliant criticism of the philosophes, the human condition in their time continued to be appallingly bad, the vast majority of the population still illiterate and in a state of serfdom or near-serfdom. But surely what counts is the fact that so many fine minds applied themselves to social problems and hoped by the application of reason to remedy abuses and prepare the way to a better life. What, indeed, could be more relevant to the situation of our own time? Many and great improvements have been made since the Enlightenment, but the need for reform remains pressing. If it is not to be accomplished by reason and knowledge, how can we anticipate anything but utter confusion?

THE ENLIGHTENMENT

PETER GAY

The proposition that the Enlightenment has anything of interest to say to our time sounds at first merely absurd. It sounds like special pleading, the effort of a cloistered scholar to establish some sort of relevance to our impatient time. The Enlightenment seems unreal, a vanished world, charming in the worst possible sense of the word, "historic," wholly remote from us and our pressing needs, as though it were five centuries away, or ten, rather than merely two. We know—are we not often told?—that the age of the Enlightenment was addicted to reason, to optimism, to humanitarianism, to secularism, to rising expectations, and that its self-appointed spokesmen, the philosophes, were a collection of irresponsible literary men, like Voltaire, or unworldly professors, like Kant, or shallow politician-philosophers, like Jefferson, all guilty of first arousing and then encouraging unjustified expectations.

If this portrait were accurate, the age of the Enlightenment would be nothing more than a condition to which it would be pointless to aspire. And the reforming program of the philosophes would be nothing better than a fantasy that once aroused false hopes, and as its inescapable consequence, produced real despair. At best the Enlightenment would be irrelevant; at worst, it would be pernicious.

But the portrait is, in fact, badly distorted. Each of its lines must be redrawn and assigned new significance. And it is important to undertake this corrective activity. Santayana once said that those who do not learn from the past will be condemned to repeat it. I may add that those who do not understand the past will be unable to learn from it.

"Enlightenment" is the name given to two distinct but interdependent entities. It is the name of an age, the eighteenth century all across Europe and the European colonies in the New World, and at the same time, the name of a movement that pervaded and came to dominate that age: a movement of philosophes. The two Enlightenments were not the same; Kant, with his customary acuteness, called his age an age of enlightenment, but not an enlightened age; there was, in other words, a great deal of work for reforming, critical philosophes to do.

It is always perilous to characterize a century with a single epithet, but, taking the risk, I will call the age of the Enlightenment an age of hope. The hope that radiated from scientists and philosophers captured the imagination of a wide public. More and more men came to feel a sense of power over their environment and over their individual destinies. This hope sprang from a number of sources, and it was this confluence of elements that made it so irresistible. And it *was* irresistible. Not merely professional optimists like Condorcet, but hardened realists and unsparing critics of optimism like John Adams, found their age a time that offered solid grounds for self-confidence. Science and its companion, technology, were opening new, exhilarating vistas into a life that might be longer, easier, pleasanter, safer, than life had ever been before. Science, too, with its spectacular successes, suggested a dependable method for acquiring knowledge outside the increasingly specialized realms of physics or astronomy. Few philosophes were presumptuous enough to deny their forebears all capacity for fruitful thinking, but the scientific thinking of their own day struck them as being a new instrument, far more powerful, far more accurate, than any intellectual instrument ever devised. Scientific thinking was unprecedented and unique in commanding the unanimous assent of informed minds. As the French physiocrats put it, a little quaintly, Euclid had been the greatest despot who ever lived —his propositions had compelled the agreement of all men of intelligence and goodwill. Philosophy, the philosophes argued, ought to imitate the exact sciences and produce ideas that could be corrected, refined, and improved upon, so that they could be universally accepted as no philosophical system or theological doctrine had ever been or could ever be accepted.

This quality of the enlightened mind deserves emphasis, for it separates the eighteenth century from its predecessors and places it into direct relation with our own. Voltaire saw history aspiring to the condition of a science; Adam Smith dismissed the "political arithmetic" of earlier economists as inadequately precise; the authors of the Federalist papers spoke proudly of the advances that the "science of politics" had made in their own time. It is characteristic of the age of the Enlightenment that the sciences of man—psychology, political economy, political science, cultural history, sociology—should take their beginning then. And the leading practitioners of these new sciences—nearly all of them philosophes —steadily reiterated that they had two related purposes: to establish objective, general truths about man and his conduct, and to establish these truths principally for the sake of improving man's lot.

The pervasive hope that animated the eighteenth century did not emerge from intellectual inventions alone. All around them men saw evidence of improvement, most of all in medicine. Eighteenth-century medicine looks unimpressive to us, even deadly; but its contemporaries found it enormously promising. We are more skeptical in assigning causal importance to a single element; we are inclined to doubt that the disappearance of pestilence and the reduction of famines, like the palpable increase in population all across Europe, were somehow the work of improved medical attention. But the eighteenth century found the scanty statistics spectacular and gratifying: they took the growth of population as a good sign, as a sign of rising hopes for all. The pessimism of Thomas Malthus came at the end—in many ways it *marked* the end—of the age of the Enlightenment.

This was not all. The conduct of all classes—even the upper classes—seemed to be improving. There was more talk and less violence; reforming causes like the antislavery crusade were receiving a serious hearing. Horace Walpole—no optimist—thought it a splendid century. Reason, he wrote, had finally begun to "attain that ascendant in the affairs of the world" that it deserved to attain; while prejudices and tyrannies survived, they had at least produced no new "persecutors or martyrs." It was remarkable, he thought: "No prime ministers perished on a scaffold, no heretics in the flames: a Russian Princess spared her competitor; even in Turkey the bowstring has been relaxed."

These improvements, and many others, were by no means universal. In recent years social historians have insistently reminded us that in the eighteenth century the poor remained as poor as they had always been; that short life expectancies remained the rule among the majority of people; that while epidemics loosened their deadly grip, the lower classes continued to die in uncounted numbers, and while famine officially disappeared, many unofficially still starved to death. Exploitation did not vanish with the new industrial techniques that spread, slowly at first and then more rapidly, through England and across Europe. It merely took new, often more savage, forms. The law, a cherished province of the reforming philosophes, grew more repressive as the possessing classes sought to protect themselves from the most petty thievery by enlarging the list of crimes for which the death penalty could be imposed. Yet, when all these allowances have been made, when we keep in the forefront of our minds that records are normally left by those who are fortunate enough to be literate, it still remains true that the general color of life was brighter and that hope grew, like a beneficent weed, unchecked.

It was in direct response to this hope that the philosophes developed their program. If the philosophes were reformers, they were so for two reasons: they had cause to think that their program had a chance of realization, and they continued to have a great deal of work to do. Far from being utopians, the philosophes sensed the mood of their century and sought to capture its public opinion and influence its direction. But it was the direction in which the century was going in any event, if a little more slowly than the impatient philosophes hoped it would. In a word, for the eighteenth century optimism was realism, or to put it another way: the philosophy of the Enlightenment was the philosophy that the age of the Enlightenment wanted, needed, and deserved.

Thus, just as the philosophes' optimism was more reasonable than many have long believed, so was it more moderate. Nothing would be easier than to compile a little library of pessimistic pronouncements by philosophes of all countries, by Germans like Wieland and Scots like Hume, by Frenchmen like Voltaire and Italians like Beccaria. All these philosophes were men of good hope, but none trusted themselves to a theory of progress. All thought well of the prospects of human reason, but none ever said, or ever believed, that it would triumph totally or for all time.

Indeed, the Enlightenment's view of reason itself was a complicated, highly nuanced affair. Far from denigrating passion, the philosophes appreciated its power and valued its work. They persistently assailed Christianity—it was their main enemy—because Christianity seemed to them the deadly adversary not merely of reason but of passion as well. Everyone recalls David Hume's remark that "reason is, and ought to be, the slave of the passions," but few have treated that remark with the seriousness it demands. With a vigor that some modern playwrights would appreciate, the philosophes honored the claims of the body and celebrated the pleasures of sensuality—within reason, no doubt, but vigorously nonetheless. Nor is this all. The Enlightenment's admiration for reason was, to use modern language, confidence in the scientific method. The philosophes' unceasing complaints against the seventeenth-century metaphysicians and their ambitious rationalist systems—coupled with their equally unceasing advocacy of Newton's "philosophical modesty"—make the men of the Enlightenment into apostles of experience, into pragmatists who insisted on testing each proposition or each institution by its works rather than by its façade.

Thus corrected, the Enlightenment appears rather more complicated and much more reasonable than before. It becomes possible to see the Enlightenment not as a fossil, to be displayed in a glass case for our distant admiration or yawning indifference, but as a force, to be used.

But how? Let us grant that the leading historians of the Enlightenment—Hume and Voltaire, Robertson and Gibbon—were the first modern historians; still their moralizing and their preoccupation with the failings of Christianity compromise the value of their histories as working models for historians of our own day. Let us grant that the leading sociologists of the Enlightenment—Montesquieu and Hume, Ferguson and Adam Smith—were the first modern sociologists; still their inadequate data and primitive theories reduce their books, fascinating as they may be, to distant ancestors of the sociology books we study today. Let us grant that the aestheticians of the Enlightenment—Dubos and Hume, Diderot and Kant—were the first modern aestheticians; still their bid for aesthetic freedom was so closely bound up with neoclassicism that their concerns are no longer ours. Perhaps most troubling of all: let us grant that the reformers of the Enlightenment (and that includes practically all the philosophes in all the countries that could boast of an Enlightenment) were the first modern reformers— they hated slavery, deplored poverty, denounced the cruelty of criminal law and the dead hand of the censor, and decried the subjection of women and children—and that their goals remain recognizable and indeed admirable; yet their specific proposals strike us as halfhearted, tepid, and indeed, irrelevant—irrelevant in part because they have already been achieved, in part because they no longer seem to matter, or to be enough.

If we could restore a philosophe to life and confront him with the distance between his time and ours, he would, I think, welcome rather than deplore that distance as a sign of his, and his movement's, success. After all, the philosophes sought to make knowledge scientific, which, as I have said, is self-corrective and progressive. If they often did not succeed, if they carried a heavier burden of unexamined assumptions and hasty conclusions than they knew, if their very procedures have required marked amendment, reformulation, sophistication, these in themselves do not make the Enlightenment irrelevant. Was it not of the very nature of their thought to invite and welcome change, even in the method of thinking itself?

It is with this question that we have reached the heart of the Enlightenment's thought and the surviving meaning of the Enlightenment for our time—its method. The secularism of the philosophes was at least partly a sectarian quarrel with Christianity. The philosophes paid a price for their bellicosity: being at war, they had no perspective on what they persisted in thinking of as the enemy; they could never fairly assess the contours of Christian thought, Christian art, Christian humanitarianism—in short, Christian civilization.

But the issue at stake in their monotonous exposures of the wickedness of priests, the presumption of theologians, and the contradictions in Holy Writ was actually of the highest importance. The philosophes sought to extend critical thinking to all areas of human life and belief, to extend it even to—especially to—those sacred precincts that had normally escaped scrutiny: the legitimacy of dominant authorities, the conduct of the ruling house, the logic of the state religion. Gibbon's cynical observations on the religious policies of the Roman emperors and Voltaire's sardonic dissection of the apologetic gymnastics of contemporary theologians may have been deficient in humanity, but they point directly to the Enlightenment's most significant contribution to its time, and if we will only listen, to ours: they are direct assaults on the formidable citadel of untested belief.

Criticism, it is often said, is not enough. One cannot live by
method alone. But the criticism of the Enlightenment was more

than destructiveness, its method was more than a method. Each implied a philosophy of man. The great critics of more recent years —Marx, Nietzsche, Freud—all in decisive ways children of the Enlightenment, exercised their critical faculties and developed their critical techniques not for some malicious private pleasure. They sought instead to penetrate beyond appearances to realities, to see through the cant of theologians, politicians—and historians —to expose man's unconscious self-deceptions for the sake of greater jurisdiction over events.

But these later critics did their thinking in their own way; they found new terrain on which to stand. This, I must repeat, was only proper. A twentieth-century thinker who sought in all ways to imitate Lessing or Voltaire or Hume would in no way be like them. He would be a slave to books; they were pupils of experience. He would be an antiquary, losing nothing of his models but their spirit. The authentic admirer of the age of the Enlightenment will show his admiration by moving beyond it.

But in what direction? Our time, it seems, in its mood, in its general temper, is the antithesis of the Enlightenment; reasonable though the Enlightenment's self-confidence may have been, our self-doubt seems just as reasonable. Both appear as appropriate responses to experience. I need not rehearse again, at length, the malaise of our age. The threat, or the temptation, of unreason is everywhere. It is not merely that we have discovered the powers of unreason; reason itself seems to have gone mad. The worst creations of our time—the manipulation of the buying public and the violation of privacy by powerful agencies, the brainwashing practiced by the Chinese Communists and the mass murder practiced by the Nazis, the abuse of our environment and the callousness of world politics—are all products of invention, of calculation, of experiment, of practical reason in the service of profit, degradation, and murder. Science, once man's great hope, has become our nightmare.

I do not mean to make light of our terrors, our victims, and our gloomy prospects when I add to this conventional catalogue of horrors a few unfashionable dashes of hope. With all our anguish, beneath the surface of our lives there are, I think, certain elements of soundness. The very weakness of Europe, the very failures of our foreign policy, suggest that amidst turmoil, ugliness, and suffering, a global civilization may be near birth. Just as four hundred years ago the French *Politiques* advanced the novel and utterly subversive notion that men of differing religious persuasions could live together in the same country, under the same sovereign, so we are witnessing the spread of the equally novel and equally subversive idea that all-out war is nonsensical, impractical, impossible. It may be cold comfort indeed in the wasteland of our century, but we are still here; and that, in the face of Nothing, is better than nothing. Similarly, the rebellions of the young and of the blacks in this country, as elsewhere, are rich in ambiguous and unexplored possibilities.

The decisive question, of course, is, what will we do with it all? Will we be victims or guides? And it is here that the Enlightenment continues to have validity for us and may still exercise a significant and beneficent influence on our civilization. For what the Enlightenment did, with its championship of criticism and its insistence on the right of uncompromising examination of everything, was to show man the way to autonomy—that is, to responsible freedom. Autonomy, Kant said, speaking for the Enlightenment in the years of its close, is the freedom to obey rational laws. This dictum looks at first glance a little obscure—what freedom is there in obedience? But in fact the dictum sums up, with splendid economy, the meaning of the Enlightenment's critical method. It holds that to obey every fleeting impulse, to follow every whim, to surrender to every passion, is not freedom but anarchy, which is merely another form of slavery. The free man follows law, but his freedom lies in his knowledge that he himself has freely made that law and that it is legislation that has emerged from his continuous and critical examination of his environment, his possibilities, and himself. Such law gives not merely self-control but control of one's fate to the extent that it lies within man's control. Only by following this method, and by rejecting easy compromises and the strangely seductive charms of despair, can man master the world he has made.

*The author of this entertaining and instructive essay rightly stresses
the importance of the Grand Tour in creating common standards of
conduct and a certain sense of solidarity among the aristocracies of the
European countries in the eighteenth century. The results of this
fantastically expensive form of education were truly impressive, but it
must be remembered that only the systematic exploitation of the lower
classes produced the wealth that made it possible. From England
to Russia the nobility consisted predominantly of great landed
proprietors, drawing huge annual incomes from the leases and
subleases of their lands to those who tilled them. The Grand Tour
should probably be viewed as a feature of the background of the French
Revolution, though it is more obviously an integral aspect of the
Enlightenment.*

*J. H. Plumb is a Fellow of Christ's College, Cambridge, and a
recognized authority on eighteenth-century history.*

THE GRAND TOUR

J. H. PLUMB

Before the end of the seventeenth century, education in England, as elsewhere in Europe, was confined to a narrow compass. At a very tender age gentlemen's sons were boarded out with
a country parson to learn their letters, their numbers, and the
rudiments of Latin grammar—like Robert Walpole, the future
Prime Minister of England, who was sent away from home at the
age of four. Holidays were sparse—a few days at Christmas and a
month at harvest time. At nine or ten the children left the vicarage
for the grammar school in the neighboring county town where they
boarded with the master. There they rubbed shoulders with local
tradesmen's sons. They dressed alike and spoke the same dialect;
in those days a difference in social rank did not inhibit close social
intercourse. At adolescence their ways tended to part: the shop-
keeper's son went to his apprenticeship, the gentleman's son left
for the university or the Inns of Court to acquire that extra knowledge of religion and law that his station required. After two or
three years at Oxford and Cambridge (and if his home were distant, there he stayed without a holiday), he returned to help his
father with his estate. Apart from a rare visit to London and a
more frequent one to the local metropolis—York, Bristol, Norwich, Exeter—his traveling days were over. He lived and died in
his neighborhood. And this, with few variations, was the pattern
of education throughout northwestern Europe; it differed only for

83

a few aristocrats attached to courts. Sir Philip Sidney was granted a passport to complete his education abroad, to perfect his languages, and to familiarize himself with different nations and governments so that he might be trained to play a part in the affairs of state. Sometimes a likely youth, noticed by a statesman, would be sent to a foreign university to be trained for a career in public administration. But generally governments regarded foreign travel as dangerous: Protestant states feared the wiles of Romish priests might corrupt their young, Catholic ones dreaded the contact with heresy.

By 1700 all this had changed. The grammar schools and universities were no longer crowded with gentlemen's sons; indeed they were emptying fast (Christ's College, Cambridge, had only three freshmen in 1733, and many of its rooms were deserted). Shopkeepers preferred the new education provided by private enterprise, the schools and academies which taught bookkeeping, languages, geography, navigation—the arts necessary for commercial life; gentlemen sent their sons abroad on a Grand Tour. By 1720, no Englishman or German pretending to a place in society could expect to be regarded as anything but a country bumpkin unless he had spent two or three years in France or Italy. The aristocracy of Scandinavia and Russia quickly followed suit. The effect was to give a remarkable homogeneity of manners and taste to the nobility of eighteenth-century Europe.

The reasons for this change are clear and simple. The ferocity of religious conflict had been assuaged by the growing sophistication of the educated classes. True, barbarities were still perpetuated in the name of God. States, however, had grown confident of their abilities to impose the religion of their choice upon their subjects, and the seventeenth century witnessed an ending of religious strife which was also civil. The disruptive powers of religion were no longer acute. The spread of philosophy, the cult of a rational deity and rational universe which became fashionable amongst the upper classes at the same time, made parents fear less the dangers their sons' souls might encounter from a sojourn abroad. Furthermore, northwestern Europe was growing rich on the fat commercial profits which the New Worlds, East and West, had brought into being. Sugar, tobacco, slaves, and spices made the guineas jingle in the pockets of nobleman and merchant from Bristol to Hamburg. Rich, they were also raw. Italians, and even Frenchmen, were aware of their magnificent heritage from the ancient world. Buildings of beauty still greeted them either in decay or in ruin. Scientists, philosophers, historians, poets all proclaimed the greatness of *their* past. But the English, the Germans, the Russians, the Scandinavians possessed no ancient glory. A broken military wall, an arch here and there merely proclaimed their ancient slavery to Rome. Apart from these, they possessed only what their age professed to regard as barbarous—the great Gothic cathedrals and the vast castles of their immediate feudal past. Their nations had grown up outside the pale of culture; they belonged to Europe's remoter provinces, to its frontiers with the outer world. They knew themselves to be uncouth. And this had been made even more self-evident to them by the splendors of the court of Louis XIV.

At Versailles Louis had created a world of sophisticated, aristocratic grandeur. His palace was vaster than any that had been built since the days of Imperial Rome. His painters and his poets constantly harked back in their pictures and their dramas to the glories of the Roman Empire, hinting that in Louis and in France, Europe had at last found an equal to the magnificence of Augustus and his age. The classical world, either in its reflection in the Italian Renaissance or in its own right, entranced Europe. No gentleman worthy of the name could be unfamiliar with the writers of antiquity, and Latin tags were bandied about in the House of Commons, the Virginia Assembly, and the Polish Diet. And throughout Europe developed the feeling that at last the long centuries of barbarism were over, and that life could be lived with that elegance combined with dignity which was the hallmark of Roman gentility. Louis XIV had achieved far more than a mere imitation of imperial grandeur. He had developed the arts of war and diplomacy to an efficiency which no other kingdom could rival, although all desired to do so. Soldiers and ambassadors in embryo could learn their trades only in France. And it was the only place where a nobleman could learn to live according to his station; there he could discover how an aristocrat should eat, dress, dance, converse, love, and fight. Yet France itself was not sufficient: taste could be properly formed only by a visit to the fountainhead of antiquity itself— Italy. Some even considered Italy superior to France in teaching the young nobleman how to make love.

To learn manners, to learn the only trades open to an aristocrat —war and diplomacy—to learn the culture of his class made a Grand Tour a necessity for the young English or German peer. Fortunately the new wealth that was seeping into Europe enabled him to afford what was the most extravagant form of education ever devised by European society. The young nobleman resided abroad usually for three, but often for four, and at times even five years. More often than not he was accompanied by two tutors: one for bookish study, the other for riding, fencing, the arts of war. Often the former were men of distinction—Adam Smith, the economist, accompanied the Duke of Buccleuch; William Coxe, the historian, tutored Lord Herbert. Usually one personal servant was taken from England, the others hired as necessary. The grandest people shipped their own coaches, but the enterprising hotelier, Monsieur Dessin of Calais, ran a highly profitable coach-hire business and had a virtual monopoly on it.

Usually the Tour started very modestly with a stay in a French provincial town, preferably where the English were few, so that the boy was forced to speak French. Strasbourg, Dijon, Lyons were favored because they afforded convenient places for short tours to Germany and Switzerland. Others preferred the towns in the Touraine because the purest French was spoken there. A boy's day was meticulously regulated. William Coxe was instructed to make "a return of the occupations of every day in the week and at what hours" to the Earl of Pembroke. Both Coxe and Captain Floyd, young Lord Herbert's second tutor, and the boy himself had to give an account of themselves on the first, tenth, and twentieth of every month. The young man's hours of riding, fencing, dancing, tennis, and billiards were as keenly regulated as his mathematics, history, and geography. He was ordered to a dentist twice a year, commanded to take a purge of camomile tea every morning before eating, and to have the tips of his hair trimmed on the second day of every new moon. This vigorous, almost remorseless system could be kept up only whilst the boy was young, the society in which he moved alien and strange, and the tutors still in awe of the noble father at home. Paris with its salons and sophistication usually proved irresistible and the tutors' resistance easily overcome.

Paris either entranced or disappointed; the incurable Anglophiles saw it as a meaner, shabbier London, but the majority were delighted by the clean streets, brilliant lighting, and the lovely royal gardens designed by Le Nôtre; gardens made for elegant lounging and discreet flirtation. Here the young Englishmen, Germans, and Russians came to gape at fashion and to grow accustomed to the new French clothes it was *de rigueur* to buy on arrival in Paris. Even Dr. Johnson, who made his Grand Tour very late in life, gave up his brown fustian and went into silk and lace the day he arrived. Naturally the wellborn were amply provided with introductions to aristocratic circles and usually they were presented at

Court. Weeks of balls and parties followed, interspersed with sight-seeing and buying luxurious gewgaws—gold snuffboxes, seals of carnelian and agate, the lovely porcelain of Sèvres; fine velvets, silks, and damasks; screens, fans, *étuis*, clocks in ormolu and marble; watches framed in diamonds; daring terra cottas by Clodion and bronzes by Bouchardon. All were boxed, packed, insured, and dispatched against the day when the exile returned home.

Before Paris endangered the morals and demolished the finances, the young nobleman's steps would be diverted towards Italy. Until 1780, the usual routes were either through Savoy and over the Mont Cenis to Turin or by boat down the Rhone and by felucca—a coastal sailing craft—from Antibes to Genoa. Both

A young Englishman, trailed by his tutors, arrives at a French inn, hoping nervously that he will survive the cooking and the bedding.

A tourist reacts to the techniques of French customs agents. The lesson was soon learned: a discreet bribe saved time and trouble.

could be exciting. The Mont Cenis route necessitated taking the coach to pieces and carrying the traveler in a chair over the steepest part of the path, a formidable undertaking in winter when bad weather might endanger everyone's life. During his passage, Horace Walpole had his favorite lap dog seized from under his nose by a wolf. The danger of the other route lay in the treacherous nature of the swift-flowing Rhone, particularly at Pont-Saint-Esprit, and after that there was always the possibility that the felucca would be seized by the Barbary corsairs that roamed the Mediterranean: rich Christians fetched a good ransom. After 1750, however, mountains became fashionable and the sea route grew neglected. The marvels of nature—particularly glaciers and above all the *Mer de Glace* on Mont Blanc—began to be admired and no Grand Tour was complete without a mountaineering adventure. So, on the way to Italy, many stopped off at Chamonix. Armed with guides and loaded with barometers, tea kettles to boil water on the glacier and so determine heights, luncheon baskets, tents, and servants (the Empress Josephine took sixty-eight guides in 1810!) they braved the mountainside. Sometimes even an artist was hired to render the scene immortal—Lord Palmerston took a famous water-colorist, William Pars; so did Beckford, who had with him J. R. Cozens. Their drawings are some of the earliest we have of roman-tically viewed mountain scenery. Amidst the towering peaks of snow and ice all felt a proper sense of fear, of man's insignificance, of the majesty and indifference of Nature. More than twenty years after his visit, Dr. Howard of Baltimore, one of the early travelers to the *Mer de Glace*, said: "I cannot even now think of some of the situations without a feeling of dread." Earlier generations, like that of Addison and afterwards of Gibbon, had ignored these mountains and concentrated on a course of comparative constitutional study for which the multiplicity of states and cities in Switzerland pro-vided ample material. But it was of the nature of the Grand Tour to increase in entertainment and diminish in education as time passed; also romanticism, through Rousseau, was making the transition easier by insisting that the feelings needed education as much as the mind.

Italy was, perhaps, the most important part of any tour and a far longer time was usually spent in it. As Dr. Johnson said: "A man who has not been in Italy is always conscious of an inferiority."

Italy was the land of marvels, the antique shop of Europe. Spec-ulators dug feverishly for Roman marbles and bronzes, and the discoveries at Herculaneum and Pompeii inflamed the imagination still further. All Englishmen were expected to return festooned with works of art and they became dilettantes overnight, talking with assurance of patina and of significant form. They ransacked palaces, abbeys, and convents, employed spies and informers, and were easily, too easily, gulled by fakes. But throughout the cen-tury an ever-increasing stream of works of art—good, bad, and indifferent—flowed into the country houses of England, Germany, Scandinavia, and Russia. Italy, however, offered more than art. "Indeed," pontificated Dr. Johnson, "if a young man is wild, and must run after women and bad company, it is better this should be done abroad, as, on his return, he can break off such connec-tions and begin at home a new man." Better an Italian countess, Catholic and married, than an English actress, marriageable but impossible. Furthermore the Italian countess was likely to improve his style not only in the arts of elegant flirtation but also in train-ing him for the marriage bed. And the worldly-wise parents ex-pected their young to lose their hearts in Italy; some like Lord Pembroke recommended their old flames to their sons and wrote

A high spot of an Italian tour was the chairlift journey up Mount Vesuvius to peer into the crater.

sentimentally about their own past. Strenuous sight-seeing days followed by nights, equally strenuous, of amorous dalliance completed the education of the young nobleman abroad. But it was a leisurely finish—Turin, Milan, Rome (the Jacobite Court carefully avoided), Naples for the ruins and the opera, and then Verona for Palladio's sake, and Venice for its Carnival. The pictures of Longhi —suggestive, raffish, elegant—recall for us the dissolute nature of Venice's charm. Here the mask permitted license.

After one or two years in Italy, the long voyage home began. The traveler had left England as a stripling unversed in the arts of life; he returned sophisticated, urbane, and a *cognoscente*. His portrait painted by Batoni, Rosalba, or Mengs; one or two pictures of the first rank, sometimes genuine, sometimes false; a collection of water colors, drawings, and lithographs; the latest volumes on Pompeii from the royal press of Naples; marbles, bronzes, Genoa velvet, and Capodimonte porcelain that would embellish his state rooms were packed in their great crates and sent home via a warship for safety's sake. On his return to Paris, the success of his

90

Grand Tour could be measured by the ease with which he bore himself in the salons. Back at home, he joined a magic circle. By turning the conversation to stories of Madame du Deffand, or by the mention of a picture in the Pitti, or the prices charged by Busiri, he could quickly get the measure of each new acquaintance and discover whether he belonged to his own aristocratic world.

This extravagant education was achieved only at considerable cost—a young nobleman abroad could easily run his father into three or four thousand pounds a year (by modern standards some sixty thousand dollars a year). Expensive though it might be, it drew more and more people into its orbit; indeed, not only the young and aristocratic but also the middle-aged and the middle class. The fascination of a European tour even began to intrigue the well-to-do in the American states and the West Indies. By the end of the century, English, Germans, Scandinavians, bourgeois as well as aristocrats, began to swarm to the warm south. Philip Thicknesse pioneered and popularized the idea of making the Grand Tour cheaply. In 1790 William Wordsworth, the poet, and his friend Robert Jones were perhaps the first undergraduates to make the tour on foot with their belongings strapped to their backs. As steamships and railways replaced the sailing ship and the coach, the swarm became a flood and finally submerged the Grand Tour. Under the pressure of middle-class values, aristocratic standards of education began to give way and the tutor and the Grand Tour were replaced by the public school and university. Entertainment became the aim of foreign travel rather than education and fine manners.

During its heyday, however, the Grand Tour had influenced social life to a remarkable degree; it also created the basic structure of foreign travel which later generations were to adopt and to extend. Some of the diaries and journals, which all travelers tended to keep, got into print; others stayed in the family archives to warn and exhort and advise youngsters. As the eighteenth century progressed, descriptive literature gave way to practical guides. Thomas Taylor's *The Gentleman's Pocket Companion for Traveling into Foreign Parts*, which provided maps, advised on roads, and gave distances, also printed tables of money and weights for conversion, listed a huge variety of information, and gave as well simple dialogues in Italian, French, German, and Spanish. It quickly became every traveler's *vade mecum* and spawned a vast brood of guides that have never ceased to pour from publishing houses.

Nor were the journalists, publishers, amateur writers the only men to see that money was to be made out of the passion for the Grand Tour. Fencing masters, dancing masters, riding masters did so excellent a trade in Paris that their professions became overcrowded. The least successful drifted to Moscow, Budapest, Edinburgh, and Stockholm to take the education in manners to the *petite bourgeoisie* who could not afford either the time or the money to leave their native heath, but wanted their sons and daughters to ape the airs of the aristocracy. Language masters often pioneered the way, for it became a mark of gentility in all countries to be able to interlard conversation with a few phrases in Italian or French. Although moralists might denounce the corruption of native manners that French and Italian airs always produced, there can be little doubt that the rage for southern European culture softened the barbarity and increased the civility of countries in the west, north, and east of Europe. Yet when carried to excess, as it was in some German courts and amongst the aristocracy of Russia, it possessed dangers. The noblemen of Russia spoke French, dressed in French clothes, sat on French furniture, mostly employed French servants, and became alien to their own people and their problems; and the cleavage between classes in Russia was immeasurably widened. In Germany the nationalistically minded *bourgeoisie* turned under the influence of the *Aufklärung* from emulation to envy and hate, and cultivated Teutonic customs—crude, absurd, cloudy with bourgeois romance—as a sort of protest against the aristocratic attitude of international culture derived from Greece and Rome and kept alive in France and Italy, of which the Grand Tour was the symbol. Perhaps both these disruptive effects were natural responses to the greatest achievement of the Grand Tour. This was to give a homogeneity of attitude to the European aristocracy, a homogeneity never achieved since by any class on such an international scale: James Boswell had no difficulty in slipping into the best aristocratic society in Utrecht, Berlin, Darmstadt, Geneva, Florence, Venice, Milan, Naples, Paris; yet he was, as Scottish gentlemen went, rather a raw youth of no great family distinction. Horace Walpole, a youth of twenty, fitted into the highest circles in France and Italy with instinctive ease: taste, knowledge, background, and education were the same—whatever their race—for young men of his birth and breeding. Their early years had been spent in learning those arts of living which the Grand Tour brought to perfection. It made for ease not only in the transmission of taste but also of ideas. Voltaire, Rousseau, Diderot, Gibbon, Hume were read about as quickly in St. Petersburg or Naples as in their native lands. Yet the Grand Tour probably had its most profound effect in two spheres—travel and taste.

The rudimentary foundation upon which the huge structure of modern European travel has been erected came into being very largely to fulfill the needs of the young aristocrats setting out on their tours. Hotels, couriers, foreign exchange facilities, specialized transport to beauty spots—the whole paraphernalia by which the aristocrats were transported, housed, fed, and informed came into being in eighteenth-century Europe. By and large these early travelers found and fixed upon what were to become the playgrounds of Europe. They discovered the delights of the Alps and made Switzerland a tourist center of Europe; they recommended the French and Italian Rivieras for their climate and their cheapness. 'Before the end of the century the old and delicate from northern Europe were infesting Nice, Menton, and San Remo; the unmarried aunts of the European peerage drifted into the resorts—throughout France and Italy—which their noble ancestors had discovered on their Grand Tours.

Yet the greatest influence of the Grand Tour was in art and taste. Every museum in northern Europe owes something to the wealth and skill of those young aristocrats who made the Grand Tour, and bought on the strength of their taste—or rather the taste of that small band of Anglo-Roman expatriates who devoted themselves to the British nobility's passion for sight-seeing and for art. Usually they were failed architects or artists like Colin Morrison, James Byres, and John Parker. They usually could be found hanging about the English coffeehouse in the Piazza di Spagna, waiting for their customers. They gave good value. James Byres took the historian Edward Gibbon on a tour of Roman antiquities that lasted eighteen weeks without a day's intermission, and left Gibbon exhausted. Even the indefatigable Boswell, who in a fit of enthusiasm insisted that he and Morrison speak Latin as they visited the Forum, discovered that he lacked the stamina and the spirit to maintain a passionate interest as Morrison remorselessly plodded in the Roman heat up and down the hills and in and out of the ruins, leaving nothing undescribed. Usually these *cicerones*, as they were called, kept a close contact with Italian painters and art dealers, collecting a double commission from the patron and the patronized. Byres was responsible for the Portland Vase reaching England, and the sale of Poussin's *Seven Sacraments* was also negotiated by him. Obviously the young noblemen felt

much safer if buying through one of their own countrymen: a weakness which a shrewd Welshman, Thomas Jenkins, turned to his own great profit. He became the leading art dealer in Rome. Often the aristocrat could not raise the huge sums Jenkins demanded for his statues, so he lent the money for the purchase and thus took a double profit. Jenkins's histrionic powers were highly developed: he wept with emotion at parting with an object on which he was making several thousand per cent profit. His head, however, was equal to his heart and no one could match him in the technique of restoration; under his skillful hands a battered antique torso quickly achieved arms, legs, and head with the finest nicotine staining to give them an age worthy of the price that he charged. Nor was he humble to his clients. He underlined their ignorance, paraded his own virtuosity, and plucked their pockets in the mood of humility so induced. And, of course, there were far less reputable sharks than Jenkins, eager to catch the gullible nobleman with a bargain at an exorbitant price. The standards of professional honesty were low and the skill in copying old masters high, and many a Raphael was born to blush when seen in the cold, critical, northern light.

No traveler came back empty-handed: pictures, statuary, and bronzes, ranging from antique Greek marbles to water colors by fashionable Italians, were brought back in thousands to enable English, Dutch, Germans, Russians, and Scandinavians to appreciate and enjoy the great aristocratic inheritance of Europe. The astonishing virtuosity of these young men can be seen from a recent exhibition held at Norwich which displayed works collected on the Grand Tour during the eighteenth century, principally by the leading Norfolk families. This not only contained old masters, but also illustrated the patronage they brought to eighteenth-century Italian artists. No Italian artist of real merit was absent and the quality of many of their works was exceptional; there were magnificent examples of Canaletto, Guardi, Piranesi, Zuccarelli, Batoni, Rosalba, Pannini, Busiri, the Riccis.

This passion for all things Italianate, whether antique or modern, forced painters and architects to make their own pilgrimages to Rome, for they stood little chance of making a living in England unless they could parade a recognizable virtuosity to the returned tourists. So off they went: some, like Reynolds, by man-of-war in

After his Grand Tour, the collector Charles Towneley had Johann Zoffany paint him surrounded by treasures from Hadrian's villa.

the luxury of great patronage; others, like Thomas Patch, on foot
in poverty. They reached Italy in droves; some died there, some
stayed, most returned with improved techniques and many splendid canvases to stimulate the powers and imagination of those who
stayed at home. Strangely, few Italian artists attempted to exploit
the English market in its homeland; the most outstanding of these
was Canaletto, whose pictures of London, Windsor, and Alnwick
Castle are amongst the finest topographical paintings of the eighteenth-century English scene.

Passionately preoccupied as tourists were with art, few developed a keen critical judgment or displayed much independence of
mind. They were willing to pay huge prices for Veroneses and
Titians, they prized Caravaggios and eagerly bought early Bolo-
gnese painters—Guido Reni, Guercino, and the Caraccis—artists
who are now regarded as far, far inferior to Tintoretto or Botticelli
whom they consistently ignored. As in painting, so in architecture:
they confined themselves strictly to the limits of the fashionable,
thought St. Mark's at Venice barbarous, and kept their praise for
Caserta by Vanvitelli or for Bernini's colonnades at St. Peter's.
Their classical education, however, gave them a profound interest
in the discoveries at Pompeii and Herculaneum. Sir William Hamilton with his lovely wife Emma, afterwards Nelson's mistress,
acted as host to a whole generation of the British aristocracy and
not only taught them the beauties of classical design, but often
secured objects for them that were both authentic and beautiful.
Indeed the pilgrimage to Pompeii strengthened considerably the
adoption of classical motives in architecture and decoration which
marks the last half of the eighteenth century. The wily Josiah
Wedgwood was quick to exploit this acquired taste of returned
aristocrats, and he manufactured for them huge quantities of pot-
tery in Pompeian shapes festooned with classical reliefs. Indeed,
he called his factory "Etruria."

The ideas, the attitudes, the tastes fostered and extended by the
Grand Tour imbued the aristocracy with more than sophistication.
They regarded themselves as the true heirs of the Augustans. They
came, in consequence, to believe passionately in the virtues of
courage and stoicism. They thought nothing became them so well
as heroic death in the service of their country, and in the wars
against Napoleon they died as well as many a Roman. Furthermore they regarded an interest in classical literature and a capacity to judge the decorative arts as essential qualities of a gentleman. At least these were the standards in which they believed,

even though many fell short of them; for all did not respond, as Adam Smith realized, to the educational values of the Grand Tour. He thought that the boy "commonly returns home more conceited, more unprincipled, more dissipated, and more incapable of any serious application, either to study or to business than he could well have become in so short a time had he lived at home." True of some, it was not the common experience. The country houses of England, its museums and galleries, the vast literature of travel, the increased urbanity and the growth of civility of English social life in the late eighteenth century, reflected in the correspondence of Horace Walpole, show that this fabulously extravagant education for a ruling class—more costly than any invented before or enjoyed since—paid fat dividends. The rich are not always remarkable for taste, wit, elegance, but the eighteenth-century aristocracy throughout Europe insisted on these virtues. Thanks to the Grand Tour, taste acquired in Italy, combined with the breeding acquired in France, brought sophistication to the remoter outposts of European society which had previously lived close to barbarism. It also gave to the Western world a love of ancient Europe and its artistic heritage that has long ceased to be confined to the aristocracy. What was once the unique privilege of a nobleman is now the common experience of the English-speaking peoples.

Rousseau, by an unknown artist.

Ironically, the first great critic of modern society was a drifter, not to say a tramp, a man averse to regular work who preferred to lie under a tree and ruminate. Because he did not fit into the society of his time, Rousseau was perhaps better able to recognize its weaknesses and to realize the extent to which civilized society inhibits basic urges of human nature. He would never have made so deep an impression on his contemporaries nor in the aftermath have exercised so strong an influence unless the arguments of his major writings had been to a large degree warranted. It is a fact, as Freud was to point out, that society and civilization require the repression of individual urges. Man is basically a social animal, but group existence is possible only through sacrifice of certain desires and impulses. Rousseau ended as a hopeless neurotic, a type all too familiar to today's even more complex and demanding culture.

Mr. Herold is well-known for his book on Napoleon's Egyptian expedition and other studies of eighteenth- and nineteenth-century history.

ROUSSEAU: THE SOLITARY WANDERER

J. CHRISTOPHER HEROLD

When, in 1778, Rousseau died at the age of sixty-six, one of the most tortured existences ever recorded came to an end. He had spent the better part of his life as a tramp. Suddenly shot to fame, he had been at the same time hunted like a criminal over the face of Europe and consulted like an oracle. He had made enemies of all his friends and had spent his final years in a state close to insanity. He had suffered from a variety of bizarre physiological complaints and from almost every conceivable form of neurosis. He had never owned a house or founded a family (he abandoned his five illegitimate children to an orphan asylum). He had been ostracized in his native land. He had published, in his lifetime, a body of works that contained the most radical and comprehensive social criticism ever formulated up to his time, a criticism whose impact on modern society was and remains incalculably great. Misunderstood and misrepresented by his contemporaries, he had written his *Confessions*—a unique act of self-exposure designed to prove to his detractors that even with all his weaknesses he was, like all men, fundamentally good. The posthumous publication of the *Confessions* only added to the misunderstanding and misrepresentation. Always his own worst enemy, and endowed with a sure instinct for making enemies of others, he saw to it that he would have a large number of them as long as people read books: the *Confessions* alone have supplied his detractors with virtually the entire arsenal of weapons they needed to attack him.

Rousseau was the victim not only of his enemies and of his mania for self-exposure, but also of his most enthusiastic followers. Indeed, like his critics, the majority of his admirers have obstinately persisted, down to our own times, in distorting his thought. They took from his writings only what they pleased, either to propagate or to attack what they chose to regard as his doctrine. He has been both claimed and damned by Marxists and conservatives, by atheists and mystics, by anarchists and totalitarians. He has been blamed with some plausibility for such disparate developments as the Reign of Terror, Hitlerism, progressive education, romantic love, liberalism, communism, nudism, momism, and the revival of square dancing. Everybody has read something about him, everybody thinks he knows what Rousseau said and preached; yet hardly anybody, whether admirer or enemy, seems to have taken the trouble to read him as attentively as he deserves. As a result, he has been almost universally credited with ideas that he either did not hold or that he held in common with most of his contemporaries, whereas the gist of his thought remains misunderstood. Before attempting to formulate what Rousseau did think, it is essential to dispose of at least five stereotyped falsehoods about him.

Falsehood 1: Rousseau preached a "return to nature." It is true that Rousseau, like Hobbes, assumed that man had lived in a state of nature before living in the state of society. Yet he insisted in his *Discourse on the Origin of Inequality* that this hypothetical state of nature may never have existed and probably will never exist; he merely used it as a critical tool, or yardstick. He did not ask man to *re*turn to nature but simply to *turn* to her, and he expressly defended himself against the imputation that he wished man to turn back on the road he had already traveled. "Human nature does not retrogress," he wrote toward the end of his life; and, referring to himself in the third person, he continued: "He has been obstinately accused of wishing to destroy the sciences and the arts . . . and to plunge humanity back into its original barbarism. Quite the contrary: he always insisted on the preservation of existing institutions, maintaining that their destruction would leave the vices in existence and remove only the means to their cure."

Falsehood 2: Rousseau extolled primitive man, the "noble savage."
The idea of the savage's moral superiority over the civilized European can be traced at least as far back as Montaigne, who wrote two centuries before Rousseau. The phrase "noble savage" occurs in Dryden; Rousseau never used it. American Indians and South Sea Islanders were extolled by Diderot and his collaborator Abbé Raynal, but not by Rousseau, who looked to Sparta, republican Rome, and his own native Geneva rather than to primitive societies. There is not a single exotic note in all his writings.

Falsehood 3: Rousseau began the cult of sensibility. He did not begin it; it was in full swing when he appeared on the scene, and though he contributed to its spread, so did the novelists Richardson and Sterne and the philosophers Shaftesbury and Diderot. The morbid sentimentality of the late eighteenth century—the fashionable fainting fits, floods of tears, suicides, romantic landscaping, and artificial rusticity—cannot be imputed to Rousseau, even though those who indulged themselves in these fads claimed him as their patron saint. Artificiality was precisely what he wished to eliminate from men's lives, and the antics of his misguided followers filled him with misgivings and scorn.

Falsehood 4: Rousseau reacted against the rationalism of his time and substituted feeling for reason as man's guide. This cliché contains two falsehoods. Far from being rationalist, the entire Enlightenment was a rebellion against Cartesian rationalism, metaphysics, and system making. It was an age of experimental science and empiricism, with Bacon, Locke, and Newton its guiding spirits. Voltaire, Diderot, and Hume no more rejected feeling than Rousseau rejected reason; what Rousseau did reject was intellectualism and the arrogance that goes with it. In assigning a primary place to feeling, conscience, or instinct, Rousseau was in complete harmony with his times.

Falsehood 5: Rousseau was the spiritual ancestor of the French Revolution. The early leaders of the Revolution looked more to Thomas Jefferson and the American Declaration of Independence than to Rousseau. Leaders of the later stages, such as Marat, Hébert, and Danton, were indifferent or hostile to Rousseau. Mme Roland and Robespierre, it is true, were fanatic Rousseauans—and two more opposed political thinkers it is difficult to imagine. All that can be said is that many revolutionists invoked Rousseau's name, and that Robespierre made the mad attempt to put his own version of Rousseau's political theory into practice; he emphasized the totalitarian features of Rousseau's *Social Contract* at the expense of its very spirit. The *Social Contract* is a theoretical blueprint for a society of equals; how such a society should come into existence Rousseau did not say, but it is quite plain that he never advocated the violent overthrow of existing institutions.

Every idea, every book, every act, has two sets of consequences —those intended and those not intended. It has just been shown that in at least five instances Rousseau is credited with an influence that he did not intend or that can be just as readily credited to others. Indeed, it may perhaps be said that no man since Christ has had more follies committed in his name. But it cannot be said that his *real* thought, the thought that was original with him, was of less consequence than were the ideas falsely imputed to him. Contemplating him from the vantage point of our own time, we see the gigantic and tortured figure of the prophet of modern man's predicament. Weak, sick in body and mind, perverted, unfit for society, he knew all the distress of the human condition, and he said, in essence: all man's sufferings are brought on him by man, not by God, who has given man the means to save himself.

"Everything is good as it leaves the hands of the Creator; everything degenerates in the hands of man"—the celebrated opening sentence of *Emile* contains all of Rousseau's thought in germ. All the conclusions he reached, no matter how mutually incompatible they may seem, can be traced to the same point of departure. And yet, for all the inner consistency of Rousseau's thought, it does not form a system; rather, it represents the application of the same emotional conviction to various fields. It is the intensely personal, subjective tone of his writings that lends them their force and that sparked the enthusiastic response they received. Regarding himself as both unique and universally human, Rousseau drew all his ideas from subjective experience. To understand what he thought, we must feel what he felt—hence the continuing emotional character of our reactions for or against him. It was the misery of his neuroses as much as the brilliance of his genius that made him the prophet of man's discontent with modern civilization. If we share his malaise (and who does not?), we should at least listen to him, though we do not have to agree with him.

Rousseau's birth, which took place in Geneva in 1712, cost his mother's life. His father, a watchmaker with a taste for travel, gave him an odd early education: he kept the boy up nights reading novels while he wept over the loss of his wife. Rousseau's elder brother ran away to Germany as a boy and was never heard of again. When Jean Jacques was ten, his father had to leave Geneva

as the result of some fracas. All in all, not a very settled family.
Shortly after his father's flight, the boy experienced his first sexual
pleasure while being spanked by the sister of the pastor with whom
he was boarding. The perverse desire to repeat that experience remained with him all his life — although, as he asserts, he was too
shy ever to ask from a woman the thing he desired most. Appren-
ticed to a watch engraver, he ran away at sixteen; became a Catholic convert (in return for a cash bonus) in Turin, where he served
for a while as a lackey in a noble household; wandered off to Savoy,
and there, in Chambéry or its environs, spent several years as the
protégé, helpmate, adoptive son, and bedmate of a strange and remarkable woman, Mme de Warens, whom he called *Maman*.

Promiscuous in a motherly and dispassionate way, Mme de
Warens was at the same time a devout Catholic in her own fashion,
unbelievably kindhearted, and unbelievably irresponsible. She did
not succeed in making Rousseau into a great lover, but she profoundly influenced his religious thought. Also, in the rustic idyll
that he shared with her, Jean Jacques experienced—as he was to
recall a few weeks before his death—the only period in his life
when he felt entirely himself, the only time of which he could say
that he had truly lived. *Maman*'s growing financial difficulties
eventually forced him back into the world. We find him in Geneva,
returning to the Protestant faith in order to regain his citizenship;
we find him at Lausanne, giving piano lessons to young girls without himself being able to read a note of music (he was later to become a thoroughly competent musician); we find him wandering
about Switzerland with a bogus archimandrite from Jerusalem,
making speeches to raise funds; we find him in Paris, trying to
make a fortune with a new system of musical notation he had invented. Everywhere his attractive looks, his obvious gifts, and the
impression he conveyed of being made for better things, earned
him the personal interest and patronage of those he met—among
them some very eminent people. It was largely with their help and
encouragement that he educated himself in the course of his wan-
derings. None of his writings betrays a lack of formal schooling.

His musical notation scheme was a fiasco, but he eventually ob-
tained the post of private secretary to the French ambassador in
Venice, where he gained an insight into the seamier sides of practical politics, had several bizarre and inconclusive love affairs, and,
above all, gorged himself with music. The ambassador was an eccentric if not a maniac; after a while a resounding quarrel between
the two men ended Rousseau's diplomatic career.

Back in Paris and now in his thirties, Rousseau still had accomplished nothing, yet the happier half of his life was behind him. He fell in with the circle that soon was to acquire universal fame as the philosophes and encyclopedists—Diderot and d'Alembert at their head, the publicist Frédéric-Melchior Grimm, and Grimm's mistress Mme d'Epinay. He also acquired a companion, Thérèse Levasseur, who worked as a servant girl at his lodgings and who was to remain by his side throughout the rest of his stormy and tragic career. In the winter of 1746–47, Thérèse bore him the first of five children, all of whom, according to his own testimony, he deposited at a foundling home, never to see them again. "In letting them become working people and peasants rather than adventurers and fortune hunters, I believed that I was acting as a good citizen and father," he explained later, without much conviction—though he may well have been right in his own case. Some have questioned whether Thérèse's children were really his; but even though Rousseau's sexual passion, extraordinarily intense as it was, remained largely confined to his imagination and to daydreams, there is no indication that he was impotent; or rather, he was impotent only with women whom he desired and loved passionately—and Thérèse was not one of them. It is certain that with his meager savings and his sporadic earnings as a literary hack and a music copyist he was scarcely in a position to support a family.

It was on a summer day in 1749, when he was entering his thirty-eighth year, that chance drove him into the career which was to make him both famous and wretched. He was walking to Vincennes to visit his friend Diderot, who was briefly and very comfortably imprisoned there. As he walked, he glanced at an announcement in a literary journal he was carrying, and read that the Academy of Dijon had proposed the following subject for its annual prize competition: Whether the restoration of the arts and the sciences has contributed to the purification of morals.

"If anything ever resembled a sudden inspiration," Rousseau wrote several years later in a letter, "it was the emotion that worked in me as I read that. I felt my spirit dazzled by a thousand lights; swarms of lively ideas presented themselves to me at once, with a force and confusion that threw me into an inexplicable turmoil; I felt my head seized with a dizziness like that of inebriation. A violent palpitation oppressed me and made my chest heave. Since I could no longer breathe while walking, I let myself drop under one of the trees by the wayside, and there I spent half an hour in such excitement that as I rose I noticed that the whole front of my jacket was wet with my own tears which I had shed without noticing it. Oh, Sir, If I could ever have written one fourth of what I had seen and felt under that tree, with what clarity I should have revealed all the contradictions of the social system! With what force I should have exposed all the abuses of our institutions! With what ease I should have shown that man is naturally good, and that it is through these institutions alone that men become bad. All I have been able to retain of these swarms of great truths that enlightened me in a quarter of an hour under that tree has been scattered quite feebly in my three main works."

Diderot afterward claimed that it was he who advised Rousseau to answer the academy's question in the negative and thus launched him on his career. Perhaps so; Rousseau later blamed Diderot for having made him insert extreme views in his *Discourse on the Sciences and the Arts* as well as in his *Discourse on Inequality*—views that indeed do not reappear in his later writings. It seems strange that the man who was just then editing the epoch-making *Encyclopedia, or Dictionary of the Sciences and the Arts*, should give such advice; but then Diderot probably felt that his friend had a better chance of winning the prize if he took the more original view, and besides he must have known that a negative answer would be more congenial to Rousseau's *farouche* temperament.

Though overrhetorical, intemperate, and slightly confused, Rousseau's *Discourse* is so passionate and incandescent an indictment of civilization and material progress that even after two centuries it cannot leave the reader indifferent. In some respects the indictment was nothing novel: it echoes Thucydides, Cicero, Tacitus, and Plutarch, all of whom denounced the debilitating effects that luxury and ease produced on the moral fiber of society; yet, at the time when Rousseau's *Discourse* appeared, the more commonly held view was that the civilizing effect of higher living standards, industrial progress, luxury, and art would also produce a beneficent influence on man's moral conduct. To Rousseau, things looked different. Paris, that apex of civilization, appeared to him like a vast and nightmarish agglomeration of some five hundred thousand people who had come there to sell or prostitute their minds or bodies, to exploit others if they could, to impress each other with their wealth, their rank, their power, or their wits; half a million people busily scurrying about either to produce superfluous goods and services for their exploiters or doing nothing with an air of busy importance; polite to each other when expedient, but ready for treachery and caring only for themselves; alienated from the sources of true happiness; wretched in their hunt for success; stripped of the proud dignity of active citizens; thinking, acting, and striving not according to their own conscience and nature but according to the artificial standards of society. "No one," he wrote toward the end of his life, "cares for reality; everyone stakes his essence on illusion. Slaves and dupes of their self-love, men live not in order to live but to make others believe that they have lived."

Rousseau's *Discourse on the Sciences and the Arts* won the first prize it deserved. Though launched on a literary career and famous virtually overnight, he never renounced what he thought was his real vocation: he continued to write about music and even composed it. His opera *Le Devin du village*, a slight but charming work, was successfully performed before the king in 1752. Yet, half against his will, his newly gained reputation drew him into philosophy. He was accused of attacking the arts and sciences and of wanting men to go back to walking on all fours. The accusation, though unfair, forced him to explain himself and to clarify his position. If the arts and the sciences had failed to make men happier or more virtuous, the fault was not theirs but must be sought in the social institutions which perverted their ends. In his discourses *On the Origin of Inequality* and *On Political Economy* Rousseau's thought takes on a sharper focus: social institutions, almost everywhere and at all times, rest not on true law but on power; laws and conventions aim to consolidate the wealth and power of the *haves* and to reduce the *have-nots* to increasing dependency. Under the existing social institutions men had renounced the freedom of the state of nature without gaining the advantages of associating as equals for the common good. The law of the jungle still prevailed, but the innocence of animals was lost: "Thinking man is a depraved animal."

How man could raise himself above this wretched state is the theme of the two great works of Rousseau's maturity—*The Social Contract* and *Emile*. Perhaps Rousseau found the key to his quest in his epistolary exchange with Voltaire concerning the latter's poem on the Lisbon earthquake of 1755. Shocked by that terrible disaster, Voltaire questioned the existence of a benevolent God or Providence: God is said to be free, just, and clement. Then why, asks Voltaire, do we suffer so much under so mild a master? In reply, Rousseau pointed out that if people did not insist on gathering in large cities and on dwelling in six-story stone buildings, disasters on the scale of the Lisbon earthquake would be statistically less likely to occur. He went further: disbelief in God, or the pos-

sibility of a cruel or unjust God, was utterly unacceptable to him.
"All the subtleties of metaphysics would not lead me to doubt for a
moment the immortality of my soul or a spiritual Providence. I
feel it, I believe it, I desire it, and I will defend it to my last breath."
And again: "In this strange contrast between what you prove and
what I feel, I beg you to relieve my anxiety and to tell me where
the deception lies—whether on the side of feeling or of reason."
(Voltaire's reply was *Candide*, which Rousseau never read and
which in fact leaves the question unanswered.)

In the words just quoted lies the key to Rousseau's religious and
moral philosophy as he developed it in *Emile* and in his novel *Julie,
or the New Héloïse*, and to which he gave expression most movingly
and succinctly in the section of *Emile* entitled "The Profession of
Faith of the Savoyard Vicar." Philosophy and theology, he con-
tends, in all the thousands of years of their existence, have led us
nowhere. We cannot be certain of anything except what we feel.
Judgment and reasoning can enter only into our correlation of
what we perceive through our senses. Yet while we can never be
wrong in feeling what we feel, we certainly can reason erroneously
in relating our sense perceptions to one another. Reason and feeling
must never be in conflict, but since reason is subject to error, it
must always be controlled by feeling. The paradox disappears if
one realizes that by "feeling," in this context, Rousseau always
means "conscience."

To Rousseau, the purposes of God were unfathomable, as they
are to most of us, and he derided as empty metaphysics any attempt to explain them. The hypothesis that the universe was the
purposeful creation of a Supreme Being seemed to him incontro-
vertible simply because he *felt* it to be true, and who could convince him that he did not feel what he felt? Why there were seem-
ing imperfections in the Creation he did not presume to say; like
Alexander Pope, he felt that "in erring reason's spite/One truth is
clear, Whatever is, is right." And yet—this is the second great
paradox in Rousseau's thought—it was plain that everything was
wrong. "Everything is good as it leaves the hands of the Creator;
everything degenerates in the hands of man" and the opening sentence of *The Social Contract*, "Man is born free, and everywhere he
is in chains," are but two formulations of the same thought. What
had gone wrong? Rousseau did not share the conviction of Voltaire's Dr. Pangloss that all was for the best in the best of all possible worlds; nor did his feeling allow him to accept the fashionable
despair of later romantics and existentialists; nor did he find it pos-

sible to ascribe the sad state of our affairs to the Fall of Adam and Eve. To suppose that God would be so unreasonable and, one might say, inhuman as to create man simply in order to punish him for acting human went counter to reason and feeling. By endowing man with reason and with conscience, God had equipped him, in Rousseau's view, with everything he needed to pull himself up by his own bootstraps. Then why did everything degenerate in the hands of man? In answering the question, Rousseau substitutes for the Devil and Original Sin a new hypothesis: man is born good, but society corrupts him.

When we say nowadays that society is responsible for many of the crimes and sufferings in the world, we usually are unconscious of being Rousseauans; yet this idea, now a cliché, did originate with Rousseau, and in fact it is the weakest part of his philosophy. Rousseau's apparent inconsistency is twofold: (1) If man is good, then why does he become evil through association with other men, who are also good? (2) If society is the villain, then why does Rousseau prescribe the social contract as man's sole salvation? The questions would be well taken if it could be shown that Rousseau said society must necessarily corrupt man. But he never says such a thing. On the contrary, his entire social-contract theory is based on the assumption that the social state (not as it is, but as it might be) is a step forward from the state of nature. What is more, Rousseau maintained not only that just and beneficent societies were theoretically possible but that they had actually existed in the past —as in Sparta and republican Rome—and even in his own times, as in Geneva. (He soon was to revise that latter opinion.)

It is true nevertheless that, in Rousseau's opinion, society tends to corrupt man because it generally rests on power and exploitation rather than on law and co-operation. In a society not governed by law the individual moral will is stunted, social conventions take the place of inner conscience, men scramble after false values, self-love and vanity drown all benevolent instincts, and the gifts of life and nature pass unnoticed. All these evils are man-made and result from society, yet they are inherent neither in man nor in society. For man, it was Rousseau's conviction, is born not only with a conscience and with reason but also with a free will. He is the author of his fate, collectively speaking. Social redemption can be found in a collective exertion of the will by which men surrender all their individual rights to the body of society. Under such a "social contract," the state would be governed solely by the law, and the citizen could function at the same time as a free individual and as a member of a society whose exclusive goal is the common good. Indeed, "each man, by giving himself to all, gives himself to nobody"; and as long as no individuals or interest groups gain ascendancy over the rest, there will be a free and responsible citizenry. Thus, in the Rousseauan state, society cannot be answerable for the crimes and sufferings of individuals, nor can there be any leniency toward antisocial misfits.

Such are the basic features of Rousseau's *Social Contract*. That a theory of this sort should have been proposed by one of the most notorious social misfits in history must seem ironical, but it is not particularly surprising, nor does it invalidate its importance in modern political thought. But Rousseau was not content with abstract theory. A perfect society, he realized, would have to be a society of gods, and all human institutions carried the germs of their own decay within them. A good society could neither come into existence nor maintain itself for long unless its members had the necessary moral will. In *Emile*, which he wrote concurrently with *The Social Contract*, Rousseau attempted to show how man's inborn good instincts could be fostered and developed through education and how citizens worthy of the good society could be formed. Since existing society is corrupting, the pupil Emile is brought up far away from urban civilization by a tutor who serves as guide rather than teacher. No ready-made knowledge or moral code is imparted to him: all his learning is derived from direct experience, all his judgments spring from his own intellect and heart. While Rousseau failed in *Emile* to prove the innate goodness of man, he undoubtedly succeeded in laying the basis for modern pedagogy. All education since his day, whether progressive or traditional, rests to a large degree on Rousseau's psychological insights and moral goals.

The Social Contract deals with the good society, that is, a collective body; *Emile* deals with the good citizen, that is, the individual. Unlike some of his critics, Rousseau could see no contradiction between the two works. Within the collective state, the individual potentialities of its members could and should be developed in all their diversity, since free and rational men willing the common good could not help but agree on all essentials. While the two books complement rather than contradict each other, they nevertheless reveal the tension between two poles in Rousseau's temperament. Rousseau the champion of civic virtue and activity was also Rousseau the contemplative, solitary dreamer; a forerunner of Marxist collectivism, he was also one of the ancestors of romantic individualism and of Thoreau's civil disobedience. In both roles—the dour patriot and the eternal adolescent who plays hookey from class—Rousseau reacted against his social environment. This soon became apparent to his friends the philosophes, who tried to enlist him in their cause only to discover that he was not one of them. Although, like him, they criticized society, society was the very air they breathed, whereas he revealed himself increasingly as a crank who shunned society and took offense at everything. The parting of the ways was gradual, but thanks to Rousseau's hypersensitive and morbidly suspicious nature, and to his radical alienation from society, it eventually became complete. "[He] makes me uneasy," Diderot wrote of their final meeting, "and I feel as if a damned soul stood beside me. . . . I never want to see that man again. He could make me believe in devils and in Hell."

The years Rousseau spent at the *Ermitage* and at Montmorency as the guest of Mme d'Epinay and, after breaking with her, as the guest of the Maréchal de Luxembourg were a period of growing isolation. To his friends, Rousseau was guilty of misanthropy, the worst crime in their eyes. To him, their devious methods to regain him for their fold appeared as persecution. At the same time he fell passionately in love with a much younger woman, the beautiful Mme d'Houdetot; since she was in love with another man, she did not reciprocate the middle-aged philosopher's ardor, and even if she had, she would have been disappointed, for, as Rousseau confesses, his passion was invariably spent in anticipation of their trysts. The ludicrous affair further envenomed Rousseau's relations with his meddling friends and undoubtedly helped to unhinge his mind. Yet it also produced a positive result. Jean Jacques, who was addicted to daydreaming and to populating (as he put it) the world with imaginary creatures, dreamed not only of ideal societies and ideal citizens but also of the ideal woman. He incorporated many of Mme d'Houdetot's features in her, called her Julie, and made her the heroine of his epistolary novel *Julie, or the New Héloïse*. With its sensuous descriptions of nature, its vibrant evocation of passion at its paroxysm, and its almost hysterical sensibility the book began a new era in literature, for better or for worse. At the same time its purpose is moral and its tone often quite preachy. Here the theme is the same as in *Emile* and *The Social Contract:* passions, pure in themselves, may overwhelm people whom society has not spoiled, but they can be transcended by the moral will.

By May of 1762 Rousseau had produced, within the space of two

years, three of the most influential works of modern times. His
later writings added nothing new and were intended only to justify
himself before his fellow men. Indeed, the publication of *Emile*
brought catastrophe upon him. It was, in particular, his merciless
attack on revealed religion and on the authority of the Church (in
the "Profession of Faith of the Savoyard Vicar") that drew him
the simultaneous anathema of the Catholic Sorbonne in Paris and
the Calvinist Consistory in Geneva. In both places warrants of arrest were issued against the author; in Paris, *Emile* was burned by
order of Parliament, and as far away as the Netherlands and Switzerland it was officially condemned.

With the connivance of some very high-placed protectors, Rousseau escaped to Switzerland, finally settling at Motiers in what was
then the Prussian principality of Neuchâtel. Though the works
that had been condemned were reprinted in innumerable pirated
editions, Rousseau saw in his fame only a new cause for persecution. The authorities denounced him as a godless rebel and a destroyer of society; his former friends, the philosophes, while osten-
sibly deploring the attacks on him, privately denounced him as a
monster of ingratitude, a hater of men, a savage. His eccentric
ways and clothes and his reputation for godlessness drew upon
him the hatred of the local population; when he was stoned by a
mob, he left Motiers and took refuge on the island of St. Pierre, in
the Lake of Bienne, in Bernese territory. Two months later the
government of Berne expelled him, although he had engaged in no
more subversive activities than botanizing and boating. He accepted David Hume's invitation to join him in England. But his
stay at Hume's country seat, at Wootton, ended with another resounding quarrel. In the eyes of the philosophes his blackness was
demonstrated; they called him a tiger, and open war was declared.

Thus far, it would seem unfair to accuse Rousseau of persecution
mania. His persecution had been very real. It is true that his isolation was due more to shyness and his exaggerated sensibility than
to any initial hostility on the part of his friends, who at worst did
not understand his neurotic personality. Even his persecution by
the authorities can be largely ascribed to himself; the authorities
had bent over backward to help him escape the consequences of
measures they themselves had been forced to take because Rousseau insisted (unlike most of his contemporaries) on signing his
most subversive writings with his real name. But that he was per-
secuted, that his friends had turned hostile and occasionally even
vindictive, there can be no doubt. After his quarrel with Hume,

however, his self-isolation and suspiciousness took on all the symptoms of paranoia.

Returning to France, where he was tolerated on condition that he refrain from publishing his writings, he wandered from place to place with his inseparable Thérèse, and finally fixed himself in Paris, living in poverty on his wages as music copyist, refusing to see anybody for long periods, brooding over his persecution. Everything that had happened to him in the past twenty-five years now appeared to him quite clearly as a universal plot for his destruction. His friends had secretly laid their traps years ago, while he was still unsuspecting; even those who had remained loyal were now suddenly revealing themselves as diabolical accomplices of the archplotter, Grimm. Occasionally he would try to defend himself against their slander by posting public notices, or would denounce their machinations in readings of parts of his *Confessions*. The second part of the *Confessions* reveals these paranoiac traits only too painfully; the dialogues entitled *Rousseau As Judge of Jean Jacques*, despite some brilliant flashes of reason, are even more tragic testimony to the growing darkness in his mind. Yet it would be bold to assert that Rousseau was demented. His last works, soliloquies really—the *Reveries of a Solitary Wanderer*—show by their serenity what a heroic victory he had gained over himself. He still believed in a universal plot against him, but reminding himself of the guiding principles of his own philosophy and of his capacity to find happiness in mere existence, he transcended his mania and found long periods of inner peace. "I laugh at the plots hatched by men," he declared, "and I enjoy my own being in spite of them." He died soon after writing these lines, at Ermenonville, north of Paris, where he was staying as the guest of one of his protectors.

Rousseau's *Confessions* probably remain his most widely read work. They are a unique, amazing, fascinating, shocking, moving, exasperating document. They have done more harm to the appreciation of Rousseau's thought than all the weaknesses that may be found in his other works put together. To psychiatrists, the document is perhaps as interesting for what its author reveals as for what—despite his genuine effort to say everything—remains concealed. It is only natural and fitting that students of the human soul should look at the *Confessions* with a clinical eye and regard the rest of his writings as the outpourings of a psychological cripple. It would be futile to deny that his attack on society was the result of resentment and social inadequacy, or that his compulsion to re-create the world in his imagination was induced by his inability to function "normally," by his sexual inhibitions and his autoerotic tendencies. Rousseau's personality was what psychologists would call immature; moreover, he suffered from a number of psychosomatic problems in addition to his psychological ones. Thus, while he was the reluctant lover of the motherly Madame de Warens, who regarded the act of love as a matter of male hygiene, Jean Jacques suddenly contracted some unusual and alarming symptoms which, according to him, lasted with undiminished intensity throughout the rest of his life; they involved a constant throbbing of his arteries accompanied by a loud noise in his ears in four different pitches. He also suffered from a malformation of the urethra, which caused urine retention. It was this condition that once made him refuse Louis XV's invitation to the Court and thus miss a chance of obtaining a royal pension. He was afraid of wetting himself in His Most Christian Majesty's presence, but he made his refusal appear the proud gesture of a citizen of a republic.

Undoubtedly Rousseau's physiological and psychological handicaps go a long way toward explaining his reaction to society, yet such clinical discussions utterly fail to explain his influence or to invalidate his diagnosis of our social ills. It will never do to brush aside *The Social Contract* because its author lost his mother at birth or suffered from enuresis as a grown man. Oddly enough, however, such criticism is standard. Not only is it irrelevant, it also misrepresents Rousseau's personality.

Far from being the antisocial recluse that he became after his contact with the world of fashion, finance, and intellect, Jean Jacques as a young man had been an exceptionally amiable and good-natured tramp. His penchant for vagrancy never left him. He loved to travel on foot, and he did not always end up at his intended destination. Though he did not shun work, he disliked working more than was necessary for his subsistence, and he treasured idleness above all things. The son of a watchmaker, he looked upon the day he threw away his watch as the beginning of his wisdom. He was fundamentally companionable, at least for the first five decades of his life. He was by no means prudish and, while no Casanova himself, was never a puritan censor of other people's sexual mores. Lacking the drives and ambitions of more settled and responsible men, he found his chief pleasure in the enjoyment of existence for its own sake, in daydreaming, in strolling through the countryside with his dog, in lying down under a tree. Until he experienced his famous illumination on the road to Vincennes, he was, unlike Saint Paul, the most harmless fellow in the world. Surely his sudden change from amiable vagabond to social and moral prophet must have had more immediate causes than a urethral obstruction.

The most obvious explanation is that the social evils which Rousseau diagnosed after his clash with Paris do in fact exist. While more robust temperaments could adjust to them, partly submitting to the inevitable, partly seeking a remedy in practical action ("Let us cultivate our garden," says Candide), Rousseau was by his nature compelled to challenge the entire system. Whether this was practical or wise is a matter for argument; it was inevitable and necessary, and it enabled him to penetrate to the very roots of modern man's dilemma. Science and material progress had not made men happy. On the contrary, in their pursuit of false values, men had forgotten to learn from nature. Rather than be themselves, they strove for the creation of a desirable image of themselves in the eyes of their fellow men. Governed by the opinions of others, they had ceased to be individuals without becoming members of a community. Sacrificing their birthright as citizens and self-determined beings for the sake of security, pleasure, and comfort, they invited the destruction of all freedom. Born free and with the gift of reason, they lived as slaves and dupes. These causes of unhappiness could be blamed neither on God nor on human nature: far from commanding man to submit to fate, God or nature had endowed him with the means to shape his fate. Nature, to Rousseau, did not appear cruel—only natural. But man had become perverse since he used his natural gifts to impress and oppress other men instead of living with them in a free and brotherly community.

Whether one agrees or disagrees with Rousseau's prescriptions, it is impossible not to recognize that his persistent theme, that man's alienation from nature is the price of modern civilization, continues to vex us. His insistence that only man can save himself, that the tools are not lacking but only the will, is truer in our technological age than it was in his own. It is because of this that Rousseau was a prophet. How to simplify man's existence in an increasingly complicated culture remains the great problem. If man is not born good, as Rousseau thought he was, at least he is born with the potentiality for good; and he has reached the point where, if he does not realize that potentiality by a collective effort of the will, he must perish.

*The romantic movement of the late eighteenth and early nineteenth
centuries remains, even at the present day, an elusive phase of the
cultural history of Western man. Though it everywhere drew
inspiration from the writings of that great "Pre-Romantic," Jean
Jacques Rousseau, it developed earlier in some countries than in
others. Beginning invariably as rebellion against tradition, it ended in
some countries in arch-conservatism. In this fervent essay, the eminent
British writer and critic, the late Sir Harold Nicolson, avows his
devotion to Romanticism and strives to say what it fundamentally was.
He recognizes its many contradictions, but extols it as a great
contribution to the liberation of the human spirit. While his essay is
primarily a study of Romanticism in European literature and art, Sir
Harold is not oblivious of its political aspects and its impact on many
branches of human knowledge. Historical study, for example, benefitted
immeasurably from the Romantic devotion to the past and the constant
emphasis on the evolution and continuity of human institutions and
culture.*

THE ROMANTIC REVOLT

HAROLD NICOLSON

"Romanticism," wrote Hippolyte Taine, "imposed itself by opposing everything that had preceded it." Later critics have
contested this pragmatic judgment and have contended that the
divergence between classicism and romanticism is not clear-cut.
They are able to show that elements of pure romanticism can be
discovered even in the works of Alexander Pope, whereas Byron,
who in the early nineteenth century was hailed as the mighty
hierophant of the romantic movement, became wearied of his own
Childe Harold and ended by advocating a more classic mode.

It has thus today become the fashion to disapprove of the terms
"classic" and "romantic" as designating a contrast between two
distinct shades of thought and feeling, and to contend that the
careless use of these two labels may obscure the essential continuity
of letters. I disagree with such assimilations. I am convinced that
in the latter half of the eighteenth century people did in fact become tired of the old doctrines of symmetry or "correctness" and
came to attach importance to freer and more individual methods of
self-expression. A similar revolution in taste has occurred in our
own century, when the old habit of direct communication of meaning has in art, as well as in poetry, been superseded by new methods
of suggesting meaning through association of ideas. The older gen-

115

eration find the new allusive method incomprehensible; the younger generation regard the literary fashions of their parents as uninteresting. The continuity of letters is of course preserved to the extent that mankind will always strive to express beauty; but what to one generation appears eternal beauty will to the next appear stupid and stale. Nor should such transitions of taste and interest, even when abrupt, be dismissed as insignificant: they represent the development, and even the progress, of the aesthetic sense. It is this progress that we have inherited from the Romantic Revolt.

I quite agree with Taine that the romantics, in Germany, in England, and in France, *did* think and feel entirely differently from their classic forebears. They preferred freedom to order, adventure to conformity, surprise to recognition, imagination to correctness, the natural to the artificial, the irregular to the regular, individual experience to tradition. They argued that their aims represented a "return to nature," although they interpreted the word "nature" in many different ways. To some it meant no more than a simpler way of life, in contrast to the rush and rattle of civilized society. To others it signified "freedom"; namely, a return to a primitive age "when wild in woods the noble savage ran," before bad laws and artificial institutions had come to corrupt the virtue of the Golden Age. To others again it suggested religious liberty, a worship of the wonders of nature as contrived and regulated by a Divine Artificer who was above theological dogma and whose relation to mankind was more intimate than anything provided by the rituals of the established churches. To some it represented the peace and quiet of natural scenery, the solitude of woods and remote valleys, the majesty of mountains and waterfalls.

The age of sensibility abolished the frigid eighteenth-century dislike of overt emotion and the contempt of men of culture for anything savoring of what they called "ugly enthusiasm." The classic contention that it was improper for any artist to reveal himself was replaced by the new habit of offering to the public "the pageant of a bleeding heart" and of revealing not only one's personal melancholy and guilt but also one's sins and passions. Rousseau regarded his *Confessions* as a portrait of "the natural man"; Byron devoted his great gift of rhetoric to depicting in *Childe Harold* a sated hedonist who sought to discover in distant countries and uncivilized surroundings the lost stimulus of passion. The satiety of Childe Harold, as the *Weltschmerz* of Werther or the distress and disgust of Chateaubriand's René, became symptoms of what has been described as *le mal du siècle*.

116

It is important to remember that Byron, on attaining incomparable success, became bored by his own romanticism; that Goethe, on becoming an excellent civil servant in Weimar, repudiated poor Werther; and that Chateaubriand ended by becoming the champion of the established church and a conventional, and extremely vain, diplomatist. Thus it can be said that romanticism, which began as a heresy, had not sufficient vitality to establish itself as a doctrine. Yet from 1760 onwards it assuredly transformed the feelings and the thoughts of man.

Since the days of Langland and Chaucer, English literature had always contained a powerful "romantic" element; and the British genius has always tended to prefer freedom to correctness, individual experience to established doctrine, the inductive to the deduc-

Byron

tive, imagination to reason, the inconsequent to the logical, the serpentine to the rectilinear. During the first great phase of English literature, the period from Spenser to Milton, British dramatists and poets reveled in the variety of human adventure and the luxuriance of a rich language. To the French, who had already been taught by Boileau that all excess of feeling or expression was an error of taste, British authors appeared to be men of unkempt savagery, as exotic as today are the Australian aborigines. Voltaire, who lived several years among the English and who acquired some respect for their political sagacity and their reverence for law, continued to regard them as barbarians in intellectual and aesthetic realms. He considered that even Shakespeare, for all his incontestable genius, was, from the literary aspect, comparable only to a Hottentot yodeling in the swamps. And Voltaire during two-thirds of the eighteenth century was the recognized dictator of literary fashion.

The teaching of Boileau, the doctrine of "correctness," crossed the Channel early in the eighteenth century, and by 1733 Alexander Pope had established himself as the high priest of reason and good sense. The British, I am glad to say, are not by nature reasonable, and it was not long before the Augustan Age of English literature produced a reaction. British writers thereafter reverted to the more natural habits of individual expression and free association.

This essay is mainly concerned with the elements of the Romantic Revolt that are operative today. It does not deal with the metaphysical and social results of the revolt, but with the cult of "sensibility" which it introduced and fostered, and with the transformation it effected in man's attitude toward "nature." If we are to understand the suddenness and completeness of that transformation, we can take as an illustration the quick change of attitude toward the art of garden design. This was not a mere by-product of the revolt. It was the earliest symptom of a reaction against the formal; the widest, most rapid, most complete, and most detailed example of the reversal of taste and awareness. Those who contend that in fact there was little difference between the classic and romantic must admit that the change from the classic to the romantic concept of garden design was abrupt, creative, and universal. It illustrates the completeness with which, within two generations, men can change their attitude toward the outside world.

Dr. Johnson was not a romantic. He had no taste for natural beauty. "A blade of grass," he remarked to Mrs. Thrale, "is always a blade of grass: men and women are *my* subjects of enquiry." Whenever Boswell displayed symptoms of becoming romantic, he was sharply snubbed by his formidable companion. Yet Boswell was a natural romantic, and we can observe in his diaries not merely all the symptoms of sensibility but even those of a Wertherlike preoccupation with melancholy (which he called "hypochondria") and guilt. These guilt sensations arose from the decline in religious faith and the growth of skepticism.

The conflict of dogma and the religious wars which followed the Reformation inevitably produced a reaction against dogmatic theology and the discipline of the churches. Voltaire taught men to regard both the tyranny of the Jesuits (which he much exaggerated) and the asceticism of the Puritans and the Jansenists as "infamous superstitions." During the Age of Reason most men of culture proclaimed themselves to be deists who regarded Jehovah as an absurd Hebrew legend and sought their deity in a Divine Mathematician who might well have been a pupil of Newton or a disciple of Locke. Yet for most men and women life without some sort of faith in the supernatural becomes arid and even alarming; they thus turned from the sardonic skepticism of Voltaire to the delights and solaces of sensibility as offered them by Rousseau. According to Rousseau (whose *Julie, or the New Héloïse* was published in 1761) man could only hope to achieve happiness if he abandoned the idea of being clever and sought to become good. He must, with this in mind, develop and exploit a lovely soul, *une belle âme*, which could be acquired only by a "turning to nature" and by a rejection of all the artifices and restrictions of this wicked world. He must give free rein to his emotions, cry frequently, be deeply moved to compassion and acutely sensitive to the majesty of nature. Rousseau, whose teaching was continually drenched in tears, was a crazy genius, gifted with great rhetorical power. His doctrine of sensibility spread throughout the world and filled the vacuum caused by Voltaire's sterile skepticism and by the dry agnosticism of the Encyclopedists and the Paris salons. Even the intellectuals absorbed the fashionable idea that feeling was more important than thought, and it required the emotional and physical excesses of the French Revolution to remind mankind of the importance of balance, reason, and reflection.

For those of us who admire the achievements of romanticism, it is embarrassing to realize that it was the child of unreason. Politically and socially the man of feeling was certainly a better individual than the man of reason and good taste; but emotionalism in politics can prove a dangerous drug, and the cult of sensibility based on individual experience may lead men to become self-centered and render them miserable by the contrast between their dreams and the facts of existence. Goethe, who in his old age regretted that *Werther* had made so many youths conscious of their own inadequacy, decided that order was preferable to disorder and that learning was a sturdier guide than feeling. He was convinced that the *Sturm und Drang* movement, of which as a young man he had been the leader, had caused more misery than happiness, and most epicureans would agree. One of the most valuable legacies of the romantic movement was that it inculcated a social conscience, a gift of compassion, and that it opened the eyes of man to the beauties of nature and to the comfort that a sensitive appreciation of these beauties can provide.

Essentially the romantic movement was a rebellion against convention and an assertion of individualism. Its insistence that all religious dogma and all state institutions were "artificial" produced revolution, agnosticism, and much personal suffering and melancholy. As a political, social, intellectual, and emotional ferment, its effect was destructive in that it weakened faith. But it assuredly enlarged the thinking processes of man and gave to the individual an importance in the scheme of things that he has ever since retained. What today we take for granted as the eternal principles of justice, liberty, and tolerance derives directly from the romantic rebellion. It is therefore pessimistic and incorrect to define its legacy as wholly destructive or negative.

It may have brought melancholy to weak characters and induced much psychological sickness. An emphasis on individualism is apt to render the individual morbidly conscious of his own isolation and inadequacy, until, as with Sören Kierkegaard, he comes to doubt the reality of his own existence. In such defeatist moods the individual may yearn for identification with a group or mass and the protection of some faith and discipline. But to stronger souls the Romantic Revolt brought enlightenment, liberation, self-confidence, and a resolve to develop and express to the uttermost their individual capacities and emotions.

The reliant individual, who was able to master his sensibility, acquired not melancholy and frustration, but an enhanced opportunity for happiness. In the first place, he was liberated from the numbing conviction of original sin, from the sense of unearned guilt, and became convinced that a resolute individual could mold his own destiny. This was a consummate gain. In the second place, it provided him with an almost pantheistic delight in nature, a solace and an enjoyment of which his forebears had been scarcely aware. When I consider the achievements of romanticism, it is not the sickness of the century that I admire, but its vigor.

Thus what I reverence in Byron is not the morbidity of *Childe Harold* or the violent rhetoric of *The Giaour*, but the humorous virility of *Don Juan* and his letters, or the final act of self-sacrifice when he left for Greece *"pour finir en héro son immortel ennui."* What I like about Goethe is not the self-distrust of Werther, but the splendid balance of his Olympian old age. Keats in his letters displays a character more resolute and more intelligent than could be suspected from the perusal of his flabbier poems. The strength and vigor of Shelley's philanthropy is not always apparent in his shrill "romantic" paeans. Lamartine to us appears a poet of exaggerated sensibility, and if we admire Hugo for anything more than his mastery of the music of the French language, we admire him for the astounding vigor which he maintained until he was over eighty years of age. I should not desire for one moment to deny or diminish the value of the contribution made to world literature by the Romantic Revolt. I wish only to assert that it is its vigor rather than its sensibility that attracts me, and that the deep gratitude I feel toward it is based on the fact that it enlarged the horizon of my enjoyment by giving me a delight in nature such as the Augustans never provided or possessed.

Who, to my mind, therefore, were the greatest poets that the Romantic Revolt produced? Not Shelley, not Keats, not even my beloved Byron, and certainly not Lamartine or Hugo. But the young Coleridge and the aged Wordsworth. Coleridge taught us the freedom of imagination. It was Wordsworth who taught us to "feel that we are greater than we know" and who preached that only by the worship of natural beauty could mankind achieve "joy in widest commonalty spread." He at least realized that individualism was not enough and that man was but a seedy animal unless he were able to "erect himself" above himself. For Wordsworth the worship of nature was something more than Rousseau's plangent yearning to escape; it was "an active principle," a grandeur in the beatings of the heart," "a primal sympathy." The intensity of his worship gave him "thoughts that do often lie too deep for tears." Rousseau was incapable of thinking, and his tears were abundant and causeless. Wordsworth has often been reproved for his optimism; yet his was not the vapid optimism of Rousseau, but was based on "the depth, and not the tumult, of the soul," on "man's unconquerable mind," on "spontaneous wisdom breathed by health, truth breathed by cheerfulness." Wordsworth in his mysticism had little sympathy with the materialists and the scientists: he called them "meddling intellects" who "murdered to dissect," and preferred the "heart that watches and receives." His passion for nature was not so much an intellectual as a soothing physical passion:

> . . . a sense sublime
> Of something far more deeply interfused,
> Whose dwelling is the light of setting suns,
> And the round ocean and the living air,
> And the blue sky, and in the mind of man.

We have all today learned the lesson of Wordsworth and are able in moments of lassitude or despair to solace our fears and to revive our hopes by the sight of wood smoke drifting across a forest or the sound of a blackbird's song. Addison, for all his complacency, never experienced such sedative or stimulating affections. The extent to which the Romantic Revolt expanded the frontier of experience is the measure of its creative achievement. It is to this aspect of the romantic legacy that we today most readily respond.

What is so interesting about the Romantic Revolt is that it rapidly infected every aspect of human sensibility and behavior. In music we can trace its stirrings in the genius of Beethoven, its development by Schubert, and finally its cumulating orgy in the operas of Wagner. In painting we have the sudden refusal to accept the classic mode and the replacement of David and Ingres by such younger revolutionaries as Géricault and Delacroix. Delacroix was

Keats   *Coleridge*

much influenced by Constable's painting and the English artist's abandonment of narrative or historical themes for the simpler realities of nature. It is to the change of feeling and method that Géricault and Delacroix introduced that we owe the rejection of all previous academic standards and the great movements that were thereafter initiated by the impressionists and the postimpressionists. Had it not been for the legacy of Constable and the French romantic painters, art would be a wholly different thing today.

The Romantic Revolt also exercised an immense influence on politics and philosophy. In his fervent reaction against all established institutions and conventions Jean Jacques Rousseau, the prophet of sensibility, preached the doctrine of "natural" rights and taught his generation to love.

How therefore should I define the essential legacy bequeathed to us by the Romantic Revolt? I should define it as *individualism.* The men of the early eighteenth century were obsessed by symmetry, by static rules of order, by established conventions, and by the principles of conduct expected of the several classes or castes of society. It was an artificial century. The romantics destroyed these compartments and insisted that every individual had the right to express his own emotions, to seek his own happiness, and to develop his own capacities, unimpeded by social or prescribed compartments. It is difficult for us to realize how compelling were these social formulas, since they have now ceased to be operative.

I believe that the liberation of human personality, both in life and in art, was the most valuable legacy that the romantics handed down. Admittedly it has its difficulties and its limitations. As was

Wordsworth   *Goethe*

shown by Goethe, Byron, and Chateaubriand, individualism may lead to self-absorption, to despair occasioned by the realization of the gulf that separates the real from the ideal, and to the self-hatred of a Werther, a Childe Harold, or a René. In extreme forms this disease leads to the utter cynicism and self-distrust of such thinkers as Schopenhauer, Nietzsche, and Kierkegaard. But in its healthier form it gives us the solemn optimism of Wordsworth or Emerson and the delight in individual effort manifested by Walt Whitman and the ardent pioneers of our vigorous and ever-changing modern world.

I believe passionately in individualism and even in the cult and exploitation of personality, provided that they retain a social conscience and an aim. For me the legacy of the Romantic Revolt is energy and joy.

The trial of Hastings, one of the longest and most dramatic on record, remains of interest today because, firstly, it involved an early attack on what became known later as imperialism, and secondly, because Hastings was accused of crimes against humanity, thus foreshadowing twentieth-century trials of political and military leaders of defeated nations for war crimes. It was Hastings's misfortune that he was attacked and charged by a brilliant and eloquent trio of political enemies. His tragedy lay in the fact that, far from being the villain pictured by his accusers, he actually contributed greatly to the development of just and responsible administration in India. His ultimate acquittal was inevitable, but came only after years of vituperation and degradation.

The late Allan Nevins was noted especially for his many studies of the American Civil War, and twice won the Pulitzer prize in history.

THE TRIAL OF WARREN HASTINGS

ALLAN NEVINS

The most famous political trial of modern times opened in Westminster Hall, London, on February 13, 1788, between nine and ten o'clock in the morning, when evidence upon charges against Warren Hastings, former governor general of India, was taken before the House of Lords. So began the seven-year ordeal by oratory and public slander of Hastings, a man who, only a short time before, had held the fate of princes and dynasties in his hands.

The scene was as imposing as the twenty articles of charge of high crimes and misdemeanors against the eminent defendant. In the middle of the historic hall was placed a large table, at the head of which sat the Lord Chancellor surrounded by the judges, the masters in chancery, the clerks, and a number of law officers. On one side of the hall were placed the green benches of members of the House of Commons. Cloaked in ermine, the peers of the realm sat in the seats of honor. They, along with the lords spiritual of the Church of England, constituted the jury in this, the highest court that English law can convene, a court that had once sat in judgment on Lord Chancellor Francis Bacon and that had sent to the

During the period of his rise through the ranks of the East India Company, Warren Hastings posed for a portrait by Joshua Reynolds.

executioner the Earl of Strafford on the eve of the Civil War. Not for sixty-three years had this high court been assembled, and amid the great crowd jammed into the visitors' circle some of the great names of the day were to be seen: among them the actress Sarah Kemble Siddons, the historian Edward Gibbon, and the painter Sir Joshua Reynolds.

The proceedings formally began at twelve o'clock noon, when the managers of the prosecution entered. The diarist Fanny Burney, who had received her ticket from the queen, describes how "I shuddered, and drew involuntarily back, when, as the doors were flung open, I saw Mr. Burke, as Head of the Committee, make his solemn entry. He held a scroll in his hand, and walked alone, his brow knit with corroding care and deep laboring thought."

"How did I grieve," exclaims Miss Burney, "to behold him now, the cruel Prosecutor . . . of an injured and innocent man!" Edmund Burke was followed by an able and famous group of men. They included Charles James Fox, redoubtable leader of the Whigs, and Richard Brinsley Sheridan, dramatist and parliamentary orator. As the members of the House of Commons took their seats on their benches, the sergeant at arms rose and commanded silence in the court. A stentorian voice rang out: "Warren Hastings, Esquire, come forth! Answer to the charges brought against you; save your bail, or forfeit your recognizance!"

At this summons the small, frail figure of Hastings was brought to the bar of the House. The moment he emerged into full view he made a low bow to the Lord Chancellor and to the court; indeed, he bowed three times. "What an awful moment this for such a man!" writes Miss Burney, "—a man fallen from such height of power to a situation so humiliating—from the almost absolute command of so large a part of the Eastern World to be cast at the feet of his enemies, of the great tribunal of his country . . ."

It is not strange that so impressive an event created a sensation among the English-speaking peoples of the world and all admirers of British law. Nor is it strange that all subsequent impeachment trials, including that of President Andrew Johnson after the American Civil War, have followed the precedents of this great trial.

The impeachment of Warren Hastings was rendered the more memorable because it took place against the background of a chapter of Asiatic history full of color and melodramatic events. An old order was dying in India, and a new one was being born. Just as the French revolutionists were soon to overthrow the *ancien régime* in France, so now a body of reformers were determined to destroy the prevailing system in India. Before the struggle ended, the old British Empire was brought under such heavy fire that its ultimate replacement by the British Commonwealth was plainly foreshadowed.

The trial was to center with cruel concentration upon Hastings, but the issues were more than merely personal. Thanks to the military genius of Robert Clive, and to the administrative talent of Hastings himself, the East India Company had recently established a dominion over India that no Asian power had been able to achieve. But the rule of the company was authoritarian, and what was more disturbing, it was pervasively corrupt.

In the first half of the eighteenth century the agents of the East India Company had been traders, determined men who braved the heat, the disease, and the sodden monotony of India for only one reason: the hope of riches. The site of Calcutta, the headquarters of the company, was repellent. Built on an ill-drained swamp, it was full of cesspools and surrounded by a malaria-ridden jungle. Englishmen like Thackeray's Jos Sedley, who went out to make their fortunes, battled with clouds of flies and mosquitoes, with the sultry heat, and with diseases more deadly than tigers or cobras. Travel in Bengal was extremely dangerous. The roads were wretched, so that most communication was by river. The country was infested with bands of *dacoits* (robbers) and by wandering thugs—the word is of Indian origin—who were religious fanatics addicted to murder. Only the hope of wealth induced men to suffer such discomforts and perils. Kipling later summed up the special character of Calcutta in a line from his "Song of the Cities of India": "Death in my hands, but Gold!"

At that time, the men who sought their fortunes in Bengal were still only traders licensed by the nominal heads of India, the Mogul emperors at Delhi. When Clive and Hastings arrived on the scene, however, the Mogul Empire was rapidly breaking up, and both the French and the British saw an opportunity to take control. Two men of more divergent gifts and temperament it would be difficult to find. Clive was a man of action, dynamic and practical; Hastings was a man of thought, energetic enough, but scholarly in his tastes and philosophical in his outlook. Clive was the harsher of the two and was subject to fits of depression and gloom (it was during one of these that he was eventually to take his own life). In 1756, when the nawab who controlled Bengal quarreled with the British, overwhelmed their forces in Calcutta, and shut his prisoners in the infamous "Black Hole," from which only a few escaped alive, Clive took masterful action. His little army of British troops and native allies overcame Mogul forces of twenty times their number at the Battle of Plassey, and Bengal dropped like a ripe pear into his hands, a country as large as France and nearly as rich.

Virtually overnight the agents of the East India Company had become territorial magnates wielding political power. They were not slow to reap the advantages. Increasingly, in the years after Plassey, reports of bribery, extortion, and vicious crimes of every nature began to pour into England, and many Britons became convinced that the fair name of England was being sullied by company agents. The very term Anglo-Indian was becoming a byword for extortionate greed. The sight of a few fabulously wealthy Anglo-Indians, the famed "nabobs" of the day, seemed proof enough to many that the rumors and reports were true. As that sprightly observer, Horace Walpole, remarked at the time, "We are Spaniards in our lust for gold, and Dutch in our delicacy of obtaining it."

In truth, the whole structure of Indian government was wrong. It was wrong that a set of merchants should hold imperial power. It was wrong that a company interested primarily in trade should enjoy such political authority. The revolt of the thirteen colonies made thinking Britons more sensitive to such considerations. Three and a half years before the trial of Hastings began, an India Act had been passed, putting the company partly under the control of the Crown and leading to Hastings's resignation as governor general. But the company agents were still the men on the scene, and they were several thousand miles from London in an age of sailing ships. To many reformers the Act itself was no guarantee of a change of spirit, nor did it establish the fundamental principle that it was wrong for one people to rule over another entirely in their own interest. This last was a new idea, and Edmund Burke was its champion. He intended, at this late juncture of his carrer, to drive this new conception home to the nation, and more importantly, to the agents of the East India Company serving abroad. The object lesson he chose for his educational task was Warren Hastings, and it was a savagely ironic choice, for Hastings believed as strongly as anyone that British rule in India must be equitable and fair.

Hastings had gone to India in 1750, at the age of seventeen, to serve in the lowly post of mercantile clerk in the East India Company at a yearly salary of £36. Ambitious, tactful, and patient, he had expected to rise step by step in the company hierarchy, earn the right to engage in trade for himself—the great perquisite of the company agent—and reap, in time, a well-earned fortune. He was

only twenty-three when the victory at Plassey launched the East
India Company into the deep and troubled waters of Indian politics. The situation was wholly new and called for new talents.
Hastings, a studious and quietly self-confident young man, possessed what was needed. A scholar among a band of narrow merchants, he taught himself Persian, the lingua franca of Mogul
India. A keen observer—and respecter—of local laws and customs,
he rose rapidly among men who looked with cold indifference on
the "natives" who had so surprisingly come under their control.

In 1772, when Hastings was named governor general of India, he
wielded more power over more people than any monarch in Europe.
It was, however, a strange kind of monarchy, for the monarch,
Hastings, was bound hand and foot by a single overriding require-
ment: he had to show a profit; for profit was what the managers of
the company at India House in London ceaselessly demanded of
him, regardless of wars, defense against invasion, or any other
costs of governing. Hastings gave them their profit and simultaneously attempted to cleanse the system of its worst defects. It
was Hastings who, almost singlehandedly, laid the basis of just and
responsible rule in India. He was a great man in a corrupt system,
and he now faced a supreme test of his spiritual endurance; the
most eloquent of adversaries were bent on portraying him as the
wicked architect of the system itself.

The constellation of great names arrayed against Hastings at the
trial requires some critical examination. By far the most illustrious
figure was Edmund Burke. One of the greatest of British political
philosophers, Burke gave unremitting support to the cause of freedom in Britain, the American colonies, Ireland, and France. Although he never held a seat in any British ministry, he was one of
the boldest and most powerful figures on the political scene. Beside
him stood Charles James Fox. Fox had brought into Parliament a
daring but, in principle, sound measure for transferring virtually
all the authority of the East India Company to the Crown. He had
not been able to carry this, and he awaited new opportunities. He
was a romantic figure, dashing and reckless, but he lacked balance.
His private life was notoriously profligate, and he was known as
one of the greatest gamblers of his time. He had drawn into Whig
politics Richard Sheridan, who had followed his successful play
The Rivals, with a still greater triumph, *The School for Scandal*.
Sheridan had been elected to Parliament from Stafford in 1780. For
his opposition to the American war, the Continental Congress had
offered him a large gift, which he had refused.

But the management of the trial, and the driving force of the proceedings, were supplied by Burke. The "member for India," as his admirers called him, was a man of principle, filled with righteous indignation over the exploitation of the Indian people and conscious of the gross impropriety of entrusting the government of the great subcontinent to a chartered commercial company. Long before the trial Burke had denounced the company and decried its rule. Where, he had asked five years earlier, were the bridges and roads, the law courts and noble monuments, that even the cruelest of conquerors leave behind them? "Were we to be driven out of India this day, nothing would remain to tell that it had been possessed during the inglorious period of our dominance, by anything better than the orang-u-tang or the tiger." But Burke's vivid imagination drove him, at times, beyond the limits of reason.

On the third day of the trial the prosecution began to introduce its charges against Hastings. In his opening speech Burke scaled the heights of interpretative eloquence:

I impeach Warren Hastings, Esquire, of high crimes and misdemeanors.

I impeach him in the name of the Commons of Great Britain in Parliament assembled, whose Parliamentary trust he has betrayed.

I impeach him in the name of all Commons of Great Britain, whose national character he has dishonored.

I impeach him in the name of the people of India, whose laws, rights, and liberties he has subverted, whose properties he has destroyed, whose country he has laid waste and desolate.

I impeach him in the name of human nature itself, which he has cruelly outraged, injured, oppressed, in both sexes, in every age, rank, situation, and condition of life.

Hastings was accused of a vast catalogue of misdeeds: fraud, treachery, robbery, murder, "cruelties unheard of and devastations almost without a name." As Burke's magniloquent descriptions and thundering denunciations rolled across Westminster Hall, two things became apparent. The first was that Burke intended to try Hastings, not so much for any individual acts, but for what a later generation would call crimes against humanity: the ruin of the innocent, the turning of lands into deserts. Secondly, it was clear that the trial would not proceed very rapidly; Burke's opening speech, which was one of the greatest of his career, lasted four days, and there was more, much more, to come.

It must have seemed then, even to an objective observer, that Hastings was guilty. To a man ignorant of the chaos and complexity, the intrigue and the dangers, that were normal conditions

of Indian politics, the actions of Hastings might well have seemed
as black as his accusers painted them. So it was with the first high
crime with which Hastings was charged, and which Fox now described in a powerful speech of his own. It was alleged by the
prosecution that Hastings had attempted, without right, and in a
spirit of vengeance, to extort an enormous sum of money from the
rajah of Benares, a demand that Hastings had backed up by trying
to imprison the rajah and then violently suppressing an insurrection of his outraged people. The court was asked to behold a man
so sunk in iniquity that he had shed the blood of a peaceful people
so that India House might write its ledgers in black ink.

The second indictment for high crime proved even more sensational, and the hall was packed with an excited mass of spectators,
for the glamourous Sheridan was scheduled to sum up the charge.
The prosecution now alleged that Hastings had forced two hapless
Indian princesses to transfer £1,200,000 worth of land and treasures to their worthless son and grandson, the vizier of Oudh, so
that he could give it over to the company in payment of his debts.
Two noble ladies set upon by a heartless rogue: Sheridan did not
waste the opportunity for dramatics. Filial piety was his grand
theme, filial piety and its ugly betrayal by a dissolute son in the
grip of an evil corrupter, Warren Hastings, whom he pictured
"now cringing on his prey, and fawning on his vengeance! now
quickening the limpid pace of Craft, and forcing every stand that
retiring nature can make in the heart! the attachments and the
decorums of life! each emotion of tenderness and honor! and all the
distinctions of national characteristics! with a long catalogue of
crimes and aggravations, beyond the reach of thought for human
malignity to perpetrate, or human vengeance to punish!"

Turning the legal charge into a Shakespearean tragedy, Sheridan
unfurled one of the greatest speeches in British history. Finished,
he fell back into Burke's arms.

By now, more than a month had passed, and with several more
charges to be read, it was obvious that at this rate the trial might
take a decade to run its course. Besides, the court did not sit in
continuous session. The peers of the realm, as Macaulay said in his
famous essay on Hastings, did not intend to let jury duty interfere
with partridge shooting, no matter how grave the case. Perhaps
they were growing restive under the onslaught of invective poured
out against the silent defendant, for it poured out with ever-increasing intensity. Again, Burke led the way. He intended to leave
no room for mercy, not even the mercy of thinking that Hastings's

131

crimes were, at least, imperial ones. They are, said Burke, "of the groveling kind, which do not usually grow upon a throne, but are hatched in dunghills." Hastings, he said, had beggared the flower of Indian nobility to fatten the company's coffers, and his own. "He could not so much as dine without creating a famine." Day after day, month after month, the onslaught continued.

Hastings, meanwhile, labored without cessation to prepare arguments stating *his* side of the case. "My days pass in incessant writing and reading, and ever close with weariness," he wrote to his devoted wife, Marian. The Mogul crown prince was on his side. Most important of all, the officers of the East India Company stood with him. As more facts came to light, the black picture painted by Burke and his allies began to take on more suffused hues. The extortionate demands upon the rajah of Benares were seen to be in accord with Mogul law, a justified act of statecraft. The two princesses, pathetic victims of Hastings in Sheridan's great speech, turned out, of all things, to look upon their alleged tormentor as their friend. The complicated charges of robbery, bribery, selling offices, and so on all fell apart, as witnesses—even prosecution witnesses—came to Hastings's defense.

It was four years before Hastings finally had a chance to speak for himself. He spoke forthrightly of the conditions in India, of the harsh necessities of rule, of the progress he had made in government, of the prosperity that existed in the alleged "desert" of Bengal, and of the beggared nobles who yet looked upon him as an honored friend. As for the allegation that he made an illicit fortune, Hastings assured the court that had greed been his motive, he could have made, with his power, a hundred times the fortune in half the time that he served. "I gave you all, and you have rewarded me with confiscation, disgrace, and a life of impeachment."

As the case progressed, it became clear that his opponents were damaging themselves by their vitriolic intemperance. A reaction was setting in. By the middle of the trial Burke and the prosecution were looked upon by many as "political banditti" and the allegedly criminal Hastings as "the Savior of India." Indeed, the weight of evidence at the trial tended to prove that Warren Hastings had done great work in organizing and maintaining all that Clive had won in India. He had shown great ability and unconquerable courage. In effect, he had saved British supremacy in India by his swift and resourceful actions. The verdict of historians is that he should have been rewarded instead of being punished. In

particular, historians have rejected as unsound the prejudiced and

The POLITICAL BANDITTI assailing the SAVIOUR of INDIA.

The "political banditti" in this pro-Hastings cartoon are, from left to right, Edmund Burke, Lord North, and Charles James Fox.

overrhetorical verdict of Macaulay in his essay on Hastings. This is also the opinion of an impartial American journalist and historian. "There is no department of government, of which he was not master," writes A. Mervyn Davies in his biography of Hastings. "The extent of his versatility, of his breadth of vision and manifold interests, is even better shown by what he did outside the scope of his ordinary duties than by what he did inside, remarkable as that was. He was, indeed, the ideal ruler, not content merely to administer and to govern but reaching out to the higher realms of the mind, working to extend the bounds of knowledge and improve the intangibles of civilization."

The outcome of the trial, which dragged on for another three years, could be predicted long before its end. Nearly everyone assumed that Hastings would be acquitted. The final scene came on April 23, 1795, before a great crowd. Hastings was ordered in and was then told to withdraw. Sixteen questions were put to each peer in turn, and each was asked to give his verdict of guilty or not guilty. Only twenty-nine peers in all appeared in their robes to give

133

formal reply. The others, who had not attended regularly, were silent; they abstained from voting. On every charge the vote was heavily for acquittal—heavily but not unanimously, leaving just sufficient room for doubt to make the entire proceedings inconclusive.

The trial had cost Hastings several years of his life and a fortune in legal fees. It ruined forever any chance he might have had for a public life or for the peerage that he had once fully expected as his reward for service in India. He retired to the country, having reclaimed with what was left of his wealth the old family estate, Daylesford House in Worcestershire, where he lived until his death in 1818. As for India, the trial led to no new legislation. Two years after the verdict was passed, Edmund Burke himself was dead, though he had proved one point at the cruel expense of Hastings. The fate of the former governor general served notice to East India agents that England would no longer tolerate vice and corruption, even among the most powerful and most firmly entrenched.

The trial may have been inconclusive, but nonetheless men would remember it for years to come. They would recall Burke's extraordinary opening speech and recall how he and Fox and Sheridan had exhausted the rhetoric of invective in their savage pursuit of Warren Hastings. They might remember, too, Hastings's murmured denial, "It's a lie," as he sat hearing himself accused of the most infamous deeds. That murmured cry history would vindicate.

*Nelson's victory over the French fleet at Abukir Bay, at the mouth of
the Nile, was, according to the author of this essay, in some respects
even more important than his later triumph at Trafalgar (1805). Not
only was the Battle of the Nile Napoleon's first major reverse and as
such a stimulus to resistance to French domination, but it sealed the
fate of the French adventure in Egypt. By blasting Napoleon's dreams
of conquest in the East, it necessitated a basic diversion in the course of
European history.*

*While the Battle of Lepanto was a battle of galleys and galleasses,
in which soldiers boarded the enemy ships and fought hand-to-hand,
as on land, the Battle of the Nile was one of huge ships of the line,
a battle of guns firing broadside. Mr. Bradford's account, taken from
his* Mediterranean: Portrait of a Sea, *gives a vivid portrait of life
on these huge gun platforms as well as a clear picture of Nelson's
tactics in his first major victory.*

THE BATTLE OF THE NILE

ERNLE BRADFORD

The French Revolutionary and Napoleonic wars, lasting from
1792 to 1815, were fought on the battlefields of Europe, on the
great oceans of the world, and on the Mediterranean Sea. It was
here, indeed, that disaster overtook Napoleon, when his expedition
to Egypt was shattered by the loss of his whole fleet in the Battle
of the Nile. Whereas on land the revolutionary ardor of the French
nation was at one time or another turned against almost every nation in Europe, at sea the conflict was largely between two nations,
England and France. In the end, although Napoleon's ambitions
were terminated on the field of Waterloo, the struggle at sea decided the issue and determined the course of the century that was
to follow. As with Carthage and Rome, it was a battle between
leviathan and behemoth, a sea empire confronting a land empire, a
nation of merchants and traders fighting against a nation of hardy
peasant farmers. In this case—and only because the British, unlike
the Carthaginians, did not forget that their existence depended
upon mastery of the sea—the issue was differently resolved. Napoleon, war lord, lawgiver, and statesman, had as great a dislike of
the sea as any ancient Roman. Lord Nelson, on the other hand,
only faltered when he stepped ashore.

Behold the man-of-war, the sailing ship of the line, which swept
the Mediterranean from the Strait of Gibraltar to the Levant. The
ship comes proudly driving toward us, as she soars, lifts, and fal-

ters over the uneasy swell of the Bay of Biscay. Bound for the
Mediterranean theatre of war, she looks as beautiful and assured
as any sea bird. Whether English or French, her composition differed only in minor points—frequently, when it came to design and
manning, to the advantage of the French. Good though the English naval architects were, the French were often their superiors,
and as for the methods of manning their vessels, the French were
certainly more intelligent. The French, for example, gave special
pay to their fishermen to induce them to train and learn in the
equivalent to a naval reserve. The English, on the other hand,
still depended largely upon "pressed men"—forcibly conscripted
sailors—to man what Admiral Mahan has described as "those far-
distant, storm-beaten ships, upon which the Grand Army never
looked, but which for ever stood between it and the dominion of
the World."

Present in the Mediterranean during the Revolutionary and Napoleonic wars was the most famous warship in history, H.M.S.
Victory. Since she was in many respects typical of the great ships of
the line that were to dominate the sea until the advent of steam,
some description of her, and of life aboard her, may help to set the
scene for certain events of the late eighteenth and early nineteenth
centuries. Launched at Old Single Dock, Chatham, Kent, in 1765,
the *Victory* was the fifth ship of the Royal Navy to bear that name.
The first had been the flagship of Sir John Hawkins in the Armada
campaign of 1588. That Elizabethan galleon had displaced 560
tons, but the new *Victory*, fairly typical of other large ships of the
line, was registered at 2,162 tons—although it has been estimated
that she displaced nearer 3,500.

This ship, of which Thackeray said, "the bones of the *Victory*
ought to be sacred relics for Englishmen to worship," was built
chiefly of English oak and elm. Her hull was more than two feet
thick; her sternpost was made of one huge oak tree, and much of
the wood used in her construction came from trees that were at
least a hundred years old. Her keel—more than 150 feet long—was
made of teak, one of the hardest and most worm-resistant woods in
the world, and this again was protected by a false keel of elm. Her
fastenings consisted of oak pins, known as trennels, and copper
bolts six feet long and two inches in diameter. Both in her materials and in the weight of her construction, she was something that

*J.M.W. Turner's painting of a three-decker provisioning con-
veys the majestic proportions of the battleships of the age of sail.*

no Mediterranean shipbuilder of the past could ever have conceived of.

Her complement was upwards of 850 men, and she had sufficient water and provisions to stay at sea for four months, while she carried enough powder and shot to last her—short of some major action—three years. The most remarkable feature of these giant sailing ships was the enormous weight of metal they carried, for by now it was well understood that the broadside determined battles, and indeed, the fate of empires. A ship like the *Victory* was known as a three-decker, after her three gun decks (there were, in fact, seven different levels on such a vessel). A ship of this kind was a floating gun platform: the lower gun deck carried the heaviest guns, 32-pounders; the middle carried 24-pounders; and the upper, 12-pounders.

The term broadside—of which so much has been written both in history and in fiction—did not mean that all the guns on one side were fired at the same moment. Strong though these ships were, they could never have withstood such a concussion. "Ripple firing," whereby the guns were fired consecutively from forward to aft, was what took place during a broadside action. By the time the afterguns were firing, the forward guns were all reloaded and ready to repeat the "ripple" fire. The upper gun deck aimed at the enemy's masts and rigging, while the two lower decks sought to blow her sides to pieces. Such actions, sometimes lasting for a number of hours, were about the bloodiest and most murderous in the whole history of warfare at sea.

Much has been said about the condition of the men who manned the galleys of the Mediterranean during this and earlier periods. The expression "like a galley slave" has passed into the English language to indicate almost insupportable toil, but the fact remains that—although he was theoretically a free man—the life of a sailor aboard a great ship of the line was as hard as any galley slave's. "Wooden ships need iron men" was hardly an exaggeration.

A large number of the seamen aboard the *Victory* and her sister ships in the Royal Navy had been forcibly pressed into service. The Vagrancy Act laid down that "all disreputable persons" (which might mean anyone found in a tavern, let alone a bawdy-house, or even walking peaceably down the streets of a fishing port) were liable for impressment. So were fishermen, merchant seamen, and canalmen or inland watermen—if they were unfortunate enough to be caught by the press gang. Since so large a percentage of a ship's company was forcibly conscripted, discipline

aboard had to be of an iron-bound severity. The citizens of England who manned Her Majesty's ships during the Napoleonic wars
were ill-clad, ill-used, and to a large extent, unwilling, seamen.

Some indication of the sailor's lot can be gauged from a book
published during this period, called *Nautical Economy; or, Fore-
castle Recollections of Events during the last War. Dedicated to the
Brave Tars of Old England by a Sailor, politely called by the officers
of the Navy, Jack Nasty-Face.* Even allowing for the fact that
"Jack" was a deeply embittered man, there can be little denying
the truth of his account, for it is substantiated by a number of
others. "Out of a fleet of nine sail of the line I was with," he wrote,
"there were only two captains thus distinguished [for their human-
ity]. They kept order on board without resorting to the frequent
and unnecessary call upon the boatswain and his cat, adopted by
the other seven; and what was the consequence? Those two ships
beat us in reefing and furling; for they were not in fear and dread,
well knowing they would not be punished without a real and just
cause."

Jack goes on to describe the discipline that prevailed aboard
those "storm-beaten ships": "The cat-of-nine-tails is applied to the
bare back, and at about every six lashes a fresh boatswain's mate is
ordered to relieve the executioner of this duty, until the prisoner
has received, perhaps, twenty-five lashes . . . [He is] conveyed from
ship to ship, receiving alongside of each a similar number of stripes
with the cat until his sentence is completed. . . . his back resembles
so much putrified liver, and every stroke of the cat brings away the
congealed blood; and the boatswain's mates are looked at with the
eye of a hawk to see they do their duty, and clear the cat's tails
after every stroke, the blood at the time streaming through their
fingers: and in this manner are men in the navy punished for different offences, more particularly impressed men who attempt to
make their escape." This was the world of the human machinery
that fought the *Victory*'s canvas in a gale or her guns in action—the
ship so beautiful to the outward eye as she buried the green rollers
of the sea beneath her dolphin striker and stumbled toward Cape
Trafalgar over the awkward Biscay swell.

Nelson himself was one of the few commanders of his time who
tried to improve the conditions of his sailors. He might well have
been one of those two captains whom Jack describes as keeping
order on board without resorting to "the boatswain and his cat."
Apart from being a genius as a sailor, Nelson was a sensitive man.
He knew—as Drake had known centuries before him—that the

seaman is every whit as entitled to fair and reasonable conditions as any other man. Since his captains, whom he called his "Band of Brothers," always sought to emulate him, Nelson no doubt played a large part in improving the lot of the British seaman.

The food of these men was simple enough. Breakfast "usually consists of burgoo, made of coarse oatmeal and water; others will have Scotch coffee, which is burnt bread boiled in some water, and sweetened with sugar." At noon, "the pleasantest part of the day . . . every man and boy is allowed a pint, that is, one gill of rum and three of water, to which is added lemon acid, sweetened with sugar." The main dish consisted of salt beef or pork with pease pudding, and for supper "half a pint of wine, or a pint of grog, to each man, with biscuit, and cheese or butter." Life aboard may have been hard, the discipline harsh, but the food in general compared favorably with that of the country laborer of the time. And the sailor always had the chance of winning some prize money.

The whole ship existed to serve the guns. In the sight, smell, service, and thunder of them the sailor lived and died. The *Victory*'s true and indomitable face was revealed as soon as she stripped for action. Even the comparatively elegant quarters of the admiral were denuded of their furniture and gear, which was sent down to the main hold below the water line. From the lower deck, where the majority of the seamen slept and fed, the men's hammocks were taken up top and lashed along the bulwarks to serve as protection against flying splinters and the bullets of enemy marksmen. (A high proportion of the casualties suffered in action was caused by splinters of wood gouged out of the ships' decks and sides by cannon balls.)

The men fought the guns stripped to the waist, with a handkerchief tied around their forehead and ears to keep the sweat out of their eyes and to protect their ears against the deafening thunder of the guns. They worked barefoot, and the decks were swilled with sea water to reduce the risk of fire, as well as sprinkled with sand to prevent the sailors from slipping. The mortally wounded and the dead were thrown overboard without ceremony. Those whose wounds were within the limited capacity of the surgeons were taken down to the afterpart of the orlop deck, the cockpit. This area was painted red so the wounded would not notice how much of that red was their own blood. There were no anesthetics, and major operations were undertaken either by stunning the patient or, if time permitted, by getting him blind drunk on brandy or rum. As often as not, the strong arms of the surgeon's mates held the wounded down. The same hot pitch that served to calk the ship's seams was used to seal amputations, while gunpowder, sea salt, and brandy or rum were used as primitive antiseptics.

The officers could expect no more than the men if they had the misfortune to be wounded. Nelson himself, who in a lifetime of action had lost both an arm and the sight of an eye, could hope for no better medical attention than that given to the humblest ordinary seaman. It was a hard life and it bred hard men, but that they were not necessarily insensitive is proved by Nelson among many others. The sea life has always had its compensations, and many sailors retained a vein of poetry that their rough exteriors belied. As one commander wrote to his wife: "To be sure I lose the fruits of the earth, but then I am gathering the flowers of the sea."

The wars with revolutionary France, in which Britain was strong at sea but militarily weak, dragged on for many years. The focus sharpened upon the Mediterranean theatre in 1793, when a young British naval captain, Horatio Nelson, who had been, in the phrase, "on the beach" for five years, received a new seagoing appointment. As he wrote his wife: "The Admiralty so smile upon me, that really I am as much surprised as when they frowned. Lord Chatham yesterday made many apologies for not having given me a Ship before this time, and said, that if I chose to take a Sixty-four to begin with, I should be appointed to one as soon as she was ready; and whenever it was in his power, I should be removed into a Seventy-four. Everything indicates War. One of our ships, looking into Brest, has been fired into."

The 64-gun ship of the line to which Nelson was appointed as captain was the *Agamemnon*—a name appropriate enough to the Mediterranean, whither she was immediately dispatched under the command of Admiral Hood. Aided by French Royalists, the British fleet enjoyed an immediate success, capturing the great port and naval base of Toulon, which was shortly retaken by the French revolutionary forces—prominent among whose officers was a young commander of the artillery named Napoleon Bonaparte. The following year, 1794, during the siege of Calvi in Corsica, Nelson lost the sight of his right eye when a shot from the French garrison landed near the battery where he was engaged, throwing up a mass of sand and splinters that stuck him in the face.

During these years, while he was learning to become, as he later put it, "An old Mediterranean man," his duties were similar to those of dozens of other sea captains engaged around the French coast, or off Corsica and Sardinia, or in the long stretches of sea west of Sicily. British convoys had to be protected, contraband runners had to be intercepted, and there was sometimes an occasional brush with the enemy. But in the main the sailor's time was spent in long, frustrating days at sea, with the ship's bottom growing foul in the warm water and the sunbaked ropes and canvas chafing and fraying in idle weather, or blowing away in one of the sudden and fierce storms typical of the area. After one engagement, in which Nelson had distinguished himself by capturing the huge 84-gun *Ca Ira* with his 64-gun *Agamemnon*, he confessed in a letter to his wife: "I wish to be an Admiral, and in command of the English fleet; I should very soon either do much, or be ruined: my disposition cannot bear tame and slow measures."

Another whose disposition could not bear "tame and slow measures" was the great Corsican, who was soon to take the French Revolution all over Europe and the East. At the age of twenty-six Bonaparte, already a general, had entered Italy with an army of about forty thousand half-starved soldiers in want of everything except the fire and spirit that their revolutionary fervor had kindled within them. In words that might have been spoken long centuries before by Hannibal, he addressed them as follows: "You are badly fed and all but naked. . . . I am about to lead you into the most fertile plains in the world. Before you are great cities and rich provinces; there we shall find honour, glory, and riches."

His promises were soon fulfilled, the Italian people hailing him as the man who liberated them from their Austrian masters. All over Europe nations were welcoming the new ideas of revolutionary France that were bursting open the old wineskins of royalist and feudal centuries. Czarist Russia, for obvious reasons, was hostile, while England was anxious not only about the threat to her own security that a united Europe might pose but also about the threat to her overseas empire. Having lost the thirteen colonies, England's great concern now was India, and Napoleon was already looking in that direction. Beyond Italy lay the sea route to Egypt, and beyond Egypt lay all the wealth of the East.

Napoleon embodied, in his concept of his mission, all the dreams of his great predecessors. He had, first of all, a vision of restoring the ancient Roman Empire. The whole of the Mediterranean area, Italy, Spain, Egypt, and the adjacent countries of the Levant, should be united within one framework under the dominance of France. Napoleon saw himself as the Caesar of this new empire, but he also dreamed of being an Alexander. Beyond a united Mediterranean he looked eastward, as had the great Macedonian, and it was this aspect of his nature that alarmed the English more than anything else. Had Napoleon confined his actions to the Continent, the English might possibly, if unwillingly, have accepted the imperial *fait accompli*. But the threat to their great Eastern empire was something they could never tolerate.

While Italy was being turned into a block of republics on the French model, Napoleon's eyes were fixed upon the islands lying to the south of him. He regarded them as steppingstones to the East. Since fertile and fruitful Sicily was barred to him by the sun-bleached canvases, the oak hulls, and the 32-pounders of the Royal Navy, he looked farther southward and saw in Malta, as so many had seen before him, the perfect harbor from which to dominate the Mediterranean. It would be some years, however, before he would make a move in that direction—years in which the French were everywhere successful on land and in which the British tried as far as possible to contain them by sea. But by the latter part of 1796 the British position in the Mediterranean had clearly become untenable—for the moment, at any rate. The French were masters of the Continent; and keeping three fleets in being—one in the Mediterranean, another based at Gibraltar and Portugal (England's only ally at the time), and the third at the western approaches to the Channel—was straining English resources.

The British therefore withdrew to Gibraltar, their one secure fortress and the key to control of the sea gates. Not long after this, in an unsuccessful attack on Tenerife in the Canary Islands, Nelson (by now an admiral) lost his right arm, which was taken off at the elbow after he was hit by grapeshot. He was convinced that his career was over, that only retirement lay ahead, and that he would never more command the ships of England against the French, for whom he felt a passionate hatred. Curiously enough, Nelson never seems to have disliked his Spanish opponents, often, indeed, expressing his admiration for them. But he hated the French and everything they stood for, which, to his conservative nature, seemed to be the destruction of all law, order, and decency.

He wrote at this time to his commander in chief, Earl St. Vincent: "I am become a burthen to my friends and useless to my Country. When I leave your command, I become dead to the world; I go hence and am no more seen." To this St. Vincent replied: "Mortals cannot command success. You and your companions have certainly deserved it, by the greatest degree of heroism and perseverance that ever was exhibited." At that moment in time neither man could have foreseen that within a year the

Nelson wears the star of a Knight of the Bath in Lemuel Abbott's portrait, painted less than a year before the Battle of the Nile.

British would be back in force in the Mediterranean, let alone that within a year Nelson would have gained one of the most outstanding victories ever to take place on that sea.

Napoleon, in the meantime, had come to realize that the French fleet was in no state to carry out the great invasion of England that had been planned. Large-scale invasion of the arrogant island was still the dream of the French Republic, but Napoleon was wise enough to see that it must be deferred. The immediate aim must be to strike in the East in order to threaten India. To achieve this objective, an immense fleet and army must be assembled as quickly as possible in the Mediterranean. He explained to the Directory in Paris that his plans were "To go to Egypt, to establish myself there and found a French Colony [which] will require several months. But, as soon as I have made England tremble for the safety of India, I shall return to Paris, and give the enemy its death-blow. There is nothing to fear in the interval. Europe is calm. Austria cannot attack. England is occupied with preparing her defenses against invasion, and Turkey will welcome the expulsion of the Mameluke."

The aims of this great expedition of 1798 were nothing if not grandiose. Napoleon was empowered by his government to occupy Egypt, exclude the English from all their possessions in the East, and seize Malta on his way through the Mediterranean. Finally, he was to have a canal cut through the Isthmus of Suez, so that France might have access to the Red Sea and, of course, to India beyond it. Napoleon's own ambitions went even further. He envisaged the day when—all the East having been conquered—he would sweep back through Turkey, smash the Ottoman Empire, and complete the encirclement of Europe. The great and revived "Roman Empire," led by France, would now encompass not only all the Mediterranean areas that had once belonged to ancient Rome but all the territories that had once fallen before Alexander the Great—as well as the extensive British possessions in India. Whatever might be said about Napoleon, he certainly never lacked ambition; even the dreams of the world conquerors of the past pale into insignificance when compared with his.

The fleet and the men were gradually assembled at Marseilles and Toulon, as well as in Genoa, Civitavecchia, and his native Corsica. Thirty thousand infantrymen were to embark on the great adventure, together with specialized companies of sappers and miners and more than a hundred fieldpieces and siege guns. The fleet would ultimately consist of thirteen ships of the line, some gunboats for bombardment, seven frigates, and about three hundred transports. Although this was a formidable armada, the number of transports was out of all proportion to the number of fighting ships designed to protect the convoy. If Nelson or any other British admiral had come upon it at sea, there can be little doubt that it would have been annihilated. What distinguished this fleet from any other that had ever crossed the Mediterranean was that it carried not only the soldiers to execute the invader's designs but a whole team of savants—some of the finest intellects in France. More than one hundred and fifty learned civilians, equipped with hundreds of books and scientific instruments, were to bring French culture to the East, as well as to discover whatever secrets lay locked in the valley of the Nile. Not even Alexander had set out with the intention of deliberately cross-fertilizing the Mediterranean basin.

The expedition finally sailed from Toulon on May 19, escaping the vigilant British only by sheer good fortune. "The Devil's children," as Nelson later remarked, "have the Devil's luck." On June 9 Malta was in sight, and Napoleon at once sent a message ashore requesting permission for his fleet to enter Grand Harbor. The Order of St. John of Jerusalem, also known as the Knights of Malta, that last surviving link with the Crusades, had long been in a state of decline, and many of the Knights were actively in league with France. Despite the fact that Malta's defenses could probably have withstood a siege for a matter of months, the island capitulated within three days. The Knights of Malta, who had guarded Europe's southern flank for two and a half centuries, were unceremoniously bundled out of their ancient home.

Napoleon had every reason thus far to be pleased with the progress of his expedition. Nelson, meanwhile, had arrived at Naples, where he heard rumors of the French landing at Malta. Pressing on furiously in pursuit, he and his ships of the line came surging down the east coast of Sicily, only to hear from the captain of a passing merchantman that Napoleon had indeed taken Malta but had already left the island for an unknown destination. Nelson, presuming quite correctly that the destination of the armada could only be Egypt, directed his course for Alexandria. The prevailing northwesterly winds served him well as he drove his ships southeastward. He reached the port on June 28, six days after leaving Sicily. There he learned to his dismay that no French ships had been sighted. To quote Admiral Mahan: "This remarkable miscarriage, happening to a man of so much energy and intuition, was due primarily to his want of small lookout ships; and secondly, to Bonaparte's using the simple, yet at sea sufficient ruse, of taking an indirect instead of a direct course to his object."

The French fleet, in fact, had taken a dog-legged route, proceeding east to Crete and thence southeast. Because of this detour, and because the heavy transports slowed the convoy's speed, Nelson, in pursuit, had unwittingly overtaken and passed his quarry. His disappointment at finding no French ships in Alexandria now caused him to abandon his original, sound judgment of Napoleon's destination. On June 29, the day after arriving, he sailed northeast on the first leg of a zigzag course that would take him to a point off the coast of Asia Minor, then south of Crete, and so again to Sicily. Watchers from the Pharos of Alexandria that day had hardly seen the sails of Nelson's squadron disappear over the horizon before the sails of the immense French fleet came in sight to the northwest. Within hours Napoleon and his soldiers were at anchor.

Within three weeks of reaching Alexandria, Napoleon had met and defeated the Mamelukes—the military order dominating Egypt—in the celebrated Battle of the Pyramids. "Soldiers, from these pyramids forty centuries look down upon you," he reminded his men. The remark is famous, so too his victory: both were hollow. As has been proved so often in the past, in the conduct of war in the countries surrounding the Mediterranean it is essential to have command of the sea.

Nelson, back in Sicily, realized soon enough that his first surmise had been correct after all, and that Napoleon must surely be in Egypt now. He kept his fleet for a few days in the famous old harbor of Syracuse. Just before weighing anchor, he wrote to the British minister in Naples, Sir William Hamilton: "Thanks to your exertions, we have victualled and watered; and surely, watering at the Fountain of Arethusa, we must have victory. We shall sail with the first breeze, and be assured that I will return either crowned with laurel, or covered with cypress."

On August 1 the English fleet was once more off Alexandria. The harbor was full of French transports, but curiously enough, there were no large warships to be seen. The French admiral, Brueys, had mistrusted the entrance to the port and had sailed fifteen miles farther down the coast to drop anchor in Abukir Bay. This was an immense, sand-rimmed bay, stretching some eighteen miles from Abukir Point in the west to the Rosetta Mouth of the Nile in the east. The French ships of the line were anchored in a long, slightly curved line at the western end of the bay, in the lee of Abukir Island, which lies just off the point. In addition, four frigates were anchored in an irregularly spaced line, roughly parallel to the bigger ships and between the latter and the shore. Admiral Brueys no doubt thought that he had made his disposition very skillfully, but he had, in fact, been somewhat negligent. The intervals between his ships were too great—about 160 yards on the average; the ships, moreover, were anchored only by the bows, and consequently swung with the wind. As it turned out, when Nelson arrived upon the scene the wind was from the north-northwest, and the French ships were lined up in such a way—the bowsprit of each pointing toward the stern of the next across a broad expanse of open water—as to provide an audacious adversary with significant tactical advantages. Perhaps Brueys's somewhat casual placement of his fleet had been occasioned by the same overconfidence

147

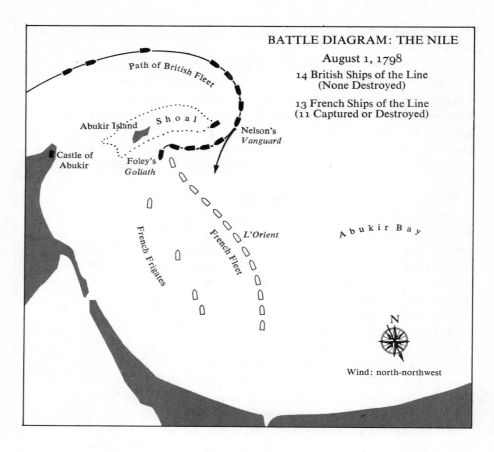

BATTLE DIAGRAM: THE NILE

August 1, 1798

14 British Ships of the Line
(None Destroyed)

13 French Ships of the Line
(11 Captured or Destroyed)

Path of British Fleet

Abukir Island

S h o a l

Castle of
Abukir

Nelson's
Vanguard

Foley's
Goliath

L'Orient

French Frigates

French Fleet

A b u k i r   B a y

N

Wind: north-northwest

that had made Napoleon write only two days before: "All the conduct of the English indicates that they are inferior in number, and
content themselves with blockading Malta and intercepting its
supplies."

At about two o'clock on the afternoon of August 1, 1798, the
English sighted the French fleet snug in its haven at Abukir Bay.
This was the moment for which Nelson had been waiting, and he at
once steered to close the distance between the ships. Brueys, for
his part, could not believe that the English would attack that day,
for the French practice would have been to make a careful recon-
naissance, decide on a plan of action, and wait for daylight. This
was not Nelson's way, for he reckoned that he and his "Band of
Brothers" would have ample time to survey the French dispositions, and prepare their plan of action, even as they drove in to
attack. During the long chase around the eastern Mediterranean

148   Nelson had been in such a fever of anxiety that he had scarcely

The brilliant British tactical stroke that opened the Battle of the Nile, painted here by Nicholas Pocock, is diagrammed at left. Goliath can be seen rounding the head of the anchored French line.

slept or taken any food other than quick snacks. Now, seeing the whole object of his ambition lying placidly awaiting him—and aware that it would be several hours before his ships would be rounding the point to commence action—he ordered dinner to be formally served.

Shortly after six o'clock in the evening the action began. Captain Foley in the *Goliath*, the leading English ship, rounded into the bay and approached the French line. Foley's trained eye quickly observed that through the failure to moor them both fore and aft, the ships had swung to the wind. This enabled him to steer between the little island and the lead French ship, to round the latter's bow, and to take up a position on the landward side of the French line—a maneuver that would have been impossible if

Brueys had made his dispositions correctly. The next four ships also passed to the landward side of the French—one, at least, boldly piercing their line between the lead ship and the ship immediately astern. The French captains were so taken aback by this unexpected move that many precious minutes passed before they could get their portside guns unencumbered and return the British fire. Nelson, in the *Vanguard*, came up just as night was falling and launched an attack from the seaward side, shortly to be followed by his next two ships. As a result, the ships in the French van found themselves engaged on both sides.

Hood, captain of the *Zealous*, in his account of the action against the French *Le Guerrier*, gives an idea of what must have been happening all up and down the line, as more and more English ships sailed up and engaged their opponents:

I commenced such a well-directed fire into her bow within pistol shot a little after six that her fore-mast went by the board in about seven minutes, just as the sun was closing the horizon; on which the whole squadron gave three cheers, it happening before the next ship astern of me had fired a shot and only the *Goliath* and *Zealous* engaged. And in ten minutes more her main and mizzen masts went; at this time also went the main mast of the second ship, engaged closely by the *Goliath* and *Audacious*, but I could not get *Le Guerrier*'s commander to strike for three hours, though I hailed him twenty times, and seeing he was totally cut up and only firing a stern gun now and then at the *Goliath* and *Audacious*.

At last being tired of firing and killing people in that way, I sent my boat on board her, and the lieutenant was allowed . . . to hoist a light and haul it down to show his submission.

The battle raged throughout the night. Nelson, who had come prepared for a night action, had given orders for his ships to show a horizontal group of lanterns so that the English could easily recognize one another. The French admiral, however, never having expected an engagement after dark, had made no such preparations. He seems to have had little knowledge of what exactly was happening, as the English slowly and methodically moved past his ships, often on both sides of them, destroying them with their concentrated fire. Brueys himself, though wounded in the head and in one hand, continued to direct the fire from his flagship *L'Orient* until a cannon ball tore off his left thigh, nearly cutting him in two. Meanwhile, a fire began to spread aboard the doomed flagship, and many of the crew started jumping into the sea to save their lives. Soon after ten o'clock the fire reached the French flagship's main magazine, and *L'Orient* exploded with a shattering crash that was heard as far away as Alexandria. The noise was so devastating that, as if by common consent, all ships stopped firing; for a brief period the action came to a halt. When the battle recommenced, it was clear that it was now no more than a tidying-up action. The French fleet, to all intents and purposes, had ceased to exist.

By daylight on August 2 *L'Orient* and one frigate were sunk, and no fewer than, nine French ships of the line were either out of action or already captured. One other ship was run aground and set afire on her captain's orders. Only the last two ships of the French line managed to escape—together with two frigates. For the French, the affair had been a catastrophe.

Many years later, when Napoleon was a prisoner aboard the *Bellerophon*, he remarked to her captain: "In all my plans I have always been thwarted by the British fleet"; later still, while sailing for his ultimate island-prison of St. Helena, he had a life of Nelson read to him by his secretary. He clearly recognized that this was the man who had done more than any other to thwart his ambitions.

The Battle of the Nile was, in a sense, more important even than Trafalgar. It was Napoleon's first major reverse, and it put new heart into the whole of Europe. It showed that the apparently insuperable conquerors were as subject to defeat as any other mortals.

"My Lord," Nelson wrote to the Earl of St. Vincent, "Almighty God has blessed His Majesty's Arms in the late Battle, by a great victory over the Fleet of the enemy, who I attacked at sunset on the 1st of August, off the mouth of the Nile. . . . Nothing could withstand the Squadron your Lordship did me the honour to place under my command. Their high state of discipline is well known to you, and with the judgement of the captains, together with their valour, and that of the officers and men of every description, it was absolutely irresistible."

The news of the victory swept through Europe like a forest fire. Its effect, in an age when emotions were less restrained than now, was almost to deprive people of their senses. Politically, the principal result of the Battle of the Nile was to bring into being the Second Coalition against revolutionary France. Nearly all that Napoleon had gained in Italy was swept away in one brief campaign, while Turkey now came into the war on the side of the Allies. Its greatest significance, however, was that although the war against France would yet drag on for many years, the English had now secured the domination of the Mediterranean. It was something that, while it was often challenged and sometimes imperiled, they never lost—until they vacated it of their own accord in the second half of the twentieth century.

To our age of high specialization, especially in all fields of technology, it seems all but incredible that in the early nineteenth century a single man should have mastered engineering to the point where he could plan and carry through the construction of great tunnels and huge suspension bridges; complete a major railway line with the fastest trains then known and only long afterward exceeded in speed; and finally build the largest and fastest ocean liners, first with wooden hulls and paddlewheels, then with iron hulls and screw propellers. Since Isambard Kingdom Brunel did all these things and did them with constant reference to beauty as well as to utility and cheapness, it is impossible not to agree with L. T. C. Rolt, an eminent authority on the history of engineering, that Brunel was "one of the most versatile and dynamic personalities the modern world has known."

THE GREAT ENGINEER

L. T. C. ROLT

In the library of Bristol University there is preserved a remarkable series of sketchbooks. Their assured draftsmanship proclaims them the work of an artist, but what is really remarkable about them is the astonishing range of subjects portrayed: steamships, locomotives, pieces of mechanism, plans and elevations of railway stations and other buildings, tunnel portals and bridges of masonry or iron. It is evident that their author was not only an artist but a civil engineer, a mechanical engineer, and, not least, an architect who was the master of a dozen different architectural styles that he delighted in adapting to new and novel purposes. Occasionally, hastily scribbled notes appear that are no less remarkable than the drawings. Thus, beside a sketch of a ship's hull, the artist has written: "Say 600 ft x 65 ft x 30 ft"—grandiose dimensions that make it difficult for us to credit the penciled date: "March 25th, 1852."

We should be right in thinking that a genius of no mean order had been at work between the covers of these books, for the artist was Isambard Kingdom Brunel, a man who was not only one of the greatest engineers in history but one of the most versatile and dynamic personalities the modern world has known. His sketches, many of them no more than the doodles of a restless imagination

Isambard Kingdom Brunel in 1858, standing before the huge anchor chains of his last and proudest work, the steamship Great Eastern.   153

throwing off ideas like sparks, were destined to be translated, by dint of the blood and the sweat of thousands of men and the expenditure of millions of pounds, into material achievements that astonished the world: a great railway system on which mile-a-minute speeds were achieved for the first time; three steamships, each in turn the largest ever built, one of which established the first regular transatlantic steamer service.

Brunel, one feels, was one of those rare mortals who could have excelled in any calling he chose to pursue. He pursued engineering as his profession because in early nineteenth-century England it offered him the most satisfying outlet for his prodigious creative powers. It is significant that his most intimate friend was not a fellow engineer but his artist brother-in-law John Horsley. Horsley knew nothing of engineering and said that what he loved in Brunel was his high courage and his artistic gifts—his love of painting, music, and drama.

Brunel himself confessed that as a youth he was forever dreaming of ambitious schemes, castles in Spain as he called them. But to have ideas, however brilliant, is one thing; to translate them into practice is quite another, and an imaginative genius often lacks the ability to concentrate upon detail and the capacity for sheer hard work that are essential before ideas can take practical shape. It was the secret of Brunel's success that he was able to do both these things. His sketchbooks reveal the meticulous attention to detail that tempered the heat of his inspiration. We notice how even the most hasty sketch is drawn upon squared paper so that, if the idea seemed promising, it could be more readily translated into a precisely dimensioned drawing. We may notice, too, how each book has two strips of glass paper—coarse and fine—pasted on the inside cover so that the fine point of Brunel's pencil could always be quickly sharpened to follow his inspiration.

In whatever task he undertook, Brunel insisted upon his absolute personal responsibility. When the directors of the Great Western Railway reprimanded one of Brunel's assistant engineers, they received this stinging retort: "I will do my best to keep my team in order, but I cannot do it if the master sits by me and amuses himself by touching them up with the whip." That he was indeed well able to keep his team in order, this letter to an erring assistant shows:

Plain gentlemanly language seems to have no effect upon you. I must try stronger language and stronger measures. You are a cursed, lazy, inattentive, apathetic vagabond, and if you continue to neglect my instructions and to show such infernal laziness, I shall send you about your business. I have frequently told you, amongst other absurd, untidy habits, that that of making drawings on the backs of others was inconvenient; by your cursed neglect of that you have again wasted more of my time than your whole life is worth, in looking for the altered drawings you were to make of the station—they wont do.

Finally, here is Brunel's working philosophy as expressed to a defeatist colleague:

You have failed, I think . . . from that which causes nine-tenths of all failures in this world, from not doing quite enough. . . . I would only impress upon you one principle of action which I have always found very successful, which is to stick obstinately to one plan (until I believe it wrong) . . . and, on the same principle, to stick to one method and push that to the utmost limits before I allow myself to wander into others; in fact, to use a simile, to stick to one point of attack, however defended, and if the force first brought up is not sufficient, to bring ten times as much; but never to try back upon another in the hope of finding it easier.

Brunel held courageously to this principle of action throughout a comparatively brief career, checkered by failure as well as triumph, in which he took the engineering world of his day by storm. Having once decided that a scheme was correct in principle, he would pursue it regardless of commercial considerations, while a single-minded quest for perfection frequently led him to ask too much of the men and the machines under his command. To put it simply, he set his sights too high, and it was this fault that drove him to his tragic death when he was at the height of his career.

Brunel's father was Sir Marc Isambard Brunel, a Frenchman of yeoman stock, whose royalist sympathies forced him to emigrate, first to New York and later to England where he married an English girl, Sophia Kingdom. Marc Brunel himself achieved considerable fame as an engineer, and at the time his only son was born at Portsea on April 9, 1806, he was installing some ingenious machines of his own design at Portsmouth Dockyard. He was thus able to give young Isambard an excellent early training and to send him to France to complete his education.

When Brunel returned to England to assist his father, it was not long before he was given the chance to prove his mettle. At the age of twenty he was appointed resident engineer of his father's last great engineering undertaking, the boring of a tunnel under the Thames from Rotherhithe to Wapping. The work was fraught with every kind of difficulty and danger. It was not only the first underwater tunnel in the world, except for certain mine workings, it was also the first in which a tunneling shield, designed by Marc Brunel, was used to protect the excavators. The miners worked in a series of cells within massive cast-iron frames, which were moved forward by jackscrew as the excavation proceeded. On a staging behind these frames the bricklayers worked, so that the brick lining of the tunnel closely followed the tail of the advancing shield.

After making trial borings, the geologists assured the Brunels that if they drove their tunnel at a certain level they would encounter only the stiff London clay. This prediction proved hopelessly wrong. As the excavation advanced under the river, the Brunels soon realized that instead of solid clay, only a few feet of gravel and mud lay between the top of the shield and the river bed. Even the shield could not ensure safety under such conditions. But although the Brunels knew full well the appalling risk they were running, the work went on. The fact that the Tunnel Company, against their advice, insisted upon admitting sight-seers to the tunnel at a shilling a time did not lighten their anxiety. "Notwithstanding every prudence on our part," wrote Marc Brunel in his diary on May 13, 1827, "a disaster may still occur. May it not be when the arch is full of visitors." Five days later the river broke in.

Young Brunel was on the surface by the head of the Rotherhithe shaft when he heard the sudden thunder of water from below and knew that the worst had happened. Soon the half-drowned miners were scrambling up the shaft stairs. Brunel shouted to them to hurry, and scarcely had the last man reached the top before a great wave carried away the stairs. It was then realized that an old man named Tillet, who looked after the pumps at the shaft bottom, was still below. Brunel seized a rope, secured one end round his waist, and slid down one of the shaft tie rods into the darkness of the drowned tunnel. Miraculously, he found the old man struggling in the water and managed to tie the rope round his waist. When rescuer and rescued had been hauled to the surface a roll call was held. No one was missing. Next day Brunel had himself lowered in a diving bell to the bed of the Thames to inspect the damage. He never wasted time.

When the hole in the river bed had been plugged with bags of clay and the workings laboriously cleared of water and silt, Brunel celebrated this victory in characteristic fashion by inviting his father and fifty of his friends to a banquet in the tunnel, at which music was provided by the band of the Coldstream Guards. This triumph was short-lived, for two months later the tunnel was drowned again.

On this occasion Brunel was in the tunnel and only escaped death by a miracle. He was working with two miners named Ball and Collins in Number One frame of the shield when the river burst in with such force that all three were swept back out of the frame into the tunnel. The bricklayers' staging was carried away, and as the water swept over him, Brunel realized that his leg was pinioned by a section of heavy timbering. By a tremendous effort he managed to free himself, but having done so, instead of immediately making for safety, this extraordinary young man stopped to gaze in admiration at the spectacle of the water pouring in. "While standing there," he wrote afterward in his private journal, "the effect was *grand*—the roar of the rushing water in a confined passage, and by its velocity rushing past the opening was grand, *very grand*. I cannot compare it to anything, cannon can be nothing to it. . . . The sight and the whole affair was well worth the risk. . . ." Brunel then turned and made for the shaft stairs, but before he could reach them he was swept off his feet and overwhelmed by an immense wave of water. This demolished the stairs and carried Ball, Collins, and four other miners to their death, but it miraculously lifted a semiconscious Brunel to the lip of the shaft.

As a consequence of this second disaster, work on the tunnel was suspended for lack of capital. It was not begun again until 1835, and it was not until 1841 that Marc Brunel saw his work completed and was rewarded with a knighthood by his queen. In this second act of the tunnel drama the younger Brunel played no part. The chief engineer of the Great Western Railway had other work to do.

It was found that Brunel had not only damaged his leg in the tunnel but had suffered severe internal injuries, which kept him to his bed for many weeks. When he had recovered sufficiently his parents sent him to Clifton, near Bristol in the west of England, to convalesce. This chance decision was to set the course of their son's future career.

The citizens of Bristol had decided that a bridge should be built over the deep and narrow gorge of the Avon River at Clifton, and the committee in charge had announced a competition for the best design. This was just the kind of dramatic project to appeal to Brunel's imagination, and the fruits of his convalescence were three designs for suspension bridges of spans varying from 870 feet to 916 feet, which would spring from lip to lip of the gorge.

To judge their competition, the Clifton Bridge Committee appointed the most eminent civil engineer of the day, Thomas Telford. Among many great engineering achievements, Telford had been responsible for what was then the largest suspension bridge in the world, his famous bridge over the Straits of Menai, in North Wales. But Telford had grown old and cautious. Unmindful of the fact that he had once designed a bridge for the Mersey at Runcorn with a span of 1,000 feet, Telford expressed the opinion that the 600-foot span of his Menai bridge could not be exceeded with safety, and on this score he rejected all the competing designs. He then prepared a design himself in which he reduced the span by carrying up two immense piers from the floor of the gorge. At first this design was acclaimed, but Brunel poured such scorn upon its timidity that enthusiasm waned, and ultimately it was decided to hold a second competition. In this Telford's design was rejected while Brunel's was accepted, and he was appointed engineer to the bridge committee.

Unfortunately, owing to lack of capital Brunel's splendid bridge —"my first child, my darling," as he called it—was not completed until after his death. Nevertheless this undertaking, and the works he undertook for the Bristol Dock Company, earned him a high reputation in Bristol. Consequently, when a group of Bristol merchants were planning a railway from Bristol to London in 1833 and wanted an engineer to carry out a survey, Brunel's was among the names put forward. He realized that this was his first great chance. Railway construction offered a boundless field of opportunity for an ambitious young engineer; but at this time the infant profession was practically a monopoly of the inventive Stephensons—George and Robert—and the engineers they had trained. Yet it was characteristic of Brunel that even with this golden opportunity dangled before him, he scorned to trim his sails to the wind. The railway committee announced that the post of engineer would go to the surveyor who undertook to survey the cheapest route. Brunel replied that he would undertake to survey only one route from Bristol to London and this would be not the cheapest but the best. He got the job, but only—as he learned afterward—by one vote.

In the opinion of many people the construction of 118 miles of railway was wildly overambitious; yet Brunel saw it as only a small beginning. In imagination he was already far ahead. Before even a sod had been cut he could see his iron road monopolizing the traffic of the west of England, stretching away through Somerset and Devon into Cornwall and along the seaboard of South Wales. So it was not as the "London & Bristol" but as the Great Western Railway that the company was incorporated.

"I am Engineer to the finest work in England," Brunel wrote in his diary after his appointment, for he had resolved to make it so. Thinking of speeds that no one had so far dared to contemplate, he laid out a superbly straight and level road, spanned the Thames at Maidenhead with two of the largest and flattest arches ever built, and drove a tunnel nearly two miles long under Box Hill near Bath. Contemporaries called the tunnel project "monstrous and extraordinary, most dangerous and impracticable"; yet it was completed in just over four and a half years. Thirty million bricks were used for its lining, and a ton of candles and a ton of gun powder per week were consumed during construction. As for the bridge at Maidenhead, its collapse under the first featherweight train was confidently predicted, but it stands fast under the main line of traffic today.

Yet the controversy that these works provoked was a gentle breeze compared to the fury of the storm that raged around Brunel when he calmly announced his intention of laying his road to a rail gauge of seven feet. The Stephensons had already standardized the gauge of 4 feet 8½ inches for no better reason, as Robert Stephenson admitted, than that they had used it before on the colliery lines of the north, which followed the tracks of the ancient wagonways. Here was a precedent that Brunel unhesitatingly threw overboard. This narrow, arbitrary "coal-waggon gauge" would never do for the speeds he contemplated on his splendid road. He wanted greater stability, and he wanted to give locomotive designers more elbow room when planning the engines to give him the speed. It is a measure of the force and the magic of Brunel's personality that in the face of the bitterest opposition from every railway engineer in the country he managed to carry his directors with him, and the broad-gauge rails went down.

Brunel argued that in practice the advantages of his broad gauge would prove so overwhelming that other railway companies would be forced to change to it. Had he been earlier in the field he might have been right, but the smaller Standard gauge was already too firmly established, and commercially the broad gauge proved a costly mistake although it was not finally banished from Brunel's main line until 1892. As an engineering tour de force the broad gauge accomplished all that Brunel claimed for it. Under the driving inspiration of his locomotive superintendent, Daniel Gooch, the Swindon shops built in thirteen weeks the *Great Western*, a locomotive with single driving wheels eight feet in diameter and a boiler of unprecedented size. At this time (1846) an average speed of 35

*Two of the handsome landmarks on Brunel's Great Western Railway
are portrayed in these lithographs. Above, the bridge over the Avon
near Bristol; at right, the entrance to Box Tunnel near Bath.*

mph was considered fast going on the Standard gauge; yet within a
month of leaving the shops, the *Great Western* had reeled off the
194 miles from Paddington to Exeter in 208 minutes, and with 100
tons behind her had covered the 77½ miles from London to Swindon in 78 minutes start to stop. She was the first of a long line of
broad-gauge flyers that carried no numbers, only the proudest of
names: *Iron Duke, Great Britain, Lightning, Emperor, Pasha, Sultan, Lord of the Isles.* These were the locomotives that hauled the
first express trains in the world, trains which themselves acquired
names that were to become immortal: *The Cornishman, The Flying
Dutchman,* and *The Zulu.*

George Stephenson called Brunel's broad gauge a humbug, and
the victory was ultimately his, but if it accomplished nothing else,
the example of the broad gauge acted as a tremendous stimulus to
railway development by breaking the Stephenson monopoly.

Brunel's extension of his broad gauge road westward through
Devon and Cornwall followed the same checkered pattern of pre-
vious successes and failures. On the South Devon Railway west of
Exeter he tried out what was called the "atmospheric" system of

160

traction. A continuous pipeline was laid between the rails, and instead of a locomotive, the trains were headed by a special carriage equipped with a piston that ran in the pipe. A series of pumping stations at three-mile intervals beside the line exhausted the air from the pipe so that the trains were driven along by the pressure of the atmosphere acting upon the traveling piston. This arrangement worked very well for a time, but then a series of troubles developed and the scheme ended in costly failure.

Once he had become convinced that the system was unworkable, Brunel had the courage to urge its immediate abandonment even though a majority of the directors of the railway company were in favor of continuing the experiment. Had he taken the easier course of siding with them in some futile effort to save face, his railway career might well have ended ignominiously, at least so far as the west country was concerned. As it was, confidence in his abilities remained unshaken, and he was able to carry the rails through Cornwall to their terminus at Penzance. The last link to be forged on this long rail route from London was Brunel's famous Royal Albert Bridge over the Tamar at Saltash. This great bridge, Brunel's final masterpiece of railway engineering, stands today as his

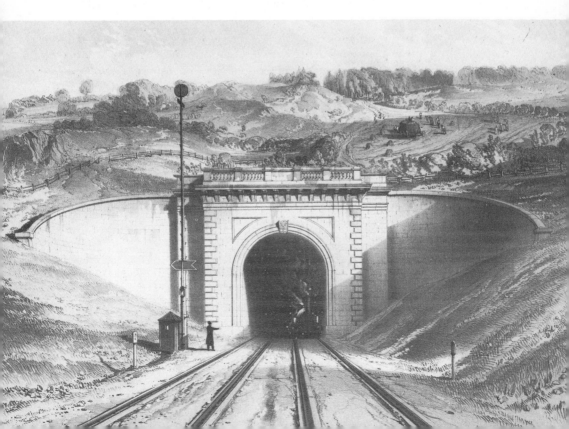

memorial. For in May, 1859, when the Prince Consort opened the bridge, and the long road from London to Penzance was complete, Brunel had only four months to live. It was from a couch carried on a platform truck that the dying engineer saw his finished work for the first and last time.

In all, about 2,000 miles of railway were built under Brunel's direction. This, one might suppose, would be more than enough for one short lifetime, but in fact it was only half of Brunel's activities. In the world of marine engineering he made a mark that was even more sensational than his broad-gauge railways.

This story began at an early board meeting of the Great Western Railway Company when someone expressed misgivings as to the length of the proposed line from London to Bristol. "Why not make it longer," suggested Brunel through the smoke of his cigar, "and have a steamboat go from Bristol to New York and call it the *Great Western?*" Those staid frock-coated gentlemen of the board accepted this sally as one of their engineer's characteristic little jokes, but that it was no joke they soon realized when a company was formed in Bristol, which began building the *Great Western*, the largest steamship in the world at the time. Once again the prophets of disaster gathered like ravens. It could be proved by calculation, they croaked, that no steamship could carry enough coal for an Atlantic crossing under continuous power. But Brunel realized that they had got their figures wrong; that whereas the carrying capacity of a hull increases as the cube of its dimensions, its area, or, in other words, the power needed to drive it through the water, only increases as the square of those dimensions. Hence, the larger the ship the greater its cruising range without refueling. This was the simple proposition which inspired Brunel to build his first ship.

As the *Great Western*, a wooden paddler with a displacement of 2,300 tons, took shape, established shipping interests began to wonder uneasily about their future if Brunel's experiment came off. To be on the safe side the British & American Steam Navigation Company of London laid down the *British Queen* on the Thames at Limehouse. But this ship was still far from completion when the *Great Western* arrived in London under sail to take on her engines at Blackwall. Determined to steal Brunel's thunder if it could, the rival company thereupon chartered the little Irish steam packet *Sirius* and began to fit her out for an Atlantic voyage. The *Sirius* narrowly won the race to get the two ships ready for sea. She sailed from the Thames March 28, 1838. With Brunel on board, the *Great Western* followed on March 31, bound for Bristol to take on passengers. Knowing that the master of the *Sirius* intended coaling at Cork, Brunel was not unduly worried by the starting handicap until, before his splendid ship had cleared the Thames estuary, smoke and flames suddenly belched from her boiler room. The boiler lagging round the base of the funnel had ignited and set fire to the deck planking. Fortunately the outbreak was mastered before any serious damage was done, but it nearly cost Brunel his life. As he was fighting the flames, the charred rung of a ladder collapsed under him and he fell eighteen feet onto the boiler room plating where, knocked unconscious, he nearly drowned in the water that had collected there. In great pain, he was rowed ashore to the care of a cottager on Canvey Island, while on his insistence the *Great Western* put out to sea after a delay of twelve hours.

It seemed that the result of the race must be a foregone conclusion, for whereas the *Sirius* left Cork on April 4, four precious days elapsed before the *Great Western* got away from the more distant port of Bristol. The little *Sirius* docked in New York after nineteen days at sea, on the morning of April 23. It had been a close call, for her coal bunkers were empty and she had had to burn barrels of resin from her cargo. A few hours later New York realized how close a race the little *Sirius* had run, for on that same historic morning the *Great Western* dropped her anchor off Sandy Hook fifteen days and five hours from Bristol. James Gordon Bennett graphically described the scene for his morning *Herald* readers when the *Great Western* arrived in New York: "The sky was clear —the crowds immense. The Battery was filled with the human multitude. . . . Below, on the broad, blue water, appeared this huge thing of life, with four masts and emitting volumes of smoke. She looked black and blackguard . . . rakish, cool, reckless, fierce and forbidding in sombre colors to an extreme. As she neared the *Sirius*, she slackened her movements and took a sweep round, forming a sort of half circle. At this moment the whole Battery sent forth a tumultuous shout of delight at the revelation of her magnificent proportions. After making another turn towards Staten Island, she made another sweep and shot towards the East River with extraordinary speed. The vast multitude rent the air with their shouts again, waving handkerchiefs, hats, hurrahing!" But these enthusiastic New Yorkers could not then appreciate the really vital point about this demonstration; this was that the *Great Western* still had 200 tons of coal in her bunkers. In that fact, Brunel had triumphantly proved the practicability of transatlantic steam navigation.

The *Great Western* was a complete success and most truly earned the honor of the Atlantic Blue Riband, which she was the first ship to wear, by making no less than 67 crossings in eight years. Her best records were thirteen days westbound and twelve days, six hours eastbound. She was followed on the Atlantic run in 1845 by Brunel's second ship, the *Great Britain*, which like her predecessor was the biggest ship afloat when she was launched. Apart from her size, the *Great Britain* was the first iron steamer and the first screw-propelled ship to cross any ocean. It is doubtful whether any other man would have had the courage to embody two such revolutionary innovations in one design.

As though to chasten his presumption, ill fortune seemed to dog Brunel and his creations, and the *Great Britain* was no exception to this rule. On September 22, 1846, the ship left Liverpool for New York with 180 passengers on board—the largest complement ever to sail in a transatlantic steamer up to that time. A few hours later she had run aground in Dundrum Bay on the coast of Northern Ireland due to a faulty chart and compass deflection caused by the iron hull. Grinding over rocks on an exposed shore, the *Great Britain* successfully withstood a battering that would have broken up any other ship afloat, and all her passengers were safely landed. The next spring, under Brunel's direction, she was successfully salvaged. The *Great Britain* continued to trade until 1886, and even now the remains of her almost indestructible hull can still be seen in Sparrow Cove, Falkland Islands.

For the greater part of her long life, the *Great Britain* was on the run to Australia, but as she had been designed for the Atlantic service, this much longer voyage involved bunkering at the Cape of Good Hope with steam coal specially sent out for her by sailing ship from South Wales. It was with the object of avoiding such costly refueling that Brunel designed the third and last of his great ships, the fabulous *Great Eastern*.

With a displacement of 32,000 tons—four times the size of any ship afloat at that time—Brunel's great ship could steam around the world without refueling. In her huge iron hull, double-skinned and immensely strong, her designer incorporated all the experience he had gained from his two earlier ships. It was his final engineering masterpiece and stands out as a landmark in the history of shipbuilding. Alas! In designing a ship which was not to be surpassed in size until 1899, Brunel jumped too far ahead of his time. Although two sets of engines were installed—one driving a screw and the other, huge paddle wheels—in those days of low-pressure steam it was impossible to provide enough power to drive so large a hull. Though her engines were the largest ever built up to that time and indicated 10,000 horsepower, the *Great Eastern* disappointed in speed.

Because the building site made an end-on launch out of the question, the *Great Eastern* had been laid down parallel with the riverbank. This meant that a hull weighing over 12,000 tons had to be pushed sideways down special launching ways until it could be floated off on a spring tide. Cruel circumstances compelled Brunel to undertake this gigantic task with inadequate equipment at the worst season of the year. Hydraulic rams burst and heavy chain cables parted like threads, but ultimately, after three months' struggle, the ship was successfully floated on the last day of January, 1858. But this success had been purchased at a terrible price: Brunel's health was ruined, and the company could not finance the fitting out of his ship.

In the spring of 1859 a new company was formed to complete the *Great Eastern*, and Brunel, though mortally ill and prematurely aged, personally superintended the work of getting his monster ready for sea. A cabin had been reserved for him for the maiden voyage that would set the seal on all his efforts, but he never achieved this last ambition. Two days before his ship was due to sail he collapsed on her deck. He had suffered a stroke that left him partially paralyzed. So, on September, 7 the *Great Eastern* left without him. She was off Dungeness on her course down channel when disaster struck. Owing to inexcusable carelessness on the part of the builder, John Scott Russell, and his men who were in charge of the paddle engines and their boilers, a feed-water heater exploded. It blew one of the huge funnels into the air, wrecked the grand saloon, and scalded to death six firemen. The ship was able to proceed to Weymouth as planned, but the effect of the disaster on Brunel, who lay waiting for news at his home, was tragic. Even his indomitable spirit was broken by the news of this crowning and final misfortune, and a few days later, on September 15, 1859, he died.

As a passenger ship the *Great Eastern* was never a success. Owing to changes in world trade and the opening of the Suez Canal, through which, as first built, she was too large to pass, Brunel's great ship could never be used on the Australia run for which she was designed. Instead she ran to New York but was too big for the North Atlantic trade of that time. It was Daniel Gooch who vindicated both the ship and her designer by equipping her for cable

The Great Eastern *under construction, from the* Illustrated London News. *The painting opposite shows the 32,000-ton steamship off the Irish coast in 1866, during the laying of the Atlantic Cable.*

laying, in which capacity she was outstandingly successful. With Gooch himself on board, the *Great Eastern* laid the first transatlantic cable from Valencia to Newfoundland, and she then went on to weave a web of cables around the world.

So ended the career of an extraordinary personality, a career of commercial failure but of engineering triumph. The man and his three great ships are now only a memory, but today his railway works still stand for later generations to marvel at. Moreover, no man contributed more than did Brunel to the task of forging those links of transport and communication that tie the two halves of the English-speaking world together.

Aside from his material achievement, what we should most admire about Brunel in our overspecialized age is the astonishing versatility of intellect and imagination that ranged so freely and

with such assurance over the whole field of art and science. He re-
minds us that there was then no gulf fixed between the arts and
sciences, and he makes us reflect a little sadly that the world might
be a better place today if that gulf had never opened and man had
not grown so specialized an animal, knowing more and more about
less and less.

The best of all memorials to Isambard Kingdom Brunel are the
words written in a dairy by that friend who had always shown him
such unswerving loyalty and who now mourned his loss. "On the
15th September," wrote Daniel Gooch, "I lost my oldest and best
friend. . . . By his death the greatest of England's engineers was
lost, the man with the greatest originality of thought and power of
execution, bold in his plans but right. The commercial world
thought him extravagant; but although he was so, great things are
not done by those who sit and count the cost of every thought and
act."

Of Darwin's Origin of Species *Ernest Mayer, one of the foremost
authorities on evolution, has said that "it ushered in a new era of
man's thought about his own nature and his place in the universe."
While earlier major discoveries in science had dealt mostly with the
physical world, Darwin concerned himself not only with man, but with
all living things. Yet his basic idea, that species evolve by the process of
natural selection, was conceivable only in the context of two other
theories, both advanced by Englishmen in the earlier nineteenth
century: Thomas Malthus' argument that population tends to outrun
the available means of subsistence and that therefore in the struggle for
existence only the fittest survive; and Charles Lyell's basic work on
geology, of which Darwin himself said that "it altered the whole tone
of one's mind" by demonstrating once and for all the great antiquity of
the earth, without which Darwin's theory of gradual change by selection
would hardly have been thinkable.*

    *The author, who teaches at a British university, has examined the
topic and the times at greater length in* Evolution and Society: a
Study of Victorian Social Theory.

CHARLES DARWIN

J. W. BURROW

Charles Darwin's body lies in Westminster Abbey, close to the
grave of Sir Isaac Newton. It is a proximity which few would
challenge, nor is there any oddity in the presence there of Newton,
devout Christian and Biblical scholar that he was. Yet the presence, in the Abbey Church of St. Peter, of Darwin, whom a Victorian clergyman had once pointed out in the British Museum to a
friend as "the most dangerous man in England," arouses more contradictory reflections: a pleased sense, perhaps, of the appropriate-
ness of the honor, and gratitude for the broadmindedness of Dean
Bradley who, on Darwin's death in 1882, permitted it? Or wry admission of the anomalies created by combining in one building the
functions of national pantheon and Christian worship? Satisfaction
at a symbol of truce between science and theology? Or simply a
sharper sense than usual of the ironies of death? Woe unto you
when all men praise you; you are probably dead.

    Yet though Darwin rests undisturbed in a Christian sepulcher,
and his place in the history of science is now as assured as that of

At the age of thirty, three years after his famous voyage aboard the
Beagle, *Darwin posed for this portrait by George Richmond.*

Newton or Galileo, his influence, the massive changes he wrought in the whole structure of men's ideas about themselves and the world they live in, is still immensely, even contentiously, alive— more alive today, perhaps, than half a century ago. The great nineteenth-century war between science and religion may indeed have subsided into cheerful reconciliation, mutual indifference, or isolated border forays. But among the numerous books and articles about Darwin and his work which continue to appear, a fair sprinkling are critical and hostile, though perhaps for slightly different reasons from those which gave that Victorian clergyman such a *frisson* when he and his friend came across the archdestroyer pottering in the Bird Room of the British Museum.

The clergyman had probably been educated, as Darwin himself had been, in that school of Christian apologetics known as "Rational Christianity," of which the work of Darwin's neighbor in death and fame, Isaac Newton, had been the chief inspiration. Rational Christianity and its close but more radical partner, deism, represented a kind of compromise, a consciously created solution to the problems raised by an earlier conflict between religion and science. This earlier conflict was less overt but more insidious than the one of which the focal point was to be Darwin's *Origin of Species*, and it was profoundly disturbing to seventeenth-century Christian apologists like Pascal, who saw in the rise of experimental science a potential threat to belief. The crisis was overcome, at least in England, at a cost of some sacrifice of the miraculous and emotional elements of Christianity. A house of intellect was established in the eighteenth century in which men of widely differing views could conduct their arguments and all feel more or less at home, though of course there were always a few defiant atheists who refused to come in out of the cold. The England into which Charles Darwin was born in 1809 was in most respects a rougher and more dangerous society than the one in which he died, more vulnerable to organized and haphazard violence, to the social effects of callous indifference, and to the accidents of nature. Intellectually, however, that world was a far cozier and more reassuring place than it was later to become, and the chief, though not the only, agent of the change was to be that peaceable Victorian family man, Charles Darwin.

Much of this apparent coziness was due to a relative lack of historical sense, which, paradoxically, helped men to feel at home with the past. Educated men could speak familiarly of Moses, Abraham, and Solomon, and derive maxims from their words and deeds with no sense of estrangement. One reason for familiarity with the past was the relatively short time span it was thought to cover. Most men at the beginning of the nineteenth century thought that the world had been created only some six thousand years before, although perhaps few would have cared to be as specific as a seventeenth-century vice-chancellor of Cambridge University, according to whom "man was created by the Trinity on October 23, 4004 B.C. at nine o'clock in the morning."

The world was not only imaginatively comprehensible, it was benevolently ordered. It is true that, ever since Copernicus and Galileo, the earth could no longer be regarded as the center of the universe; the music of the spheres was stilled. But God presided every instant, through the invisible filaments of gravitation, over the perfectly ordered harmony of the planetary motions. And if the earth was not the center of the universe, man was still emphatically the center—the end and purpose—of life on earth. This life had issued, fully formed in all its variety of fish and flesh and fowl, directly from the hands of the Creator, to be subject to a man quickened into life, as in Michelangelo's famous fresco, by the outstretched finger of God.

In harsher climates and in times when man's control over nature was more precarious, this doctrine often needed supplementation. The Fall was necessary to explain the tiger, and men wondered whether there were insects in Eden. By the eighteenth century, however, nature was sufficiently tamed to be idealized, at least by those who did not themselves labor on the land, and educated men were sufficiently leisured and urban to be sentimental about it. The eighteenth century was the heyday of the cult of a benevolent and edifying nature, while the Fall receded more and more into the theological background.

Moreover, men were beginning to have some understanding of the complex interactions in nature, of the contribution to the animal and vegetable "balance" of even the noxious and disagreeable. To pursue in any detail the pleasing evidences of divine purpose and harmony in the Newtonian heavens required some rather abstruse mathematics; to trace the same evidences in each leaf, stamen, and insect was well within the scope of any country clergyman with a pair of good legs and a collecting basket. To follow the workings of nature was to explore the mind of its Creator and to receive renewed assurances of His benevolence. The proudly displayed "collection" was almost the equivalent of a Bible laid open on a table. God was sought, not in mystical exercises in one's

171

chamber—that would have been "enthusiasm," which was both morbid and ungentlemanly—but at the bottoms of ponds and in the middle of hedges. "Natural Theology," as it was called, was the mainstay of Rational Christianity. Natural history became something of a craze in the first half of the nineteenth century and works on it outsold popular novels. When *The Origin of Species* appeared in 1859, it went quickly through three editions and found a readership which was far better prepared, both by the trend of contemporary theology and by the taste for natural history, to appreciate arguments relating to the nature of species, plant life, and animal behavior.

Darwin himself was a lover of nature, a collector and sportsman, before he was a man of science. He grew up with the tastes of an English provincial gentleman at a time when hunting, shooting, and the breeding of horses and dogs formed a staple amusement of upper-class Englishmen. In his father's unsympathetic words: "You care for nothing but shooting, dogs, and rat-catching, and you will be a disgrace to yourself and all your family." Darwin, in fact, belongs to the gallery of famous men whose school days were undistinguished and profitless. After he had shown no more aptitude for medicine, the family profession, than for the classical curriculum of Shrewsbury School, his father prepared wearily to follow the established English custom of bestowing the fool of the family on the Church, and so Darwin was sent up to Cambridge in 1827. He seemed destined to become yet another botanizing Victorian clergyman. From this he was rescued by an accident which seems almost to have been sent by Providence in a fit of self-destructiveness, for from it was to flow the work which so rudely shook men's belief in divine superintendence of human affairs. In 1831 H.M.S. *Beagle*, commissioned by the Admiralty to make a surveying voyage in the southern hemisphere, was in need of a naturalist. Darwin was recommended by his friend and mentor J. S. Henslow, Professor of Botany of Cambridge, and after some hesitation, he accepted. He was away for five years.

The voyage of the *Beagle* was, as he said himself, the formative experience of Darwin's life. He lived hard, working in the cramped conditions of a sailing ship, rounding Cape Horn and making expeditions hundreds of miles inland through dangerous and difficult country, collecting, observing, and interpreting the flora, fauna, and geological formations of South America and the islands of the Pacific and the southern Atlantic, and visiting also Australia and South Africa. The forty-thousand-mile voyage of the *Beagle* gave

Darwin, at first hand, a bird's-eye view of the natural world, from the tropical vegetation of the Brazilian jungle to the peaks of the Andes.

Darwin took with him on his voyage, besides his own knowledge and aptitudes, one indispensable tool for interpreting what he saw. Before sailing, Henslow pressed upon him the recently published first volume of Charles Lyell's *Principles of Geology*, with instructions to read but on no account to believe it. Darwin obeyed the first injunction but not the second. Lyell was foremost among those geologists who refused to accept that the crust of the earth had been formed in a few thousand years by earthquakes, floods, and volcanic eruptions far more vast than anything now observable. He insisted that changes in the earth's formation must be accounted for only by geological events similar to those with which men were familiar, which entailed an increase in the estimated age of the earth of many millions of years. There are few more dramatic episodes in the history of thought, not even the acceptance of Darwinism itself, than the change within a few decades from a prevailing view of geological time that could be imaginatively grasped to one that, like astronomical distances, could be comprehended only scientifically and mathematically. The corresponding debate in biology, however, remained unsettled. Could biology, like geology, dispense with the sudden interventions of Providence, accountable for by no natural law, and explain the formation of species by the ordinary laws of nature? Noah's Flood was no longer a necessary scientific hypothesis. Could Adam be similarly dispensed with?

The folklore of scientific invention and discovery has left no striking tale of the revelation to Darwin of the clue to the origin of species, like Newton's apple or Galileo dropping weights from the leaning tower of Pisa. It was too gradual and subtle a process for that. Darwin had begun the voyage of the *Beagle* believing, like most people, in the fixity of species. During the voyage, and while writing up his notes on it, he underwent two conversions. He became converted to Lyell's interpretation of geology, and he began to doubt the fixity of species. The latter, however, was to remain for years a secret confided only to a chosen few, as Darwin wrestled with objections, accumulated evidence, and prepared his friends for the revelation that—as he wrote to Joseph Hooker in 1844—"I am almost convinced (quite contrary to the opinion I started with) that species are not (it is like confessing a murder) immutable. . . ."

The theory of evolution in biology was already an old, even a

Skepticism about evolution, from a pre-Darwin cartoon. A seminar of crocodiles studies the skull of a "lower order of animals."

discredited, one. Darwin, in his preface to *The Origin of Species*, listed more than thirty precursors—and was accused, in spite of this, of serious omissions. Greek thinkers had held the view that life had developed gradually out of a primeval slime. Diderot, Buffon, and Darwin's own grandfather, Erasmus Darwin, in the eighteenth century had held more or less fully worked out theories of the origin of species by evolution, or transformism, as it was called. The objections to pre-Darwinian theories of evolution were partly based on the assumption of a short geological time span, which did not allow evolution time to operate, and partly on the speculative and puzzling explanations of how the process worked. In the most noteworthy pre-Darwinian evolutionist works—Erasmus Darwin's *Zoonomia* (1794) and J.-B. Lamarck's *Philosophie zoologique* (1809)—it was supposed that the new needs of an organism somehow gave rise to new organs which were then transmitted to offspring, or even that some inner impulse toward perfection caused the new organs to develop. This was merely to explain one mystery by another. True, the same might at the time have been said of Darwin's own explanation, which assumed variations in offspring (though the explanation of these variations was still not understood), but if it was a mystery, it was at least one of everyday occurrence, which was not true of the development of new organs by mature organisms.

It was the unscientific character of earlier evolutionary theory that made scientists like Lyell and Huxley, and Darwin himself, skeptical. All the same, their predecessors made some telling points. There were the improvements made in some domesticated animals and plant species by artificial selection—of which Darwin was to see the full significance. There were embryonic changes: the development of tadpole into frog and larva into butterfly. There were vestigial organs—noted by Erasmus Darwin—which seemed once to have served a purpose but now served none, suggesting that the modern species might be radically different from the ancestral one to which such an organ was useful. And there was the fossil record, unmistakable evidence of the *extinction* of species. The giant bones which lay embedded in the earth proved that the Creator could change His mind. Struggle and waste in nature were familiar to the nineteenth century long before *The Origin of Species*; Tennyson's "Nature, red in tooth and claw" is a pre-Darwinian quotation. But what naturalists did not see was that this could be used to explain the formation as well as the extinction of species.

Darwin had been struck during his voyage by a number of facts which seemed at odds with the special creation of each species. The organic life he studied so intensively and collected so assiduously seemed littered with clues, odd similarities, juxtapositions, and discontinuities, all surely significant, all part of some larger pattern if only one could discern it. Why did closely allied animals replace one another as one traveled southward? Why did extinct fossil species show such a close structural relation to existing animals? Above all, why, in the Galápagos Islands, did the birds and the famous Galápagos tortoises show slight variations from island to island, so that the local inhabitants could always tell from which island a tortoise had come? None of these things seemed to fit in with the special-creation theory. They began to tell an intelligible story once one doubted the fixity of species.

Ten months after his return to England, Darwin in 1837 opened his first notebook on "The Transmutation of Species"—the forge in which man's whole conception of the natural world was beaten into a new and enduring shape. The cause of change, Darwin was sure, must lie in reproduction, in heritable variations rather than in spontaneous changes in the living organism itself. By the end of 1838 the key was in his hand: natural selection of favorable variations in offspring. Because of these variations, and changes in the environment, nature was unstable, variable, not static, "those forms slightly favored getting the upper hand and forming species." Later, in the *Origin*, he was to describe in detail the "war between insect and insect—between insects, snails, and other animals with birds and beasts of prey—all striving to increase, all feeding on each other, or on the trees, their seeds and seedlings, or on the other plants which first clothed the ground and thus checked the growth of the trees!"

Darwin's own account suggests that in part he owed the inspiration for his theory to reading Thomas Malthus's *Essay on Population* (written in 1798), though the dates in Darwin's journal throw some doubt on this. Malthus's essay purports to show that population growth will always tend to outrun food supply unless checked by war, famine, or disease. Malthus's principle could obviously be extended in an evolutionary direction by concentrating on the struggle for existence and the question of why some survived rather than others. Seven years before the publication of the *Origin*, Herbert Spencer had already given Malthus such an interpretation in his brief essay on "The Theory of Population," but he applied it only to human beings, not to the problem of species as such.

Darwin was still planning a much longer work than *The Origin of Species* was in fact to be, when his hand was forced by the dramatic coincidence of the arrival of a paper from Alfred Russel Wallace in which the theory of natural selection was clearly set out. Darwin, in anguish, remarked, "I would far rather burn my whole book than that he or any other man should think I had behaved in a paltry spirit." But Darwin's priority was acknowledged, and the presentation of the Darwin-Wallace thesis as a joint paper to the Linnaean Society on July 1, 1858, was one of the most unsordid episodes in the history of science. It was more than twenty years since Darwin had begun his first notebook on "The Transmutation of Species." The Linnaean Society paper caused little stir; not so the publication in the following year of *The Origin of Species*. The "murder" Darwin had confessed to Hooker fifteen years earlier was out.

As a book, *The Origin of Species* gains enormously from the range of interests that a natural scientist could still, in the mid-nineteenth century, allow himself. It is a work of original research

—as original as anything ever published—yet it is also a vast panorama of the natural world seen in the light of natural selection and in the almost endless perspective of geological time as it was now understood. Its author was not merely another evolutionist, or even one who, like Wallace, had seen where the key to evolution lay. He was a geologist who had produced the modern theory of the formation of coral reefs, and explained, on geological grounds, the gaps in the fossil record. He was a painstaking research worker, one of the world's leading authorities on barnacles, who devoted much of the latter part of his life to the fertilization of orchids and the activities of earthworms. His equipment as a student of nature was virtually complete. The former undergraduate beetle-collector was geologist, botanist, zoologist, and later, physical anthropologist. He was a paleontologist who had himself dug up a fossilized Megatherium (an extinct ground sloth), an ecologist who had observed the interrelations of organic life in tropical forests and in the grounds of Down House, his Kent home.

The furor created by the publication of *The Origin of Species* was not due simply to the fact that it contradicted the literal word of the first chapter of Genesis. Many Christians had already reconciled themselves, for example, to interpreting the seven days allotted to the Creation in an allegorical sense. Religious doubt, that characteristic Victorian malaise, with its crop of social and spiritual catastrophes, of "dangerous" books and clerical resignations, had become almost a commonplace of the intellectual scene since the first impact of the new German Biblical criticism in the 1830's.

The *Origin* owed its notoriety primarily to two things. First, it destroyed at one blow the central tradition of rational Protestant religious apologetics—Natural Theology. All the beautiful and ingenious contrivances in nature, which Natural Theology had explained as the benevolent design of an Almighty Clockmaker, Darwin's theory explained by the operation of natural selection: the struggle for life, preserving random hereditary variations.

Second, the *Origin* became notorious for something it did *not* say, though anyone who read it intelligently could not fail to be aware of the implication: that man was first cousin to—*not* descended from, though this was an error often made—the ape and the orangutan. As Darwin had written in his notebook, "animals may partake from our common origin in one ancestor . . . we may be all netted together." Darwin only completed this aspect of his work in his later books—*The Descent of Man* (1871) and *The Expression of the Emotions in Man and Animals* (1872)—but the public seized on it at once. Darwinism was "the monkey theory," though monkeys are mentioned in the *Origin* no more frequently than other species. This was, however, the crux of the great Oxford debate in 1860 between T. H. Huxley and Bishop Wilberforce, at which Huxley made the famous retort, in response to the bishop's gibe, that he would prefer to have an ape for a grandfather than a man "possessed of great means and influence" who used his influence to bring an important scientific discussion into ridicule.

This episode was characteristic in many ways: of Wilberforce, whose nickname was "Soapy Sam"; of Huxley; of what was to the layman the central issue of Darwinism; and of the reasons why Darwin's supporters were victorious. They won not only because the weight of argument was on their side, but because they were always more righteous than the righteous. Intellectual infidelity had hitherto been equated with immorality and lower-class radicalism. It was an argument that died hard; Darwin was rebuked for publishing *The Descent of Man* "at a moment when the sky of Paris was red with the incendiary flames of the Commune." Hence it was of the utmost importance that the leading Victorian agnostics—Darwin, Huxley, Leslie Stephen (who resigned from holy orders as a result of reading the *Origin*)—were gentlemen and family men of unimpeachable sexual and financial respectability. They turned the tables on their opponents by taking a higher moral line. It was *immoral* to believe without proof, to refuse, as Huxley said, borrowing the language of religion, "to sit down before the facts as a little child."

Of course, Darwin's theory was not immediately accepted by all scientists, either. In England its opponents were led by Sir Richard Owen, superintendent of the natural history department of the British Museum, while in America the chief protagonists for and against Darwin were Asa Gray and Louis Agassiz. Darwin himself played little part in the controversies that surrounded him, devoting his time to his orchids and earthworms and contenting himself with boyish shouts of applause from the sidelines. He was not interested in metaphysics and was not by nature combative. He was, moreover, by now an invalid.

There has been much speculation about Darwin's malady. Was it the aftermath of some tropical illness, caught during the voyage of the *Beagle*, which confined the mountaineer and explorer of the 1830's to his sofa at Down House for a large part of his later life? Or was it, as has been suggested, psychological in origin, due to a feeling that in removing God from His part in the Creation he had committed a kind of parricide? Much has been made, too, of Darwin's confession of the withering, in later life, of his feeling for beauty. He has been called "the fragmentary man," "the anesthetic man," and so on. It has been remarked, not altogether unfairly, that he debated whether to marry—he married his cousin, Emma Wedgwood, in 1839—rather as a man might decide whether to keep a dog, but it is difficult not to find something attractive in his reflection: "charms of music & female chitchat, good for one's health; but forced to visit and receive relations, *terrible loss of time*." There was always a childlike simplicity about Darwin, which has endeared him to some commentators and irritated others.

To some the implications of Darwin's theory were negative and desolating. The whole earth no longer proclaimed the glory of the Lord. Paradoxically, in revealing the closeness of man's links with the rest of creation, Darwin seemed to have cut the emotional ties between man and nature. The world was not, apparently, the rational creation of a Being whose purposes, though infinitely beyond man's full comprehension, were in some sense akin to the purposes and feelings of man himself (at least they *were* purposes). Nature, according to Darwin, was the product of blind chance and man a lonely, intelligent mutation, scrambling with the brutes for his daily bread. To some the sense of loss was irrevocable; an umbilical cord was snapped. Faced with "a cold, passionless universe," the only appropriate attitude seemed, at best, a dignified resignation "with close-lipped patience for our only friend." Unlike the beliefs of the Greeks and the Stoics, the eighteenth-century Enlightenment, and the Rationalist Christian tradition, Darwinian nature held no clues for human conduct, no answers to human dilemmas. The modern ethics of the void—existentialism and all ethical creeds that make goodness not an innate property of things but a matter of human decision—have as an underlying assumption the purposelessness of the material world. So too, probably, did the rejection of "nature" as the prime subject for art by the aesthetes of the late nineteenth century. Man no longer characteristically expects to find nature suffused with divinity; he must create it out of his own visions.

But there were others for whom the two-thousand-year-old tradition of seeking prescriptions for human action in nature was hard to break. They found—and they were mostly the strong, the successful, or the embittered—the prescription they were looking for in "the survival of the fittest." They adopted natural selection as the key to "progress," though Darwin had not spoken of progress, only of adaptation. There were many fields, in the late nineteenth and early twentieth centuries, to which this formula seemed conveniently to apply. In Europe the nations watched each other, trained their young men, and waited for the day of reckoning. In America there were still great industrial and financial empires to be won by buccaneering methods. In Asia and Africa and the Pacific there were backward peoples to be brought within the orbit of the world's markets and taught their necessary subordination to the white man.

It is a strange paradox that Darwin, who gave up shooting because of the cruelty it entailed, should have been one of the begetters of the strident power philosophies of the later nineteenth century. The notion of the struggle for existence was not invented by Darwin, but the tendency to apply it to social relations was enormously reinforced by the apparent "scientific" backing given by Darwin's theory. Even Marx and Engels adopted Darwinism as the biological counterpart to the class war, though Darwin respectfully declined the honor of having the English edition of *Das Kapital* dedicated to him. "The survival of the fittest" in a human context could be all things to all men. Everything depended on what you took as the competing units: individuals, classes, races, or nations. It even invaded academic sociology, in the work of Herbert Spencer and Walter Bagehot in England and Ludwig Gumplowicz in Austria, the Russian anarchist Prince Kropotkin, and William Graham Sumner in the United States. To Sumner "millionaires are a product of natural selection"—an argument which appealed to Andrew Carnegie. The doctrine of the survival of the fittest also recommended itself to Theodore Roosevelt and to the British imperialists of the late nineteenth century. The belief that war was "a biological necessity," as one of Germany's leading military thinkers put it, helped to shape that country's military and political thinking before the First World War; filtered through innumerable hack popularizations, it formed a vital ingredient in the pseudoscientific mess of racialism, nationalism, and anti-Semitism swallowed by the young Hitler in the public reading rooms of Munich and Vienna. Racial doctrines had entered European thought before Darwin, as an offshoot of developments in anatomy and philology, and Darwin himself did not endorse the application of his theory in social contexts—Huxley, indeed, explicitly repudiated it—but inevitably it provided a kind of crucible into which the fears and hatreds of the age could be dipped and come out coated with an aura of scientific authority.

The bloodletting of two world wars, and the prospect that organized human aggression, far from improving the species, may actually eliminate it altogether, have dampened interest in this application, or rather misapplication, of Darwin's theory. Public attention now concentrates either on theological interpretations of evolution, in the manner of Teilhard de Chardin, or on the implications of the new factor which the development of human intelligence, with its powers of storing and communicating knowledge and hence of purposive control of the future, introduces into the evolutionary picture.

Seen in this way, evolution becomes a great adventure in which man, product of random mutations and of a suffering, blindly struggling creation, becomes, at least in part, the arbiter of his destiny. If this is to be so, a major contribution to control of the future will be the chief development in biology since Darwin: understanding the mechanism of heredity. Genetics places the thread of life in men's hands, the chemical ribbon linking past and future. In his notebook Darwin had written: "Given transmutation theory, instinct and structure become full of speculation and line of observation. My theory would lead to study of instincts, heredity and mind heredity."

When the *Origin* was written, the science of genetics did not exist. Evolution was the result of natural selection acting on heritable variations in offspring, but, as Darwin admitted, "Our ignorance of the laws of variation is profound." The gap had begun to be filled by the experiments of the Moravian monk Gregor Mendel, but Mendel's work was rediscovered only at the beginning of this century. At first Darwinian natural selection appeared to have no application in the new science, and Darwin's reputation sank somewhat. Later, however, genetic theory began to explain variations as a consequence of environmental selection acting on the results of mutations of genes, and today selection is a controlling concept in the study of genetics, with its incalculable prospects, exhilarating and appalling, of insight into the nature of life and its possibilities for good and evil in the molding of man's physical and intellectual make-up.

Darwinism was a nineteenth-century *cause célèbre*, a fashionable formula, like Hegelianism, for applying scholarship or prejudice to the results of science. It was also, like the work of John Dalton or Michael Faraday, a permanent contribution to men's knowledge of the natural world. Yet even this comparison diminishes Darwin's real stature. As with Copernicus and Newton, before and after Darwin are different intellectual territories.

181

Karl Marx was so impressed by Darwin's Origin of Species *that he offered to dedicate the first volume of his major work,* Capital, *to the eminent naturalist. Though Darwin, who was anything but a radical, declined the honor, Marx nevertheless liked to think of himself as the Darwin of the social sciences. The two men were roughly contemporaries and both, strangely enough, had hit upon the fundamentals of their theories at about the same time, in the mid-1840's. But while Marx's masterpiece was not published until 1867 he had, in the famous* Communist Manifesto *of 1848, advanced his leading ideas in capsule form and provided the radical working classes with a handbook of social revolution that must be counted among the most influential publications of modern times. However, as Mr. Burrow here points out, Marx was a man of many faces, making him, if not the most appealing, at least one of the most impressive figures of the past century.*

THE MANY FACES OF KARL MARX

J. W. BURROW

One can imagine few greater shocks to our sense of the fitness of things than a revelation that Karl Marx without his beard had the face of a romantic poet, another Byron or Shelley. We are used to seeing him in the guise of an angry prophet, beard bristling with outrage at the iniquities of his opponents; or nobly marmoreal in profile, with a similar profile of Engels or Lenin apparently adhering to one of his ears, as one sees them on innumerable communist posters. The beards of the saints of European communism seem a part of their roles: Marx's leonine and denunciatory; Engels's brisk and worldly; Lenin's a jutting icebreaker, forging forward toward the happy land over the always-receding horizon.

Yet the suggestion that the young Marx might have had a face of dreamy, romantic sensitivity—though literally speaking highly improbable, to judge from the clues among the bristles—is not altogether symbolically inappropriate. Marx was an idealistic young man, born into a romantic environment, whose early ardors bear unmistakably the marks of a youth of the generation of Hector Berlioz and Victor Hugo—a generation to which Byron and Na-

Marx was fifty-seven when he posed for this photograph in 1875 in London, where he lived almost half his life as a political exile.   183

poleon, Prometheus and Faust, were the symbols of their own thwarted aspirations, pent up by the stuffy reaction that gripped Europe in the years after Waterloo. To many of that generation "revolution" was a holy word, and the spirit of freedom appeared, as in Delacroix's famous painting, as a beautiful bare-breasted woman leading the workers at the barricades. The years of Marx's youth and early manhood were the years before the European revolutions of 1848, when it seemed that with one final titanic effort humanity might throw off all its oppressors at one blow and create from the ashes of the old social order a new world of justice and freedom. Paris was revered by young men as the holy city of revolution. As the Russian socialist Aleksandr Herzen put it, "I entered the city with reverence, as men used to enter Jerusalem or Rome."

The fate of captive countries like Italy and Poland, ruled by oppressor nations whose domination had been reaffirmed at the Congress of Vienna, touched liberal consciences as Spain was to do in the 1930's and Hungary in the 1950's. Not only proletarians but artists and intellectuals of all kinds felt, during these years, the revolutionary itch; when revolution came to Europe's capitals in 1848–49, they went with the workers to the barricades.

It was to this generation that Karl Marx, born in 1818, belonged. There is no cause for surprise that he became a revolutionary; it would almost have been surprising if he had not. What distinguished him from most of his contemporaries was that in Marx youthful fervor soon became transmuted into scientific rigor, without abating its revolutionary character. Marx's revolutionary zeal thus acquired a staying power, while that of most of his contemporaries—vaguer, more hazily idealistic—faded with age and disillusionment. Nevertheless, Marx's "scientific" socialism never altogether lost a visionary, apocalyptic aureole that occasionally gives a lurid glow to the gray pages of *Capital* and recalls the ardent years before the false dawn of 1848. In his personal tastes, too, Marx remained a man of his generation; he shared that passionate love of Shakespeare that struck the intellectual youth of France and Germany in the early nineteenth century with the force of a revelation. For him, too, Prometheus, the archetypal rebel, the Titan who had defied Zeus, was a potent symbol, as he was for Shelley, Goethe, and Beethoven. Marx's taste in novels, again, was not chiefly for realistic novels of industrial England or Flaubert's brutal dissection of the French bourgeoisie, but for Sir Walter Scott and Alexandre Dumas the elder. Karl Marx, economist and visionary, German scholar and international revolutionary, contemptuous as he was of revolutionary phrasemakers and conspiratorial play-acting, was yet himself a powerful rhetorician and prophet of doom and regeneration, a romantic realist, a man of many faces.

The paradoxes begin with his birth. He was born of comfortably-off middle-class parents, not in one of the great centers of population and industry whose portentousness for the future he was so vehemently to proclaim, but in the ancient city of Trier. Marx was to experience poverty, but after, not before, he became a revolutionary. He never gained the firsthand experience of factory conditions possessed by his partner Friedrich Engels, the son of a Bremen manufacturer. Trier is a city of ancient monuments, set among the castle-dotted, vine-clustered terraces of the Moselle valley, only a few miles from the Luxembourg border and the forest of Ardennes. In one respect only was it an apt birthplace for Karl Marx. Trier, or Treves, which at the time of Marx's birth formed an outlying part of the dominions of the king of Prussia, had once been the gateway between the Latin and the Teutonic worlds. The great gate that marked the limits of the power of imperial Rome still stands, like a grandiose, abandoned Checkpoint Charlie, in the midst of Trier's traffic, a suitable reminder of a German to whom Paris and London were not only homes but the focus of his thoughts as the breeding grounds of revolution, a man who looked always to the West and has been honored in the East.

Marx's dreams were imperial in scale, ecumenical in scope, and grounded on a panoramic view of world history. Such cosmopolitanism, too, is characteristic of his generation. The French Revolution, the great beacon, extinguished yet still smoldering in the minds of men, especially of those too young to remember it, had been an ecumenical event; the fall of the Bastille, of little importance in itself, became a universal symbol, welcomed as eagerly in Britain and in Germany as in France itself. The nineteenth century is the classic age of the émigré intellectual, the cosmopolitan revolutionary, and the ideological *condottiere* fighting in a foreign land because liberty is every man's cause or because the proletariat has no fatherland. Besides the prototype, Byron, there were Mickiewicz, Polish poet and professor at the Collège de France, who raised a Polish legion in 1848 to fight for Italian independence against the Austrians; the Russian anarchist-nobleman Bakunin, later to be Marx's archenemy in the First Workers' International; and the aged Garibaldi, leading an irregular and somewhat undisciplined column of volunteers against the Prussians in 1870 on behalf of the newly reborn French Republic. When Friedrich Engels and a handful of fellow communists stood by the graveside of Karl Marx in Highgate cemetery, London, in 1883, they were honoring one of the last, as well as one of the most intransigent and least fraternal, of that unofficial fraternity of revolt, dating from the days when romanticism and revolution were almost synonymous terms.

In his secure niche in the placid, comely, preindustrial world of Trier and the German university towns, it was not personal oppression or the sight of proletarian misery and industrial squalor that first turned Marx into a revolutionary. Rather, it was the enthusiasms of his generation and the theories of his elders, the intellectual diet he encountered as a student. Marx the philosopher and the romantic humanist preceded Marx the politician and Marx the anatomist of industrial society. The philosophy Marx imbibed at the universities of Bonn and Berlin taught that man is truly himself, truly human, only when his activities are willed by himself and not manipulated by others or by blind forces. Only when he chooses, rationally, to act as his own human essence dictates is he free. The young Marx, applying this philosophy with his own uncompromising rigor, came to the conclusion that however free men might be in the abstract, legally speaking, as workers the majority were not free at all. Labor was, or should be, the highest expression of humanity, the activity by which men freely shaped and changed the world, subjecting *things* to the creative power of man. But labor, the essence of man's humanity, his godlike creative power, had itself been degraded into a thing and was bought and sold as a commodity. Instead of productive labor being used by humanity, human beings were used to produce products. The workers, the proletariat, were not free in practice, whatever the law said. The State was not their state, nor was it impartial, because it upheld the domination of the property owners. Man could only be free if labor was an assertion of men's own wills and creative power, rather than a commodity that they were forced to barter for wages, and this could only happen by the proletariat overthrowing the existing property relations and creating a state of real, as distinct from merely abstract, freedom. As Marx wrote at this time: "Philosophy finds in the proletariat its material weapons." Marx the philosopher had become Marx the revolutionary politician.

He had also become a radical journalist, and it was this that led to his first self-enforced exile, to Paris and Brussels. In Paris Marx, now a committed socialist, saw for the first time the visible reality of the urban proletariat—which he had invoked as the savior of society—on a far larger scale than anything Germany could yet show. There, too, he found groups of other socialists. He learned from them, particularly from their critiques of capitalist economics. But chiefly it was in his intellectual struggles with them, his attempts to define his own position as a way of repudiating what he saw as the mistakes and eccentricities of theirs, that the "Marxism" of the *Communist Manifesto*, published in 1848, was born. The historian and social scientist was taking over from the idealistic philosopher of freedom.

The *Communist Manifesto* differs from most political pamphlets precisely in the breadth and grandeur of its historical perspective. The message is that history both promises victory and imposes conditions. From the ringing opening ("The history of all hitherto-existing society is the history of class struggles") to the final celebrated call to action ("The proletarians have nothing to lose but their chains. They have a world to win. Working men of all countries, unite!"), the idea is hammered home that capitalism is not the permanent state of mankind but simply the latest phase of historical development. The bourgeoisie is not respectable and law-abiding; it is dynamic and rapacious; it has won its way to power by smashing the ancient privileged regime of feudalism. Seldom has a political movement received such a gift as the *Manifesto:* at once an indictment, an analysis, and a promise of victory. Marx and his collaborator Engels, in the *Communist Manifesto*, join Jean Jacques Rousseau and Abraham Lincoln among the rare few who have given to a political attitude a classic rhetorical form. Like Magna Carta and the Declaration of Independence, the *Manifesto*, especially in its concluding sentences, has the resonance and power of myth; like *The Social Contract* and the Gettysburg Address, it gives definitive form to a hunger of the human spirit.

In the short run the prophecy was false, nor has the ensuing century done much to make it valid. The specter of communism, which Marx and Engels had declared to be haunting Europe, proved in 1848, not for the last time, to be a wraith. The masses in France, enfranchised by the new Republican government, voted overwhelmingly for property and order; the resistance of the Parisian workers was trampled into the gutters of the capital by the government's cavalry. Marx, doubly exiled now that he had made France too hot for himself, arrived penniless in London, the grimy citadel of capitalism itself, where he was to spend the rest of his life. For Marx, the would-be man of action, the best years of his life were already behind him; the years of patient research had begun. Here in London he was to work, mole-like, dogged by poverty, exasperated by the political moderation of the English working class, laboriously documenting his thesis of the inevitable downfall of capitalism. Here he added to the philosophy of human emancipation and to the incandescent rhetoric of the *Communist Manifesto* the technical apparatus of economic analysis, the patiently accumulated facts of a massive indictment of a whole social system, and detailed analyses of the failure of the recent revolutions on the Continent.

It is the last that, together with the economic sections of *Capital*, establishes Marx as a great historian—probably, in terms of sheer intellectual power and penetration, the greatest historian of the nineteenth century, one to whom modern historians, no matter how hard they try, can scarcely avoid being indebted. His most masterly work of detailed history, a study of the rise to power of the new French emperor, Napoleon III, by a *coup d'état* over the ruins of the short-lived Republic established in 1848, is only an extended essay, yet it contains a revolution in the writing of history. Using the concept of a socioeconomic class not merely as part of a political indictment but as a tool of historical explanation, Marx provides what is still the most penetrating and stimulating analysis of the character and the success of Napoleon III—and also gives the classic account of the situation of the fascist dictator who claims to be "above" class and politics and to represent symbolically the unity of the nation.

Marx's essay is outstanding for the subtlety and minuteness with which he lays bare the ironies of history and the intricacies, the agitated twists and turns, of the various sections of French society, particularly the French bourgeoisie. Parodying its cult of "order," Marx represents it as capitulating to Napoleon III by its bleating: "Only theft can still save property; only perjury, religion; bastardy [Louis Napoleon's legitimacy was doubtful], the family; disorder, order!" Marx's contempt is tellingly balanced by the glimpses he gives of the perspectives of world history; they are, in a sense, his justification for treating Napoleon's regime as a comic masquerade. The spectacle of the great Napoleon's nephew stepping into his uncle's boots offered opportunities that Marx was not the man to miss. The note is struck in the first sentence: "Hegel remarks somewhere that all facts and personages of great importance in world history occur, as it were, twice. He forgot to add:

the first time as tragedy, the second as farce." This tone, sometimes of polished irony, sometimes sheer vaudeville, is maintained throughout.

The essay on Louis Napoleon is not only the work of a profound and original historical and sociological intelligence; it also has the verve and impact of first-class journalism. It was a talent Marx was to need in his exile, not merely as a political weapon but as a means of staying alive. One of the many ironies in Marx's career is that he quarried his indictment of capitalism from the British government's reports in the scholarly security of the British Museum Reading Room. Another is that in the 1850's he saved himself and his family from destitution partly by becoming the respected London correspondent of the New York *Tribune*. The managing editor, Charles Anderson Dana, had met Marx in Germany when the latter was winning notoriety as the crusading editor of the *Neue Rheinische Zeitung*. After Marx fled to London, Dana asked him for regular articles, at five dollars apiece. At first Engels wrote them for him, but when Marx's English improved he took heart from Engels's declaration that the *Tribune*'s own English was appalling and began to write them himself. Fortunately Marx's attitude toward British imperialism and the British governing class was pretty much the same as that of his American employers, and the relationship was a moderately harmonious one.

The meager pay of the *Tribune* and the subsidies of Engels enabled Marx and his family to survive the first bitter years of exile in London. Turned out of their first lodgings into the street because of a mix-up over the rent, the family settled in two small rooms at 28 Dean Street, Soho Square, in a poor exiles' quarter, where the house is now surrounded by restaurants and strip-clubs. There they endured the hardships of genteel poverty. Marx wrote to Engels in 1852: "For a week past I have been in the pleasant position of being unable either to go out for want of my overcoats, which are at the pawnshop, or to eat meat because the butcher has stopped credit. The only good news we have here comes from my sister-in-law, the minister's wife, who announces that my wife's uncle is ill at last." In these circumstances, most witnesses agreed the Marx family created something very like a domestic idyll. Of the many faces of Karl Marx not the least surprising or remarkable is Marx the family man, a devoted husband, a jovial and indulgent father.

In 1843 Marx had married Jenny von Westphalen, the beautiful daughter of a Prussian government official. When they came to

189

London, there were already three children, Jenny, Laura, and Edgar. Shortly after their arrival Guido was born and inevitably was nicknamed Fawkes, after the would-be dynamiter of the British Houses of Parliament; Marx's own nicknames were "the Moor" —a reference to his dark hair—and "Old Nick." Two more daughters, Franziska and Eleanor, were born later. The household was completed by "Lenchen," the Westphalens' family servant, who was said to be the only person who could subdue Marx. There may have been a reason for this. There were rumors at the time that Marx or Engels was the father of Lenchen's illegitimate son Frederick, and subsequent evidence points to Marx. Whether this was the result of an isolated lapse from fidelity to Jenny or of a protracted liaison, we do not know.

Details of Marx's family life are preserved by another exile and a disciple, Wilhelm Liebknecht, in a series of descriptive scenes that have the slightly comic naïveté of the sentimental paintings of domestic scenes of the period: pictures of a benign Marx patting urchins' heads like a Mr. Pickwick and giving them pennies and apples, or of the family picnics on Hampstead Heath. Liebknecht, who was obviously often hungry, recalled with particular tenderness a "substantial joint of roast veal . . . consecrated by tradition for the Sunday outings to Hampstead Heath. A basket of a size quite unusual in London, brought by Lenchen from Trier, was the tabernacle in which the holy of holies was borne. . . . Bread and cheese could be bought on the heath, where crockery, hot water and milk were also to be had, just as in a Berlin *Kaffeegarten*." After lunch the adults would sleep on the grass, read the Sunday papers, or give piggyback rides to the children, Marx being, according to his daughter Eleanor, a splendid horse. On the walk home they would sing German folk songs, or Marx would recite Shakespeare or Dante from memory.

Three of the children died, Guido and Franziska before reaching their first birthdays, so that Marx was especially agonized by the death of Edgar at the age of nine. To his daughters he was an indulgent and fascinating companion, joining in their horseplay and telling fantastic stories in the manner of E. T. A. Hoffmann. To his daughter Eleanor he was "the cheeriest, gayest soul that ever breathed . . . a man brimming over with humor and good humor, whose hearty laugh was infectious and irresistible . . . the kindliest, gentlest, most sympathetic of companions. . . . His kindness and patience were really sublime."

Marx's political opponents would have been intensely surprised to hear it. They knew Marx in another of his incarnations, as a practical politician, a man of domineering temper, brutal speech, and implacable rancor. His opponents were, of course, not only the bourgeoisie, which was virtually unaware of his existence, but his fellow socialists. Many of Marx's key works are polemics against the errors of some erstwhile comrade. A long succession of socialist theorists and leaders felt the edge of Marx's scorn and the crushing weight of his erudition as he fought them for control of the socialist parties and movements to which he at various times belonged. Marx was a formidable political opponent, but he had no conception of consensus politics; again and again he showed himself ready to abandon or wreck a promising movement rather than allow it to fall into the hands of those he regarded as doctrinally in error. His deliberate destruction of the First Workers' International to save it from the Russian anarchist Bakunin and his followers was only the most notable of these fatal self-administered purges.

Marx's irritability was no doubt exasperated by persistent ill health. When writing *Capital* he was severely troubled with hemorrhoids. As he wrote plaintively to Engels, "to finish I must at least be able to *sit down*," adding grimly, "I hope the bourgeoisie will remember my carbuncles." Utterly dedicated to the idea of revolution, Marx spent his life as an exile, despite his attempts to organize the German exiles and to collaborate with English working-class leaders, essentially as a scholar. He would have nothing to do with merely conspiratorial politics; there was no substitute for the travail of history and the political education of the workers by the class struggle. Marx's rejection of conspiracy was not due to moral objections or to natural coolness of temperament, but to a massive intellectual self-restraint, a contempt for impractical revolutionary dreaming and frothy oratory. He was in fact a man in whose nature aggression and revolt ran deep. In a questionnaire composed by his daughter Laura he once gave the answers: "Your idea of happiness: *To fight.* The vice you detest most: *Servility.* Favorite hero: *Spartacus, Kepler.*"

The official name of Marx's circle was the German Workers' Educational Society, and the educational aspect was taken seriously even when it had nothing to do with politics. There was nothing narrow about his intellectual interests. He could read all the main European languages and taught himself Russian when he was in his fifties. He read Greek and regularly reread Aeschylus. He was interested in the natural sciences and, of course, technology; he acclaimed Darwin and became highly excited when he saw a model of an electric train engine in a shop window. For relaxation he would do mathematics; during his wife's last illness he could find solace only in working on calculus. In his dealings with his young followers one sees not only Marx the political doctrinaire but also, more surprisingly, Marx the pedagogue. On the whole the latter sounds a good deal more intimidating: "How he scolded me one day," Liebknecht lamented, "because I did not know—Spanish! . . . Every day I was questioned and had to translate a passage from *Don Quixote*. . . ." Educational bullying was obviously part of Marx's nature, even apart from politics, and one can see in these reminiscences the professor he at one time seemed destined to become.

But ultimately, of course, the politician and social scientist were uppermost. Marx had already, before he came to London, developed his characteristic theory of history: that a society's legal and political institutions are an expression of its economic substructure. But it was in England, in the British Museum, that Marx did his fundamental research as an economist and social scientist and prepared his most celebrated work, *Capital*. Marx's book is a strange amalgam: it is a highly abstract theoretical economic analysis designed to show that the capitalist annexed all the surplus value produced by the worker, leaving the latter nothing but his bare subsistence, and himself contributing nothing. There is a good deal of detailed economic history, of which Marx was a pioneer, analyzing the earlier stages of capital accumulation, the dispossession of the European peasantry, and the development of European industrial and mercantile civilization. And there is the statistical demonstration of the human cost of early industrialism, compiled chiefly from the evidence of the British government's own commissions and the reports of its factory inspectors. Marx here joins Dickens, Disraeli, Carlyle, and other Victorians appalled by the conditions of industrial and urban life. These pages of *Capital* are, for all Marx's attempts to refrain from mere denunciation, the work of an angry moralist who could see in the cold figures "the motley crowd of workers of all ages, and sexes, that press on us more insistently than did the souls of the slain on Ulysses."

Finally there is prophecy, deduced from a model of capitalist competition and production—intended to show the inevitability of increasingly frequent and disastrous economic crises and the ultimate revolt of the masses. In the *Communist Manifesto* Marx had called for this revolt and predicted its success. Now in *Capital* he thought he had demonstrated its inevitability, the result of the self-destructive character of capitalism, doomed to perish by its own inherent contradictions: "The centralization of the means of production and the socialization of labor reach a point where they prove incompatible with their capitalist husk. This bursts asunder. The knell of capitalist private property sounds. The expropriators are expropriated."

Marx thought that his conclusion was the verdict of social and economic science. More evident to us is the face and voice of the angry Hebrew prophet, denouncing the worship of the golden calf and the human sacrifices to a mechanical Moloch and trumpeting the wrath to come in the careless ears of the unrighteous. Capital is a "fetish," a false god. Marx's intellectual career comes full circle; the face of the economic theorist melts into that of the young idealist philosopher, to whom the ultimate evil is the subjection of mind and spirit to the domination of brute *things*.

The age of imperialism has come and gone within hardly more than a century. In retrospect it seems hardly credible that in half a century a few European powers should have established their control over most of Africa and much of Asia, to say nothing of the Pacific world. They were able to do so, of course, because their advanced technology provided them with weapons against which the underdeveloped peoples had no defense. It was a thrilling period, punctuated by reports of impressive victories and important conquests. Yet now the world is deluged with writings about the evils of imperialism and its inevitable decline and fall. Within a second half-century the whole elaborate structure of European domination has been liquidated. No doubt there were many seamy sides to imperialism, but in the last analysis it may well appear as necessary preparation for the undeveloped areas of the world to enter and participate in the world community.

The British were pre-eminent among imperial nations and combined the faults and the virtues of foreign administrators. In this essay Mr. Morris, a well-known commentator on British affairs, passes in review a remarkable galaxy of empire builders, from Stanley and Rhodes to "Jacky" Fisher of dreadnaught fame. These men may have lacked human sympathy, but they had courage in abundance, faith in what they were doing, and the authoritarian temperament without which a handful of men cannot hope to rule over millions.

THE IMPERIALISTS

JAMES MORRIS

When, on June 22, 1897, Queen Victoria of England celebrated her sixtieth year upon the throne, her ministers of state looked around them at the world of the day, contemplated Her Majesty's place in history, and decided to celebrate the event as a festival of Empire.

It was an obvious focus, to symbolize a reign of such unexampled success. Britain might still be the Two Nations that Disraeli had descried; its slums might still be fetid, its back streets still violent, its industrial cities satanic; but it was in a condition of rare exhilaration all the same, for it was gripped by the excitement of power. The British Empire was the greatest agglomeration of possessions the world had ever known—nearly a quarter of the earth's land mass, nearly a quarter of its population. Given a head start by their original industrial revolution and sustained by the re-

Queen Victoria in 1876, the year that she became Empress of India, seated on an ivory throne donated by one of her subject princes. 195

British troops at the Great Sphinx in 1882 during the Egyptian war.

markable social and political stability of their kingdom, the British had ringed the globe with their wealth, strength, and pedigree. The lost American colonies had long since been replaced: half of Asia; half of Africa; half of North America; all of Australia; scattered islands, fortresses, and coaling stations—all these were red on the map, and made Britain the supreme power of the time.

There were sages who understood that this was a kind of historical inflation—too much consequence chasing too little reality. Britain was an overcrowded island with no natural resources, living by its wits. The circumstances that had made it pre-eminent could not last forever, and one day it must inevitably return to normal. For the moment, though, the British were making the most of their climax. The amorphous creed called the New Imperialism, whose meanings were innumerable, had taken the Conservative-Unionists to a slashing electoral victory over their Liberal opponents, and even the Elgars and Kiplings of the decade were dazzled by the imperial colors. The Empire itself, which patriots of classical tastes liked to call the *Pax Britannica*, was growing all the time like a monumental snowball, one distant acquisition leading inexorably to another as the fleets and armies of the Crown pressed into another economic market, another strategic hinterland, or another field of Christian endeavor. Asked to define his notion of paradise, Alfred Austin, the poet laureate, probably spoke for the people in his reply: to sit in a garden receiving news alternately of British victories by land and by sea.

And yet, although there was inevitably arrogance in the British air, racial bigotry and vulgar jingoism, still this was a good-natured moment of imperial history. Success had not soured this nation, and behind the gasconade gentler national qualities awaited their turn—humor, toleration, and above all fairness. The queen herself, grandest of all old ladies though she was, perfectly expressed these

196

simpler characteristics, and it was a relief that her message on that Diamond Jubilee morning shrilled to no chauvinist trumpets and did not even pander to the national grandiloquence. She was addressing four hundred and ten million subjects occupying thirteen million square miles of British territory, but all she said was this: "From my heart I thank my people. May God bless them."

They Took England with Them

When Rudyard Kipling first went east from India, he noted that though the stinks of Lahore and Calcutta had something in common, the stink of Burma was different; he was struck by the numberless energies of the Chinese and the startling vigor of Japan, but wherever he went in the eastern Empire, he observed that the British appeared to be exactly the same. "It was just We Our Noble Selves," he wrote sardonically of a party in the barracks above the botanical gardens at Singapore. "In the center was the pretty Memsahib with light hair and fascinating manners, and the plump little Memsahib that talks to everybody and is in everybody's confidence, and the spinster fresh from home, and the bean-fed, well-groomed subaltern with the light coat and the fox-terrier. On the benches sat the fat colonel, and the large judge, and the engineer's wife, and the merchantman and his family after their kind —male and female met I them, and but for the little fact that they were entire strangers to me, I would have saluted them all as old friends."

Nobody, of course, runs as true to type as that. The subaltern probably cherished a passion for the poetry of Baudelaire, the spinster may have spoken fluent Cantonese, the merchant and his kind perhaps were Seventh Day Adventists. To the stranger, nevertheless, the British in their Empire do seem to have been instantly familiar, whether they were the stiff pomaded or parasoled representatives of the gentry or irrepressible soldiers of the line. Britishness was very strong in Victoria's later years, and British people were recognizably British.

For the most part they were bigger and fitter than other Europeans. A prosperous century had made even the poorer classes so, and several hundred years of success had filled out the gentry. The tall stature and upright bearing of the English gentleman are confirmed in every old photograph of regiment, First XV, or Union Committee. Five members of Lord Salisbury's patrician cabinet were more than six feet tall. Salisbury himself was six feet four

inches, and Henry Chaplin, his president of the Local Government
Board, weighed two hundred and fifty pounds. The average height
of army recruits in 1897 was five feet seven inches, and their average chest measurement was thirty-four inches—substantially
bigger than the conscripts of the Continental armies. The public-
school idea of *mens sana in corpore sano* was percolating, in a desultory way, into the upbringing of the masses, and no other people in
Europe were so keen on sport.

These physical advantages were sustained by a detachment of
bearing. The most rabid of the new imperialists were quite proud
of the fact that the British were not liked: certainly, to be loved
was no part of the national ambition. The British were aware that
of all the peoples of the earth they were the most commonly re-
sented, but a shell composed of pride, duty, shyness, and a sense of
membership protected them. G. W. Steevens, traveling to Egypt
in 1897, describes the all-British company on the mail train to
Brindisi: "Fair-haired, blue-eyed, spare-shouldered and spare-
jawed, with puckered brows and steadfast eyes that seemed to look
outwards and inwards at the same time, they were unmistakably
builders—British Empire builders." Can one not imagine them,
this trainload of bronzed aliens, sharing their private jokes, exuding
their particular smells of tweed, tobacco, and lavender, as they
presented their baggage to the customs officials at Modane? It is as
though they were encapsuled there, snug in their own ways, honoring their own club rules. Foreigners and subject peoples alike recognized this separateness; it was essential to the character of the
Pax Britannica. This was not so much a haughty empire as a private one.

The aristocracy of Empire was the official class, together with
the landed gentry of British planters, and in crown colonies the
two classes often intermarried. It was not a very aristocratic aristocracy. Viceroys and governors were often noblemen, and their
wives society beauties—Lady Horton, wife of a governor of Ceylon
in the 1830's, was the subject of Byron's "She Walks In Beauty
Like the Night." British regiments posted overseas contained their
quota of young bloods, but the great mass of the imperial service,
like the officer corps of the colonial forces, was pre-eminently upper
middle class.

They were the children of a unique culture, that of the English
public schools, with its celibate discipline, its classical loyalties, its
emphasis on self-reliance, team spirit, delegated responsibility,
Christian duty, and stoic control. One did not cry when one said

good-bye to Mama at Paddington Station. One did not, as a general rule, wish to appear too clever, or too enthusiastic. One loyally upheld the prefectorial system, while realizing that certain rules were made to be broken. The public schools, greatly expanded in the second half of the century and ever more dedicated to their own code of conduct, lay somewhere near the heart of the imperial ethic. "It would be terrible to think of what would happen to us," wrote Eustace Miles, amateur tennis champion of the world, "if our public school system were swept away, or if—and this comes to very much the same thing—from our public school system were swept away our Athletics and our Games."

A man's best proof of fitness to rule in India, Miles thought, was to have been a captain of games, and certainly the public school system was well suited to the imperial needs. It produced men of high spirits, courage, and assurance, ready to rough it and unafraid of responsibility. If it was intellectually narrowing and chauvinist, well, this was an empire that survived by the separateness of its rulers, their conviction that what they did was right and that all else was second best. The public-school man was generally able to see the other person's point of view, provided it reflected his own values—*civilized* values, he would say. His inability to grasp the aspirations of Indians, Africans, or Malays stemmed from his absolute certainty that their whole manner of thought or way of life was, through no real fault of their own, misguided. At his worst the public-school man was a snobbish hearty; at his best he combined authority with Christian kindness and what he would have called grit; the rarest of his virtues was human sympathy, the rarest of his vices, cowardice.

And the most irritating of his traits, at least in the imperial context, seems to have been smugness. From the memoirs of the imperial civil services there generally breathes an air of conscious rectitude—disguised often in jollity and boyish dash, but seldom altogether absent. "How is it," one Anglo-Indian asked of himself and his colleagues in a rhetorical question addressed without a blush to his fiancée, who must have loved him dearly, "how is it that these pale-cheeked exiles give security to a race of another hue, other tongues, other religions which rulers of their own people have ever failed to give? Dearest, there are unseen moral causes which I need not point out. . . ."

The imperial protocol was strict and all-embracing (in India sanitary commissioners and inspectors general of jails shared seventy-sixth place in order of precedence), and Baron von Hübner, an

Australian traveler of the time, tells us that if ever "members of the lower classes," other than grooms, showed up in Singapore, the government found means of returning them to Britain. White prestige must be maintained, and caste was in the air of Empire.

People of grander imagination often disliked these official airs. Lord Bryce thought the average Indian civil servant pretty boring: "a good deal of uniformity . . . a want of striking, even marked individualities . . . rather wanting an imagination and sympathy . . . too conventionally English." Winston Churchill, who was in India in 1896 and 1897, did not take to Anglo-Indian society. "A lot of horrid Anglo-Indian women at the races. Nasty vulgar creatures all looking as though they thought themselves great beauties. I fear me they are a sorry lot. . . . Nice people in India are few and far between. They are like oases in the desert. . . ."

Poor Anglo-Indians! Twenty-one and very clever, Churchill was applying to their provincial attitudes the standards of his own background, glittering with the wealth and genius of London and New York. Life in the official circles of Empire may not have looked exciting to him, but it pursued a staid and comfortable course, much in the tennis-party tradition of the lesser British gentry at home. The scale of things was often grotesquely swollen, though, so that a married couple in India might easily have a staff of twenty-five servants, imposed on them by a caste system even more rigid than their own: bearer, children's nurse, cooks, table servers, a tailor, a laundryman, a water carrier, gardeners, grooms, and grasscutters. In camp, if a fairly senior official took his wife on tour, this establishment might grow to fifty or more dependents. Living in what was virtually a private village with this immense ménage, the imperialist forfeited any kind of privacy—the servants knew everything—and the manner of life remained supremely orthodox. In Ceylon, for example, people were normally "at home" once each week, and there were frequent calls and dances at the Queen's in Kandy and golfing weekends at Nuwara Eliya. The bungalows were lofty and cool and lapped in lawns, and there was an English vicar at the church up the road; all seemed changeless, useful, and very agreeable.

The family tradition was strong in the imperial service. The same names appear repeatedly in the honors lists and church memorials, and fathers' footsteps were loyally followed. General Henry Rundle, Kitchener's chief of staff in the Sudan in 1897, was the son of Joseph Rundle, who had first planted the British flag on Aden soil in 1839. Generations of Stracheys had served in India, and there had been a Skinner in the 1st Bengal Lancers ever since Lieutenant Colonel James Skinner founded the regiment as Skinner's Horse in 1803.

This imperial elite was, as conquerors go, very well behaved. Its values were solid. Its rules were mostly sensible. Corruption was rare, and what Churchill thought vulgar was often no more than a dogged determination to stick to the habits and traditions that gave the Empire its stability. There are worse sins for a ruling class than thinking yourself more beautiful than you are.

The Explorers: Stanley and Eyre

The age of the great explorers was almost over by 1897, but there still lived in England one or two of the giants. Sir Henry Stanley, deliverer of Livingstone, first man to cross Africa from coast to coast, namer of lakes and discoverer of mountains, was an inconspicuous Liberal-Unionist back-bencher whose election platform had been "the maintenance, the spread, the dignity, the usefulness of the British Empire." He was fifty-six, a bullet-headed man with a truculent mouth and a walrus mustache, broadly built and very hard of eye. Nobody in England had led a more extraordinary life. Born John Rowlands in Denbighshire, North Wales, he spent nine years of childhood in the St. Asaph workhouse, his father dead and his mother uninterested, under the care of a savage schoolmaster who later went mad. He ran away and worked on a farm, in a haberdasher's shop and a butcher's, and in 1859 sailed as a cabin boy from Liverpool to New Orleans. In America he was adopted by a kind cotton broker and took his name, only to be left on his own again when the elder Stanley died. A life of staggering adventure followed: war, on both sides of the American Civil War, in the Indian campaigns of the West, in the United States Navy; journalism, with Napier in Abyssinia, in Spain during the 1869 rising, in search of Livingstone for the New York *Herald;* African exploration of the most sensational kind; wealth, fame, and the long struggle for recognition and respect in England.

By the late nineties his fighting days were over and he had become an eminent citizen of mild benevolence, reassuming British nationality and marrying very respectably. Though the British Empire had not yet recognized his services with a knighthood, he was loaded with honorary degrees, and Queen Victoria had herself commissioned a portrait of him, to hang in Windsor Castle. We hear nothing of him in the Diamond Jubilee celebrations, though we may assume he joined his fellow M.P.'s to watch the procession go by. But it is enthralling to think of him there at all, with his memories of workhouse and celebrity; the colossal journeys into the heart of Africa; the meeting with Livingstone that was to become a part of the folklore; the expedition to rescue Emin Pasha, beleaguered by the Mahdi in the Sudan, that cost five thousand lives. Stanley's journey across Africa in the 1870's had led directly to the "scramble for Africa" that was the mainspring of the new imperialism. He was the greatest adventurer of the age, an imperial monument in himself.

Edward Eyre was still alive, too, an imperial specimen of a different sort, whose name had been given to a large bump on the southern Australian shoreline, Eyre Peninsula. Eyre was a Yorkshireman who emigrated to Australia, aged seventeen, with £400. He farmed for a time, served as a magistrate and "protector of aborigines," and discovered a livestock route from New South Wales to the new settlements in South Australia. Then, in 1841, he set off on one of the most desperate of all exploratory journeys, from Adelaide around the Great Australian Bight to King George Sound in the extreme southwest. One white man and three native boys started with him, but presently two of the boys murdered the white overseer and fled with most of the supplies.

Eyre was left with a single aborigine, forty pounds of flour, some tea, and some sugar, with five hundred miles of waterless desert behind him and six hundred ahead. For eight weeks the two men labored across that terrible slab of country. Often they were reduced to gathering the morning dew in a sponge and sucking it. At Thistle Cove they were picked up by a French whaler and rested for ten days on board, but Eyre insisted on finishing the journey and after five months on the march stumbled at last into the settlement at King George Sound. It was a perfectly useless adventure, as it turned out. Nothing was discovered and nothing proved;

but Eyre had made his name as one of the most intrepid of the imperial explorers.

By 1897 he was unfortunately best known in England for other
reasons. Eyre became lieutenant governor of New Zealand, governor of St. Vincent, and finally governor of Jamaica; and there, in
1865, he put down a black riot with unusually ferocious zeal, killing or executing more than six hundred people, flogging six hundred more, and burning down a thousand homes. He became a
figure of violent controversy at home. Ruskin, Tennyson, and
Carlyle were among his supporters; John Stuart Mill and T. H.
Huxley were members of a committee that secured his prosecution
for murder. The Eyre Defense Committee called him "a good,
humane, and valiant man." The Jamaica Committee, supported
by a strong body of what Carlyle called "nigger-philanthropists,"
hounded him for ten years with accusations of brutality. The legal
charges were dismissed, but Eyre was never offered another post.
In 1897 he was living in seclusion in a Devonshire manor house, a
strange, always dignified, and self-contained man. Through it all
he had hardly bothered to defend himself—as though the sandy
silence of the outback had muffled his soul.

The Soldiers: Wolseley, Roberts, Kitchener

There were only three British soldiers whose personalties had
caught the fancy of the public. None had held command in a major
war against equal enemies; but they had all distinguished themselves in campaigns against black, brown, or yellow men, and their
fame was raised to theatrical height by the new martial pride of
the British.

The first was Garnet Wolseley, commander in chief of the British Army, who had been fighting small wars, on and off, for forty-
five years. He was Anglo-Irish and loved a good fight—"all other

pleasures pale," he once wrote, "before the intense, the maddening delight of leading men into the midst of an enemy, or to the assault of some well-defended place." The first business of any ambitious young officer, he thought, was to try to get himself killed, and this intent he pursued himself, in the Burma War of 1852, the Crimean War, the Indian Mutiny, the China War of 1860, the American Civil War, the Canadian rebellion of 1869, the Ashanti War of 1873, and the Zulu War of 1879. In 1882 his supreme moment came. Arabi Pasha rose in rebellion against the Egyptian government. The British intervened, and in a brilliant, brief action Wolseley, attacking Arabi from the Suez Canal, defeated him handsomely at Tell el-Kebir, occupied Cairo, and established the British presence in Egypt. He was given a government grant of £30,000, created Baron Wolseley of Cairo and Wolseley, and became a popular hero. It was Wolseley who was celebrated as "The Modern Major General" in Gilbert and Sullivan's *Pirates of Penzance*, and in the slang of the day "all Sir Garnet" meant "all correct." Even his failure to reach Khartoum in time to rescue Gordon in 1884 did not cost him his public popularity, though it made him enemies in the army.

Wolseley was the late Victorian soldier par excellence. Technically he was a reformer and something of a prophet. Temperamentally he was arrogant, snobbish, insensitive. Intellectually he was not only exceedingly methodical but also deeply religious, with a sense of dedication never quite fulfilled. He relied on favorites in the army, erecting around himself a "Wolseley ring" of officers who had served with him in old campaigns. Some military critics thought him a fraud, some believed him to be the only great commander of the day who would, in action in a great war, have proved himself a Marlborough or a Wellington. By 1897, at sixty-four, Wolseley was a disillusioned man. He thought his luck had turned with his failure before Khartoum, and he was very conscious of his waning powers. Even his reforming zeal, once so virile and direct, seemed to have lost its bite.

He rode along in the jubilee procession, his long, melancholy face rather like the White Knight's, sagging a little at the jowls—its mustache, its eyebrows, the shape of its eyes, the hang of its mouth, all drooping sadly with advancing age, beneath the plumed cocked-hat of a field marshal. He was commander in chief of the British Army but not, as he was once said to have imagined himself, Duke of Khartoum.

The second soldier of the Empire was Field Marshal Lord

Roberts of Kandahar, commander in chief in Ireland and the most popular man in the British Army. Where Wolseley was daunting, Roberts was endearing. Where Wolseley pressed for change and efficiency, Roberts stood for the old traditions. Wolseley's professional appeal was to experts or to his own tight circle of intimates; Roberts was above all beloved of his private soldiers, who called him Bobs. Wolseley was tall and overbearing. Roberts was small, simple, sweet-natured.

Roberts was another Anglo-Irishman, the son of a general, educated at Eton and Sandhurst and destined to spend his entire life in the imperial service. Until he assumed his Irish command in 1895, he had never served in Europe—such was the range of a British military career in those days. He was old enough to have taken his commission in the East India Company's Bengal Artillery. He served in the Indian Mutiny, in a campaign obscurely remembered as "the Umbeyla campaign against the Sitana Fanatics," in the first Afghan War of 1814, in Napier's Abyssinian expedition, and in 1878 he commanded the army that occupied Afghanistan in the second British attempt to master that intractable power. When, in 1880, the Afghans fell upon the British garrison at Kandahar, Roberts took ten thousand men on an epic relief-march from Kabul.

As Tell el-Kebir was to Wolseley, the march to Kandahar was to Frederick Roberts. It caught the public imagination. Mounted on his white Arab charger. Vonolel, the trim little image of Roberts rode through the imperial sagas, smiling and imperturbable under the gaunt Afghan hills, with ten thousand faithful tommies at his heels and a horde of brown savages waiting to be routed at the other end. Roberts became commander in chief in India, devoting several years to the problems of imperial defense against the Russians, and after forty-one years of Indian service he came home a hero—devout, happily married, victorious, and teetotal.

Behind the two aging marshals stood the third of the imperial soldiers, and the most formidable: Herbert Kitchener. He was yet another Anglo-Irishman, another soldier's son, but in no other way did he resemble his peers. Set beside Wolseley's languid elegance, or the neat genial precision of Roberts, Kitchener looks a kind of ogre. He was only forty-eight in 1897, but around him a mystique had arisen, a glamour that set him apart from other soldiers and made him one of the figureheads of the new imperialism. He was huge in stature—six feet two inches in his socks—and terrible of visage, and his life was powered by an overriding and ceaseless ambition. He was aloof to women. He did not care whether his colleagues, his subordinates, or his common soldiers loved or loathed him. He had made his early reputation by a series of romantically mysterious adventures among the Arabs—first in Palestine, then in the Sudan—in which he improbably passed himself off as an Arab and undertook various dashing intelligence missions. He had fought under Wolseley in the unsuccessful campaign to relieve Gordon in 1884; he had become sirdar of the Egyptian army; in this jubilee year he was now, with heavy-footed thoroughness, slowly moving up the Nile, month by month, cataract by cataract, toward the capture of Khartoum.

Kitchener was not, like Wolseley and Roberts, a familiar figure in England. His allure was remote and enigmatic. He fascinated some women by his cold detachment; he maddened many colleagues by his ruthless determination to succeed. He was a great organizer but a plodding and sometimes irresolute general, and seen over the perspective of the years he appears, far more than the two field marshals, to have been emblematic of his times. He was too large for life. He was like a great idea somehow overplayed, so that it has lost its edge. He had never in his life fought against white men, and there was to the ferocity of his eye, the splendor of his mustache, his immense bemedaled figure, and his utterly humorless brand of imperialism—there was to Kitchener, though one might hardly dare say it to his face—something faintly absurd.

The Sea Lord: "Jacky" Fisher

Alone among the admirals of the imperial navy stood Sir John Fisher, "Jacky," third sea lord and controller, but about to raise his flag in the battleship *Renown* as commander in chief of the North American and West Indies station. Fisher was the most brilliant, the most disliked, the most beloved, and the most extraor-

dinary of the many remarkable officers who led the late Victorian
navy.

He was a raging individualist in a service full of eccentrics. He was one of the few British naval officers to approach the problems of his profession intellectually, to interest himself in the higher strategy as well as in the new technology, in the social structure of the service and its part in the *Realpolitik* of the times. Fisher was at once a violently enthusiastic reformer and a sentimental traditionalist. His personal saint was Nelson; one of his many slogans was "Think in oceans, sink at sight."

Fisher's life had been inextricably imperial. He was born in Ceylon, where his father, having retired from the Ceylonese police, had a small coffee estate; and his yellowish complexion and mandarin features seemed to give substance to the legend that his mother was a Singhalese princess (she was in fact the granddaughter of a Lord Mayor of London). His godmother was the governor's wife—that Lady Horton whom Byron had apostrophized. His godfather was commander of the garrison. Two of his brothers entered the Ceylon civil service, and two more became naval officers. Before he was forty-one Fisher had served in the Mediterranean, the West Indies, and the Channel Squadron, had attacked the Taku forts on the Peiho River in China, and had commanded the battleship *Inflexible*, the greatest of her day, in the bombardment of Alexandria in 1882.

But though the Empire had made him and he was fast becoming one of the most powerful men in the kingdom, he was hardly a new imperialist. His ebullience was tauter than the rather rambling enthusiasms of the greater Britain school. He thought of Britain essentially as a European power, faced always by potential enemies across the Channel, as it had been in Nelson's day. The imperial duties of policing the seas, showing the flag, and overawing petty potentates did not excite him, for he knew that when the *Pax Britannica* was finally challenged, it would survive only by the most modern naval expertise. He wanted to concentrate the navy's scattered strength in three or four massive fleets. He gave the destroyer its name. He was concerned always with gunpowder, speed, new kinds of boilers, with the menace of the submarine and the aircraft. He had blatant favorites and bêtes noires, devoted disciples and unforgiving enemies. He frequently made shameless use of the press.

Wherever he went, whatever command he assumed, he turned things topsy-turvy and shook officers out of their comfortable lethargy. When he commanded the cruiser *Northampton*, so his second-in-command complained, "we had 150 runs with Whitehead torpedoes in the last ten days, and the whole Navy only had 200 last year."

Yet in his person this marvelous man, so obsessed with the severe techniques of his profession, represented almost better than anyone the style of the British Empire, its pungent mixture of quirk, arrogance, and good nature. Fisher was a man of tremendous personal charm. He had a passion for dancing: if no women were present, he would dance with a brother officer, whistling his own music. He loved sermons and was often to be seen in garrison churches hunched formidably in the front pew, eye to eye with the quailing preacher. He gloried in show: the flurry of foam at the stern of the admiral's barge, as it reversed to the gangplank, the splendor of British battleships sliding into Malta at daybreak, the boyish pleasure of things biggest, fastest, newest. "The Royal Navy always travels first class," he liked to say; it was the best navy in the world, serving the best of countries, and Fisher was never ashamed to show it.

And so transparent was this patriotism, so bluff its expression, and so fascinating Fisher's personality, that to foreigners he seldom gave offense. He was an admiral of the Royal Navy, and that was that. Even more, by the expression on his face, the effortlessly peremptory pose of his body, and the irresistible twinkle in his eye, he seemed to exemplify in his person all that the navy meant to the world. The sultan of Morocco, once paying a visit to Fisher's flagship, was asked afterward what had most impressed him and replied without hesitation: "The Admiral's face." To anyone meeting Fisher for the first time, the British Empire must have seemed perfectly impregnable. The pictures show a thickset man, a cluster of medals on his chest, his face an indescribable mixture of sneer, defiance, and humorous bravado. His thick-lipped mouth turns down at the corners. His hair is carefully brushed in a cowlick across his forehead. His nostrils appear to be dilated, like a bull's, and the diagonal creases running down from his nose make him look as though he is finding life perpetually distasteful. Yet if you place your hand over the lower half of the face, you will find that the upper half is alive with laughter: there are laugh lines all around the eyes, the big, clear forehead looks sunny and carefree, and there is something about the expression that makes you feel even now, across the gulf of so many years, that if Fisher's aboard, all's well.

The Proconsuls: Lugard and Cromer

Of the proconsuls in the field of Empire that summer of 1897, two in particular would long be remembered: Cromer of Egypt, then in his prime; and Lugard of Africa, still awaiting bigger things —the one a Baring of the banking Barings, the other the son of a chaplain in the Madras establishment.

Frederick Lugard was thirty-nine and already famous. Born inside Fort St. George in Madras, he had failed the Indian civil service examination and, helped by his Uncle Edward, permanent undersecretary at the War Office, joined the army instead. But he was not cut out for soldiering. A small, wiry, nervous man, he was adventurous in a solitary way, a fine shot and an irrepressible big-game hunter, and the first ten years of his adult life were unsatisfying. He served under Roberts in Afghanistan, but was ill and saw little fighting. He fought with Wolseley in the Sudan and in Burma in the campaign to unseat Thebaw, the last of the Burmese kings. He tried unsuccessfully to join the Italian forces preparing in 1887 to fight the Abyssinians for the possession of Massaua. He was short of money and in poor health when in 1888 he was invited to join a force raised by the African Lakes Company to protect its interests on Lake Nyasa against the raids of Arab and Swahili slave traders.

At a stroke Lugard became a convinced and dedicated imperialist. He never went back to the army. Instead he joined the British East Africa Company and at thirty-two became virtually the father of British Uganda. He defeated the slavers, established a series of stations from the coast to the Nile, ended the wars between Moslems and Christians, made treaties with the local chiefs, and finally persuaded the British government to assume responsibility for the whole country. He became the trouble shooter of British Africa. In Nigeria he forestalled the French in the occupation of a place called Nikki, beating them to it in a lightning march and securing the British position in western Nigeria. In Bechuana-land he made a fearful journey across the Kalahari Desert, seven hundred miles through country devastated everywhere by the rinderpest, to explore a mineral concession.

Through all this derring-do he was evolving a new theory of imperial government, a concept of indirect rule that would enable the natives to maintain their own social and political forms, refined rather than destroyed by the imperial authority. Under his inspiration indirect rule was carried in Nigeria to a pitch of subtlety and complexity never equaled elsewhere. Lugard began as a mercenary of Empire; but he was already acquiring the habits of an apostle, a dedicated champion of imperial trusteeship, of a paternal imperialism that would allow the native peoples to develop—not in their own time but at least according to their own cultures—while ensuring that the resources of their territories were developed for the benefit of the world as a whole. He was a kind and lonely man, bad at sharing responsibility, excellent at shouldering it. He was one of the very few British theorists of Empire to apply his ideas in the field—the very antithesis of the unobtrusive bureaucrat the Indian civil service might have made of him.

What a world away was Cromer of Cairo, who was now, at fifty-six, in his fourteenth year as proto-Pharaoh! Cromer was born to authority, the son of a Member of Parliament, the grandson of an admiral, and a member of one of London's most distinguished banking families—German, probably Jewish, by origin. He was a ruddy-faced man, with short white hair and trimmed mustache, wearing gold-rimmed spectacles and rather nattily dressed. He looked like a surgeon or perhaps a reliable family solicitor, a serious, calm, and balanced man. The wild vagaries of Egyptian life only threw his composure into greater relief. It was Cromer who, without prejudice and without excitement, had been at the receiving end of Gordon's feverish hates and enthusiasms, telegraphed downriver from the palace at Khartoum; Cromer who stood halfway between Gladstone and Lord Wolseley during the tragic campaign of 1884; Cromer to whom the great Kitchener had sent an urgent cable, only a month or two before the jubilee, asking what he ought to do next, when faced with a tricky military situation up the Nile.

Cromer had started life as a soldier himself, serving first in the Ionian Islands in the days when they were a British protectorate, then in Malta and in Jamaica. He went out to India as private secretary to the viceroy, his cousin Lord Northbrook, and spent a few years in Egypt before the British occupation. Then, in 1883, he followed Wolseley into Cairo and began his life's work—the reformation and reconstruction of Egypt. He was very grand indeed. In India they had called him Overbaring. In Cairo they nicknamed him Le Grand Ours. Wilfrid Blunt, then resident in Cairo, said Cromer's reports were written in a "first chapter of Genesis style." He moved with an air of ineffable superiority and disapproved, as D. G. Hogarth wrote, of "fantasy, rhapsody and all kinds of unstable exuberance."

It was his fate to live in a country where every kind of exuberant instability was part of the very climate. The longer he stayed in Egypt, the loftier Cromer became. "The Egyptians," he wrote, "should be permitted to govern themselves after the fashion in which Europeans think they ought to be governed"—and when he spoke of Europeans, he unquestionably thought first of himself. His mandate of power was indeterminate. His use of it was masterly. He was in practice the absolute ruler of Egypt, in whose presence nationalist aspirations repeatedly withered; giving office to any leading nationalist, Cromer thought, would be "only a little less absurd than the nomination of some savage Red Indian chief to be Governor-General of Canada." Cromer knew what was best for the country, and to the intense irritation of many of his contemporaries, generally seemed to be right. Under his command Egypt escaped from bankruptcy and actually produced a surplus. Great irrigation projects were launched. The Aswan Dam was begun. The Egyptian courts were reformed, the ancient practice of forced labor was abolished, the railways were rebuilt, the army was disciplined.

It was paradoxical that in Egypt, the most tenuously indirect of British possessions, British imperialism should have come closest to the classic form of the ancient conquerors: a personal despotism, that is, characterized by the imposition of a new order upon a demoralized people and the building of great engineering works. Almost alone Cromer left this mark upon Egypt, like an off-stage Alexander; for from first to last his official rank was that of consul general of Great Britain, and his modest palace was only the British consulate. The Egyptian princess Nazli Fazil was once visiting her cousin the khedive of Egypt when they heard a shout far down the street and the rattle of wheels. The khedive paled. "Listen," he said, "I hear the cry of the runner in front of Baring's carriage. Who knows what he is coming to tell me?"

The Adventurer: Cecil Rhodes

Rhodes in the field during the 1896 Matabele Rebellion in Rhodesia.

There was something almost unreal about the scale of Cecil Rhodes. He was nicknamed the Colossus, of course; and of all the new imperialists, he most looked the part. He had a Roman face: big, prominent of eye, rather sneering—just such a face as a police reconstruction might compose if fed the details of one who was both a diamond millionaire and a kind of emperor. There was a shifty look to Rhodes, but it was shiftiness in the grand manner, as if he dealt in millions always—millions of pounds, millions of square miles, millions of people.

Rhodes scarcely figured in the celebration of the jubilee. By the summer of 1897 he was nearly discredited by his sponsorship of the Jameson Raid, carried out by his assistant and protégé, Leander Starr Jameson. In a premature rehearsal of the Boer War, Jameson had led a band of five hundred men on an expedition to seize the government of the Transvaal. This raid failed, and Jameson was sent to jail, but only after he had charmed half of England by observing with candor: "I know perfectly well that as I have not succeeded the natural thing has happened. I also know that if I had succeeded I should have been forgiven." To many new imperialists he and Rhodes were heroes still, and the raid was seen only as an endearing excess of boyish dash. They expressed for many Britons the grand fling of Empire, skullduggery and all.

Rhodes was first of all a money-maker. A millionaire before he was thirty-five, he took five years to get his pass degree at Oxford because he spent so much time supervising his diamond interests in Kimberley. The fifth son of an English country parson, he first went to South Africa to help his brother grow cotton in Natal, where the climate was thought to be better for his asthma; it was only in the second half of his life that he conceived a vision of empire in some ways more naïve, in some ways nobler, and in all ways more spacious than anyone else's. To Rhodes the British Empire was to be one of the revelations of human history, a new heaven and a new earth. In 1877, at twenty-four, he made his first will, leaving his money for the formation of a secret society to extend British rule across the earth; he foresaw the occupation by British settlers of the entire continent of Africa, the Holy Land, the whole of South America, the islands of the Pacific, the Malay Archipelago, the seaboard of China, and Japan. The United States would be recovered, the whole Empire would be consolidated, everybody would be represented in one imperial parliament, and the whole structure would form "so great a Power as hereafter [to] render wars impossible and promote the best interests of humanity."

Rhodes's achievements fell pitifully short of these Olympian prospects. He failed to build his Cape-to-Cairo railway, or even to unite South Africa under the British flag. His one great political creation, Rhodesia, was presently to prove a disastrous anachronism—a white state set impossibly in a black continent. In 1897 he was forty-four and had fallen to the nadir of his affairs. He was seen by more restrained imperialists as a mere shady speculator, extending his unsavory activities from diamond mining to statesmanship and masking all in high talk. His grand idea, though, survived it all. He really thought of the Empire as an instrument of universal peace. Through all the fluctuations of his fortune, he was perfecting his scheme for the Rhodes Scholarships, which would take "the best men for the world's fight" from the English-speaking countries, send them to Oxford to be polished in England's civilization, and distribute them through the Empire to fulfill his dreams. Of all the new imperialists, Rhodes was the most genuinely inspired. William Blane, the South African poet, wrote truly of this misleading man:

Not from a selfish or sordid ambition
Dreamt he of Empires—in continents thought:
His the response to that mystic tuition,
From the great throb of the universe caught.

Requiem

There were other exceptional imperialists, of course, waxing or waning in Britain then—the politicians like Dilke and Rosebery; future proconsuls like Curzon and Alfred Milner; George Goldie, the Rhodes of the Niger basin; and Frank Swettenham, the Raffles of Malaya. Our chosen celebrities, though, may stand as champions for them all, the stars of the imperial show, a strange and gaudy company of performers above whose nodding plumes and ruthless ambitions there sat only the one supreme imperial presence, Victoria RI.

The queen empress was the image and summit of Empire, revealing in herself many of the strains of the British imperium—proud and often overbearing, but with an unexpected sweetness at the heart; suburban and sometimes vulgar; sentimental; in old age less beautiful than imposing; girlishly beguiled by the mysteries of the Orient, maternally considerate toward the natives, stubbornly determined to hang on to her possessions; seduced by high words, dazzling persons, lofty projects, colors; impatient of things small, meticulous, or self-effacing. A formidable lady indeed, but old, very old, and portly in her long dresses, so that when she sat sculptured on her throne in the public gardens of Aden or Colombo, Kingston or Melbourne, she seemed less a person than some stylized divinity—a goddess inescapable, glimpsed through screens of banyan trees or rising, tremendous, above banana groves; a goddess of wealth, age, power, so old that the world could hardly remember itself without her and had already given her name to an era. She *was* the *Pax Britannica*, and geography recognized the fact with towns called Victoria in South Africa, Labuan, Guiana, Grenada, Honduras, Newfoundland, Nigeria, Vancouver Island; with Victoriaville in Quebec, the Victoria Nile in Uganda, the state of Victoria in Australia; with six Lake Victorias and two Cape Victorias; with Victoria Range, Bay, Strait, Valley, Point, Park, Mine, Peak, Beach, Bridge, County, Cove, Downs, Land, Estate, Falls, Fjord, Gap, Harbor, Headland, Island, and Hill—setting such a seal upon the world, in cartography as in command, as no monarch in the history of mankind had ever set before.

The Diamond Jubilee was an immense success. The queen herself was "deeply touched," so she wrote in her diary, and thought the whole festivity "truly marvelous."

So it was, but soon the immense illusion was to fade; the imperialists would retreat to their northern islands again, and Britain would return to size. Two years later the Boer War broke out, and the certainty of Empire was cracked. Two years after that the queen died, and an era ended. Within twenty years the forces of the Crown were engaged with enemies far more real than any legendary Pathans or Zulus, and regiments that had bestrode the world lay mutilated in French mud. Seventy years later only the rump of Empire remained—a few islands, a fortress or two, a legacy of responsibilities.

All the great glory had gone, and the panoplies had been dismantled. The great queen's statues, emplaced with such fanfare, were quietly removed—sometimes, as at Aden in 1967, in the dead of night. Imperialism had lost its power to move men's hearts, and the British generally had no regrets as they put the dazzle of it out of their minds, packed away the pith helmets and the camp baths, and returned to a smaller world.

The circumstances attending the assassination of Austrian Archduke Franz Ferdinand at Sarajevo in June, 1914 are still obscure and the crucial question whether the Serbian government was privy to the plot still awaits a satisfactory answer. But Mr. Stillman, who has written much on Balkan and Near Eastern affairs, is less concerned with these moot questions than with the larger problems evoked by the ghastly world war which ensued. He recalls the brilliance and promise of the immediate prewar years, when so many important departures were made in science, literature, and art, and when the standard of living even of the common man was constantly rising. He argues cogently that many spiritual values as well as material goods were destroyed in the holocaust. Furthermore, there emerged from the four years of slaughter the ruthlessness and violence characteristic of the following period, to say nothing of innumerable specific problems with which the world is still wrestling.

SARAJEVO: THE END OF INNOCENCE

EDMUND STILLMAN

A few minutes before eleven o'clock in the morning, Sunday, June 28, 1914, on the river embankment in Sarajevo, Gavrilo Princip shot the Archduke Franz Ferdinand and brought a world crashing down.

After a half-century and much pain, Sarajevo is worth a pilgrimage, but to go there is a disappointing and somehow unsettling experience: this dusty Balkan city, in its bowl of dark and barren hills, is an unlikely setting for grand tragedy. Blood and suffering are endemic to the Balkans, but Sarajevo is so mean and poor. Why should an age have died *here*? Why did the double murder of an undistinguished archduke and his morganatic wife touch off a world war, when so many graver pretexts had somehow been accommodated—or ignored—in the preceding quarter-century? It was an act that no one clearly remembers today; indeed, its details were forgotten by the time the war it engendered was six months old. Nowadays, even in Sarajevo, few pilgrims search out the place where Princip stood that morning. Nearby, on the river

June 28, 1914: Franz Ferdinand and his wife arrive in Sarajevo on a good-will tour. Within hours they were assassination victims. 217

embankment, only a dingy little museum commemorates the lives and passions of the seven tubercular boys (of whom Princip was only one) who plotted one small blow for freedom, but who brought on a universal catastrophe. Within the museum are faded photographs, a few pitiable relics of the conspirators, a fly-specked visitors' book. A single shabby attendant guards the memorials to a political passion that seems, well, naïve to our more cynical age. "Here, in this historic place," the modest inscription runs, "Gavrilo Princip was the initiator of liberty, on the day of Saint Vitus, the 28th of June, 1914." That is all, and few visitors to present-day Yugoslavia stop to read it.

There is so much that goes unanswered, even though the facts of the case are so well known: how the failing Hapsburgs, impelled by an unlucky taste for adventure, had seized Bosnia and Herzegovina from the Turks and aggravated the racial imbalance of the Austro-Hungarian Empire; how the southern Slavs within the Empire felt themselves oppressed and increasingly demanded freedom; how the ambitious little hill kingdom of Serbia saw a chance to establish a South-Slavic hegemony over the Balkans; and how Czarist Russia, itself near ruin, plotted with its client Serbia to turn the Austro-Hungarian southern flank. But there is so much more that needs to be taken into account: how Franz Ferdinand, the aged Emperor Franz Josef's nephew, became his heir by default (Crown Prince Rudolf had committed suicide at Mayerling; Uncle Maximilian, Napoleon III's pawn, had been executed in Mexico; Franz Ferdinand's father, a pilgrim to the Holy Land, had died—most improbably—from drinking the waters of the Jordan); how the new heir—stiff, autocratic, and unapproachable, but implausibly wed in irenic middle-class marriage to the not-quite-acceptable Sophie Chotek—sensed the danger to the Empire and proposed a policy that would have given his future Slav subjects most of what they demanded; how the Serbian nationalists were driven to panic, and how the secret society of jingoes known as "The Black Hand" plotted Franz Ferdinand's death; how seven boys were recruited to do the deed, and how one of them, Gavrilo Princip, on the morning of June 28, 1914, shot Franz Ferdinand and his Sophie dead.

But why the mindlessness of the war that followed, the blundering diplomacies and reckless plans that made disaster inevitable once hostilities broke out? It is all so grotesque: great and shattering consequences without proportionate causes. When the inferno of 1914–18 ended at last, the broken survivors asked themselves the same question, seeking to comprehend the terrible thing that had happened. To have endured the inferno without a justifying reason—to be forced to admit that a war of such terror and scope had been only a blind, insouciant madness—was intolerable; it was easier to think of it as an unworthy or a wrongful cause than as a ghastly, titanic joke on history. After the event Winston Churchill wrote: "But there was a strange temper in the air. Unsatisfied by material prosperity the nations turned restlessly towards strife internal or external. . . . Almost one might think the world wished to suffer." Yet if this opinion had been widely accepted, it would have been a judgment on human nature too terrible to endure. And so a new mythology of the war grew up—a postwar mythology of materialist cynicism almost as contrived as the wartime propaganda fictions of the "Beast of Berlin" or the wholesale slaughter of Belgian nuns. It embraced the myths of the munitions manufacturers who had plotted a war they were, in fact, helpless to control; of Machiavellian, imperialist diplomacies; of an ever-spiraling arms race, when in fact the naval race between England and Germany had, if anything, somewhat abated by 1914. But no single cause, or combination of such causes, will explain the First World War. Neither the Germans, the Austrians, the Russians, the French, the Italians, nor the British went to war to fulfill a grand ambition—to conquer Europe, or the world, or to promote an ideology. They did not even seek economic dominion through war. The somber truth is that Western civilization, for a hundred years without a major war and absorbed in a social and technological revolution—progress, in short—turned on itself in a paroxysm of slaughter.

On both sides the actual war aims, so far as they were articulated at all, were distressingly small. Merely to humiliate Serbia and to "avenge" a man whose death few particularly regretted, the Austro-Hungarian Empire began a war which cost it seven million casualties and destroyed its fabric; to prevent a senile Austria-Hungary from gaining a precarious (and inevitably short-lived) advantage in the poverty-stricken western Balkans, imperial Russia lost more than nine million men—killed, wounded, or taken prisoner. To support an ally, and to avoid the public humiliation and anxiety of canceling a mobilization order once issued, Germany lost almost two million dead, Alsace-Lorraine, a third of Poland, and its growing sphere of influence in Central Europe and the Middle East. England, to keep its word to Belgium, committed eight million men to the struggle, and lost nearly one million dead. France, to counter its German enemy and to avenge the peace treaty it had accepted in 1870, endured losses of 15 per cent of its population and initiated a process of political decline from which it may not yet have emerged.

This was the price of World War I. Two shots were fired in Sarajevo, and for more than four years thereafter half the world bled. At least ten million soldiers were killed, and twenty million were wounded or made prisoners. But the real legacy of the war was something less tangible—a quality of despair, a chaos, and a drift toward political barbarism that is with us to this day. We have not recovered yet.

In the summer of 1914 the armies marched out to Armageddon in their frogged tunics, red Zouave trousers, and gilded helmets. Five months later they were crouching in the mud, louse-ridden, half-starved, frozen, and bewildered by the enormity of it all. "Lost in the midst of two million madmen," the Frenchman Céline was to write of the war, "all of them heroes, at large and armed to the teeth! . . . sniping, plotting, flying, kneeling, digging, taking cover, wheeling, detonating, shut in on earth as in an asylum cell; intending to wreck everything in it, Germany, France, the whole world, every breathing thing; destroying, more ferocious than a pack of mad dogs and adoring their own madness (which no dog does), a hundred, a thousand times fiercer than a thousand dogs and so infinitely more vicious! . . . Clearly it seemed to me that I had embarked on a crusade . . . nothing short of an apocalypse."

The savagery of the war and the incompetence of the military commanders quickly became a commonplace. The generals proved wholly unprepared for quick-firing artillery, machine guns, field entrenchments, railroad and motor transport, and the existence of a continuous front in place of the isolated battlefield of earlier centuries. They were helpless in the face of a combat too vast, too impersonal, too technical, and too deadly to comprehend. Quite aside from their intellectual shortcomings, one is struck by the poverty of their emotional response. Kill and kill was their motto. No one in command was daunted by the bloodletting, it seems. No more imaginative battle tactic could be devised than to push strength against strength—attacking at the enemy's strongest point on the theory that one side's superior *élan* would ultimately yield up victory. Verdun in 1916 cost the French some 350,000 men and the Germans nearly as many; the German penetration was five miles, gained in a little more than three months. The Somme cost the Allies more than 600,000 casualties, the Germans almost half a million: the offensive gained a sector thirty miles wide and a maximum of seven deep in four and a half months.

*Dutch artist Louis Raemaekers'
comment on the carnage in Flanders
in 1914:* The Harvest is Ripe.

That it was an insane waste of lives the combatants realized early, but no one knew what to do. The waste of honor, love, courage, and selfless devotion was the cruelest of all: at the first Battle of Ypres, in the opening days of the war, the young German schoolboy volunteers "came on like men possessed," a British historian records. They were sent in against picked battalions of British regulars who shot them to pieces on the slopes of Ypres with the trained rifle fire for which they were famous. The incident has gone down in German history as the *Kindermord von Ypern*—"the Slaughter of the Innocents at Ypres." No other phrase will do.

It was a strange world that died that summer of 1914. For ninety-nine years there had been peace in Europe: apart from the Crimean War, only eighteen months of all that time had been spent in desultory and petty European wars. Men apparently believed that peace was man's normal condition—and on those occasions when peace was momentarily broken, war was expected to be comprehensible and salutary, an ultimately useful Darwinian selection of the fittest to lead. To us, after the profuse horrors of mustard gas, trench warfare, Buchenwald, the Blitz, Coventry, and Hiroshima, to name only a few, this is incomprehensible naïveté. But that we have been disillusioned and have awaked to our condition is due to the events of 1914–18.

In the nineteenth century the belief in progress—automatic progress—went deep. The American anthropologist Lewis Morgan had sounded a note of self-confident hope for the entire age when he said, in 1877, "Democracy in government, brotherhood in society, equality in rights and privileges, and universal education, foreshadow the next higher plane of society to which experience, intelligence and knowledge are steadily tending." The emphasis here was on *steadily*: nothing could stop the onward march of mankind.

And the progress was very real. The age that died in 1914 was a brilliant one—so extravagant in its intellectual and aesthetic endowments that we who have come after can hardly believe in its reality. It was a comfortable age—for a considerable minority, at least—but it was more than a matter of Sunday walks in the Wienerwald, or country-house living, or a good five-cent cigar. It was an imposing age in the sciences, in the arts, even in the forms of government. Men had done much and had risen high in the hundred years that came to an end that summer. From Napoleon's downfall in 1815 to the outbreak of war in 1914, the trend had been up.

Removing casualties and prisoners on the Western Front. Overleaf is the blasted landscape around Passchendaele, Belgium, in 1917.

"As happy as God in France," even the Germans used to say. For France this was the time of *la belle époque*, when all the world's artists came there to learn: Picasso and Juan Gris from Spain, Chagall and Archipenko from Russia, Piet Mondrian from the Netherlands, Brancusi from Romania, Man Ray and Max Weber from America, Modigliani from Italy. All made up the "School of Paris," a name which meant nothing but that in this Paris of the *avant-guerre* the world of the arts was at home.

"Paris drank the talents of the world," wrote the poet-impresario of those years, Guillaume Apollinaire. Debussy, Ravel, and Stravinsky composed music there. Nijinsky and Diaghilev were raising the modern ballet to new heights of brilliance and creativity. The year 1913 was, as Roger Shattuck puts it in *The Banquet Years*, the *annus mirabilis* of French literature: Proust's *Du Côté de chez Swann*, Alain-Fournier's *Le Grand Meaulnes*, Apollinaire's *Alcools*, Roger Martin du Gard's *Jean Barois*, Valéry Larbaud's *A. O. Barnabooth*, Péguy's *L'Argent*, Barrès's *La Colline inspirée*, and Colette's *L'Entrave* and *L'Envers du music-hall* appeared that year. "It is almost as if the war *had* to come in order to put an end to an extravaganza that could not have been sustained at this level." That was Paris.

Vienna was another great mongrel city that, like Paris, drank up talent—in this case the talents of a congeries of Austrians, Magyars, Czechs, Slovaks, Poles, Slovenes, Croats, Serbs, Jews, Turks, Transylvanians, and Gypsies. On Sunday mornings gentlemen

strolled in the Prater ogling the cocottes; they rode the giant red Ferris wheel and looked out over the palaces and parks of the city; or they spent the morning at the coffeehouse, arguing pointlessly and interminably. It was a pleasure-loving city, but an intellectual one, too. The names of the men who walked Vienna's streets up to the eve of the war are stunning in their brilliance: Gustav Mahler, Sigmund Freud, Sandor Ferenczi, Ernst Mach, Béla Bartók, Rainer Maria Rilke, Franz Kafka, Robert Musil, Arthur Schnitzler, Hugo von Hofmannsthal, Richard Strauss, Stefan Zweig— these hardly begin to exhaust the list. (There were more sinister names, too. Adolf Hitler lived in Vienna between 1909 and 1913, an out-of-work, shabby *Bettgeher*—a daytime renter of other people's beds—absorbing the virulent anti-Semitism that charged the Viennese social atmosphere; so did Leon Trotsky, who spent his evenings listening contemptuously to the wranglings of the Social Democratic politicians at the Café Central.)

England was still gilded by the afterglow of the Edwardian Age: the British Empire straddled the earth, controlling more than a quarter of the surface of the globe. If the realities of trade had begun to shift, and if British industry and British naval supremacy were faced with a growing challenge from the United States and Hohenzollern Germany, the vast British overseas investments

tended to hide the fact. England had its intellectual brilliance, too: these were the years of Hardy, Kipling, Shaw, Wells, the young D. H. Lawrence and the young Wyndham Lewis, Arnold Bennett, Gilbert Murray, A. E. Housman, H. H. Munro (Saki)—who would die in the war—and many others, like Rupert Brooke, Robert Graves, Siegfried Sassoon, and Wilfred Owen, who were as yet hardly known.

As for the Kaiser's Germany, it is melancholy to reflect that if Wilhelm II himself, that summer in 1914, had only waited—five years, ten years, or twenty—Germany might have had it all. But Wilhelm was shrewd, treacherous, and hysterical, a chronic bully whose mother had never loved him. His habitual style of discourse was the neurotic bluster of a small man who has had the bad luck to be called upon to stomp about in a giant's boots. Wilhelm II lived all his life in the shadow of "the Great Emperor," his grandfather Wilhelm I, who had created a united Greater Germany with the help of his brilliant chancellor, Prince Otto von Bismarck; he wanted to make the world stand in awe of him, but he did not know, precisely, how to go about it.

If only he could have been patient: Austria-Hungary was really a German satellite; the Balkans and the Middle East looked to Berlin; Germany's industrial hegemony on the Continent was se-

cure, and might soon have knocked Britain from her commanding place in the world's trade. By 1914, fourteen Germans had won Nobel Prizes in the sciences (by contrast, their nearest competitors, the French, had won only nine).

But the lesson is something more than a chapbook homily on patience. Wilhelm's personal anxiety merely expressed in microcosm the larger German anxiety about the nation's place in the world. Something strange lay beneath the stolid prosperity of the Hohenzollern Age—a surfeit with peace, a lust for violence, a belief in death, an ominous mystique of war. "Without war the world would quickly sink into materialism," the elder Von Moltke, chief of the German General Staff, had proclaimed in 1880; and he, his nephew the younger Von Moltke, and the caste of Prussian militarists they represented could presumably save the world from that tawdry fate. But this belief in war was not a monopoly of the Right: even Thomas Mann, spokesman of German humanism, could ask, in 1914, "Is not war a purification, a liberation, an enormous hope?" adding complacently, "Is not peace an element in civil corruption?"

There had been peace in the world for too long. From Berlin, in the spring of 1914, Colonel House wrote to Woodrow Wilson: "The whole of Germany is charged with electricity. Everybody's nerves are tense. It only requires a spark to set the whole thing off." People were saying: "Better a horrible ending than a horror without end." In expressing this spirit of violence and disorientation, Germany was merely precocious. It expressed a universal European malaise.

The malaise was evident everywhere—in the new cults of political violence; in the new philosophies of men like Freud, Nietzsche, and Pareto, who stressed the unconscious and the irrational, and who exposed the lying pretensions of middle-class values and conventions; and in the sense of doom that permeated the avant-garde arts of the prewar years. Typical of this spirit of rebellion was the manifesto set forth in 1910 by the Italian Futurist painters: it declared that "all forms of imitation should be held in contempt and that all forms of originality glorified; that we should rebel against the tyranny of the words 'harmony' and 'good taste' . . . ; that a clean sweep be made of all stale and threadbare subject matter in order to express the vortex of modern life—a life of steel, pride, fever, and speed . . ."

In England and France, as in Germany and Italy, the darker strain was there, seemingly only waiting for release. When the war came, a glad Rupert Brooke intoned:

Now God be thanked Who has matched us with His hour.

A fever was over Paris as the spring of 1914 slipped into summer. Charles Péguy—Dreyfusard, Socialist, man of good will and reason, to his intellectual generation "the pure man"—had caught this other darker spirit as well. That spring he had written:

Happy are those who have died in great battles,
Lying on the ground before the face of God . . .

By September of that year he himself was dead.

No doubt we shall never understand it completely. What is absolutely clear about the outbreak of the First World War is that it was catastrophic: the hecatombs of dead, the appalling material waste, the destruction, and the pain of those four years tell us that. In our hearts we know that since that bootless, reckless, bloody adventure nothing has really come right again in the world. Democracy in government, brotherhood in society, equality in rights and privileges, universal education—all those evidences of "the next higher plane of society" to which experience, intelligence, and knowledge seemed to be steadily tending—gave way to mass conscription and the central direction of war, the anonymity of the trenches, the calculated propaganda lie: in short, between 1914 and 1918 Europe evolved many of the brutal features of the modern totalitarian state. And twenty-one years after the last shot was fired in the First World War, a second war came: a war of even greater brutality, moral degradation, and purposeful evil, but one where the issues at last matched the scale on which men had, a quarter-century earlier, blindly chosen to fight. Here was a deadly justice. That such a war should be fought at all was the direct outcome of the spiritual wasteland that the first war engendered.

Woodrow Wilson, greeting the Armistice, was able to proclaim to his fellow Americans that "everything" for which his countrymen had fought had been accomplished. He could assert that it was America's "fortunate duty to assist by example, by sober, friendly counsel, and by material aid in the establishment of a just democracy throughout the world."

But today we know that the poet Robert Graves more truly expressed the spirit of the nightmare from which the world awakened in 1918 when he wrote, "The news [of the Armistice] sent me out walking alone along the dyke above the marshes of Rhuddlan . . . cursing and sobbing and thinking of the dead."

Keynes expounding from the depths of his characteristic slouch; a caricature by cartoonist David Low for the New Statesman.

It is probably no exaggeration to say that Keynes, a man trained as a mathematician, has been the most influential thinker in the field of economics since Adam Smith. Reading about him one cannot help but marvel at the keenness of his insights and his audacious originality. In a world stricken with depression and rapidly sinking into utter despair, he was able to point the way to master unemployment and initiate recovery. His revolutionary teaching entitles him to be ranked with Einstein and Freud among the great innovators of the twentieth century. Mr. Malkin, whose career has been devoted to reporting and analyzing economic conditions and economic thought, sees Keynesian doctrine in the setting of its time and notes the ways in which it is being gradually transcended.

THE ECONOMIC IMPACT OF MAYNARD KEYNES

LAWRENCE MALKIN

Almost everyone who knew Maynard Keynes—he disdained the banality of his first name, John—remembered him as just about the cleverest man in England. Lytton Strachey once remarked that "his common sense was enough to freeze a volcano." Leonard Woolf, Bloomsbury's judicious liberal conscience, said that Keynes had "absolutely the quickest brain of any man I've ever met, except perhaps Bertrand Russell's." But Russell himself admitted that he seldom emerged from an argument with Keynes without feeling something of a fool. Russell was demolished by Keynes as one successive age demolishes another: "Bertie . . . sustained simultaneously a pair of opinions ludicrously incompatible. He held that in fact human affairs were carried on after a most irrational fashion, but that the remedy was quite simple and easy, since all we had to do was to carry them on rationally." Let Keynes's loyal biographer, the economist Sir Roy Harrod, have the last of our opening words: "No one in our age was cleverer than Keynes, nor made less attempt to conceal it."

Inside this intellectual dandy was a genius crying to get out. When it finally did, in the depths of the depression, Keynes's brilliant intelligence devised a technique for steering capitalism off the rocks on which it was then stuck fast. He demonstrated beyond a doubt that the forces of the free market would not automatically bring prosperity if allowed to work themselves into balance in the

long run; for, as Keynes said, "In the long run we are all dead."
Adam Smith's "invisible hand" was simply not there to moderate
mankind's self-interest.

Keynes's classifications of aggregate income and expenditure,
savings and investment, are as basic to modern thought as Freud's
discovery of the emotional forces by which we are individually
driven. The discovery of what was essentially a neutral fact—that
there was no God in the economic machine—had an impact as
forceful as the awesome discoveries of the atomic scientists. The
scientists showed man that it was possible to harness the raw
energy that runs the physical universe; Keynes showed him that it
was possible to regulate and offset the greed that drives our capitalist world. He overturned Victorian economic morality at a
stroke: "The engine which drives Enterprise is not Thrift, but
Profit." These discoveries about ourselves and our environment,
whether emotional, physical, or material, share one message: if
man will be master of his fate, he must seize the power to control
it. But Keynes, like the atomic scientists, was never quite at home
with this brute fact of power. Politics, he said, is "a fairly adequate
substitute for bridge." The clever Whig aristocrat, the gray eminence to two wartime governments, the patron of the arts, the
prolific pamphleteer, the academic economist who outguessed the
markets and made a fortune as a speculator, composed a life that
was truly Mozartean in its grace, elegance, and success. But like
Mozart and the Mysterious Stranger, Keynes at last came face to
face with the irrational power of the self-perpetuating modern
superstate, and his weak heart collapsed.

Keynes was born in 1883 and died in 1946. Fathered by an age
of rational moralists (his parents were Cambridge dons), he grew
up in an age of clever people. They were the fragile gadflies who
led us out of Victorian certainty but not quite into the modern
world; we know them as Bloomsbury. His life spans the period of
change from individual enterprise to mass capitalism, and he was
among the first to see the inevitability of this change in *The Economic Consequences of the Peace.* The book is seldom read nowadays because its conclusions are so obvious to us. Written in
1919, in the heat of resigning as Treasury representative to the
British delegation at the Versailles Peace Conference, the book was
a sensation and made Keynes internationally notorious at the age
of thirty-six. Perhaps its most famous passage describes the capitalist system that gave birth to Keynes's class and sustained its
self-confidence. It is worth quoting at length, to sample both his

penetrating style and his reformist view of a system that Marx wanted to destroy as passionately as Keynes wanted it rebuilt.

. . . this remarkable system depended for its growth on a double bluff or deception. On the one hand the laboring classes accepted from ignorance or powerlessness, or were compelled, persuaded, or cajoled by custom, convention, authority, and the well-established order of Society into accepting, a situation in which they could call their own very little of the cake, that they and Nature and the capitalists were co-operating to produce. And on the other hand the capitalist classes were allowed to call the best part of the cake theirs and were theoretically free to consume it, on the tacit underlying condition that they consumed very little of it in practice. The duty of "saving" became nine-tenths of virtue and the growth of the cake the object of true religion. . . . I seek only to point out that the principle of accumulation based on inequality was a vital part of the pre-war order of Society and of progress as we then understood it, and to emphasize that this principle depended on unstable psychological conditions, which it may be impossible to re-create. It was not natural for a population, of whom so few enjoyed the comforts of life, to accumulate so hugely. The war has disclosed the possibility of consumption to all and the vanity of abstinence to many. Thus the bluff is discovered; the laboring classes may be no longer willing to forgo so largely, and the capitalist classes, no longer confident of the future, may seek to enjoy more fully their liberties of consumption so long as they last, and thus precipitate the hour of their confiscation.

It took a depression and another world war for the capitalists and the workers to come to terms, with Keynes as their mediator. He was writing then under the shadow of the Bolshevik revolution, which he feared. When he visited Russia six years later, he came away horrified at this new and to him utterly drab religion: "Leninism is absolutely, defiantly non-supernatural, and its emotional and ethical essence centers about the individual's and the community's attitude towards the Love of Money." He asked himself: "How can I adopt a creed which, preferring the mud to the fish, exalts the boorish proletariat above the bourgeois and the intelligentsia who, with whatever faults, are the quality in life and surely carry the seeds of all human advancement?"

Now here is a curious type of economist, one who places personal development above material prosperity and assumes that others will, too. This is the key to Keynes; it was to be his triumph as an economist and at the same time his chief failing as a social thinker. He had grown up in an Edwardian late afternoon that cast deep and distinctive shadows on the personalities of those permitted to flourish in it. It is nice to be nostalgic about that age, but in fact it favored only the few. In 1910 poor-law relief in England reached a fifty-year high. Domestic servants in the middle-class London sub-urb of Hampstead outnumbered all other residents. Three-quarters of Britain's investment went overseas instead of building up home industry. The empire had not yet started running down, but its heart was; England made up its trade deficit with banking profits. British capitalism, once vigorously productive, had become essentially manipulative. Upper-class Philistinism, with its shootin' and huntin' types, buried emotions and could be cruel to outsiders who seemed to violate the natural order of things. A Manchester industrialist might be a vulgar upstart, but he and his social betters shared a vast insensitivity for those trapped on the wrong side of the double bluff.

From their earliest days Keynes and his friends had gathered in secret sects to shut out this thick-skinned world. Perpetuating the individualism, even the eccentricity, of this life was one of his goals as an economist. His method was not mass organization but the intelligence of the precious few. Woolf and Strachey came to his rooms at King's College in 1903 to invite him into the Apostles, a society of Cambridge's intellectual elite that met secretly on Saturday nights. Their guiding philosophy was a kind of didactic aestheticism. The ideas were those of the Cambridge philosopher G. E. Moore, or at least their interpretation of him. They built on Moore's *Principia Ethica*, a work sweet and confident in its assumption of the existence of beauty and goodness and practical in its calculations of how to attain them. As Keynes later described their version of Moore, good was an attribute as morally neutral as, say, green. A little logical analysis—Keynes's father was a logician, the son's first theoretical work was a *Treatise on Probability*—leads quickly to a philosophy of finding the greatest good (as Keynes said he did) in the enjoyment of beautiful objects and the pleasures of human intercourse. The gravest sin seemed that of bad taste.

It certainly was in Bloomsbury—the group that took its name from the district of London where so many of its members lived. Much has been written about that ingathering of intellectual self-exiles that makes it seem a sort of conspiracy, at least to those who remember being withered by its conversation (unacceptable or insipid beliefs were quashed with a single word: "*Really!*"). But in fact it was a shepherd's reed hardly strong enough to be sinister. Years later, Keynes described its youthful genesis: "I can see us as water-spiders, gracefully skimming, as light and reasonable as air, the surface of the stream without any contact at all with the eddies and currents underneath." Bloomsbury was the original of the Beautiful People. The set gave famous parties, and one masquerade ball at which Keynes danced the can-can in 1923 has gone into the history books. The two Stephen sisters, who became Virginia Woolf and Vanessa Bell, were its queens, although their husbands were definitely not its kings. This honor was disputed, as was much else, between Keynes and Strachey. When Keynes defied Bloomsbury's positively Ptolemaic tradition of intermarriage and picked a bride from outside the set, the Russian ballerina Lydia Lopokova, Strachey dismissed her as "a half-witted canary."

But there was more involved. Keynes and Strachey had been lovers years before, then Strachey took up with the beautiful young painter Duncan Grant. Maynard stole Duncan away. Lytton was desolate. The two remained friends, but Strachey seemed able to get close to Keynes only when Keynes was unhappy. After his marriage he fell away from the set, although never completely. Lydia, it appears, protected him from the depredations of Bloomsbury and the outside world alike.

To this day, the surviving members disagree on who belonged to this Upper Bohemia, where it met, even when it existed (roughly between 1910 and 1930, with time out for a detestable war in which Keynes was one of Bloomsbury's few participants, as a Treasury official managing external finance). The catfights of the memoir writers are of minor importance. What matters is Bloomsbury's essentially static sense. It was a kind of terminal moraine to the great Victorian glacier, the morality leached out; Stephen Spender described it as "the last kick of an enlightened aristocratic tradition." Bloomsbury was indeed the last of the Whig aristocracy, and except for Keynes, these intellectual oligarchs deliberately stripped themselves of public power. Keynes was Bloomsbury's man of action and adviser on the outside world, with a typical Whig zest that disdained all zeal. He would help arrange the finances for that Room of One's Own, which cost a neat £500 a year. He would advise Strachey where to go in the Mediterranean for the best value in "bed and boy." His homosexuality helped reinforce his sense of social separatism. Today we would call it alienation. But Keynes was never alienated from his society, except perhaps when he attacked it for sheer economic stupidity. He mastered society from above and quite naturally built his personal elitism into his economic techniques.

Reminiscences of Keynes's life make it a fine, sunlit, effortlessly spun web. His characteristic manner was sitting sunk deep in an armchair, each hand tucked into the opposite coat sleeve like a mandarin. His face was not handsome. He had a large spoonbill nose, which earned him the nickname "Snout" at Eton. But he allied his modulated, musical voice to his persuasive powers and delighted in argument for its own sake. "Like Dr. Johnson, he would talk for victory," recalled Noel Annan, a Cambridge colleague.

Keynes speculated on both money and commodity markets with the same languorous confidence. Operating from his bed every morning, equipped only with telephone, newspapers, and an uncanny knowledge of long-range trends—"my diversion," he wrote his mother—he built his personal fortune from an initial capital of £4,000 (most of it borrowed after losing his own savings in a first plunge on the markets). "The dealers on Wall Street could make huge fortunes if only they had no inside information," he once said. He beat them at their own game in the 1930's by investing heavily in American utility stocks. Wall Street believed Roosevelt would show his true socialist colors by nationalizing the public utilities. Keynes knew better. When the stocks eventually rose, he made a killing.

By 1937, when a heart attack curtailed his activities, his fortune was £506,450. His art collection was valued at £31,419 at his death. In the public interest he had also laid the foundations of the National Gallery's impressionist collection by attending a wartime Paris art auction armed with £20,000 of government money and Duncan Grant's advice; it was the spring of 1918 and the German ultra-long-range cannon, Big Bertha, was shelling the city, fortuitously depressing prices. "We have great hopes of you and consider that your existence at the Treasury is at last justified," Vanessa Bell wrote patronizingly, and indeed, ungratefully, for Keynes had risked his public position to testify for Bloomsbury's conscientious objectors. When his own call-up notice came, he replied on Treasury stationery that he was simply too busy to attend. For a man of such sheer practical genius life was a game, and the greater the intellectual or financial risk the better.

Keynes was a true Whig. This curious type of aristocracy is not found outside England. They did not accept the Victorian view of progress and the perfectability of human nature, and they also rejected the Tory extreme of an Augustinian belief in the utter corruptibility of human nature. Keynes held to the skeptical Whig belief in tolerance and human intelligence as a way out of the thicket. But instead of democratically according these qualities to the citizenry at large, he transferred his faith in an intellectual elite to the government, to that supposedly sensible leadership beloved of the Whigs. He believed that an elite intelligence could manage things better than the citizens themselves, or more precisely, that it could define the arena for the play of individual interests. What he failed to recognize, until too late, was that in our time the government's own huge interests in that same arena would extend its role far beyond that of pure arbiter and that it would be equally subject to the deep irrationalities of the nation as a whole. The disinterested elite is ground to dust in the ring.

Every economist, like any social scientist, is a product of his times. Adam Smith observed and favored an agricultural society in which unemployment was impossible. Industry, cushioned by agriculture and fueled by thrift, operated from what Smith saw as a natural propensity to bargain. Of course this had its ups and downs; in the aggregate it was known as the trade cycle. When demand was slack, the farm families worked less at their cottage looms, sold less, ate less. But they survived, and national accumulations of capital slowly bettered their lot. (Bagehot said Smith believed there was a Scotsman inside each of us.) Malthus described an expanding urban society, and his predictions were consistently overturned by advancing technology. Ricardo and Mill described an early industrial economy of heavy saving and cutthroat competition. The dominant character was the Dickensian entrepreneur plowing his profits back into the firm; the subservient one was the worker robbed of his share of the reinvested profits and forced to sell his labor to the highest bidder.

All their speculations were turned into something close to science by Alfred Marshall, Keynes's teacher at Cambridge. This nineteenth-century mathematical economist devised calculations of supply and demand down to a hairsbreadth, and the more precise they became, the further they were from real life. These economists believed instinctively in the law of the eighteenth-century Frenchman Jean Baptiste Say: supply creates its own demand. Whatever could be produced—and this was natural in an economy of scarcity—would be bought. When the system got out of balance, it could be righted by cutting prices to increase demand, and that included a brutal cut in the price of the worker's labor. The system was beautiful in its self-regulating automaticity. Cheaper labor was supposed to encourage the capitalists to start up their idle factories and put people back to work.

Marx had already realized that the workers wouldn't play and would one day refuse to cut their wages. Keynes looked around him and saw that the capitalists wouldn't play either. They refused to risk cutting their prices—and risk is the essence of capitalism. When it faced its crisis in the 1930's, it had lost the nerve to employ the tremendous resources lying idle in Europe and America. With populations declining and technology stuck fast, capitalism seemed to have lost its creative drive. There was a closing of economic frontiers. The Marxists thought the system was at last in its death throes, but Keynes restored its vigor by repealing Say's unworkable law of supply and demand and replacing it with a system that could make man a master of the economic machine instead of its slave.

But Keynes belonged nevertheless to the rationalist tradition of his predecessors, and out of this tradition came *The General Theory of Employment, Interest, and Money* (1936). This seminal work of the twentieth century is not in fact a general theory (Keynes never suffered from excessive modesty), but a system of short-run techniques for manipulating the economy, and in particular the level of employment, which was then capitalism's most serious threat. Their proof was in their practice: the techniques worked. Keynes depended primarily on his eclectic intuition and experience. A collector of Newton's papers, he quotes with approval a dialogue between Halley and Newton about planetary motion. Halley: "How do you know that? Have you proved it?" Newton: "Why, I've known it for years. If you'll give me a few days, I'll certainly find you a proof of it." By now we know Keynes's discoveries in our bones, and unless we want to return to a situation in which one man out of every five or six is out of work through no fault of his own, we forget them at our peril.

Keynes introduced the concept of a national balance sheet to regulate the level of employment and the level of consumption plus investment. The balance was not between individual supply and demand, which never worked anywhere outside the daily cabbage market, but between the size of a nation's total resources and the demand for them. In short, what everyone produces and earns must equal what everyone saves and spends. If we earn less, we also spend and save less. We also produce and invest less. Then the machine begins to run more slowly, and resources are not used, human ones especially. Keynes demonstrated that nothing decreed the machine would ever start up again and call those resources back into use. It could idle along at half-speed for years, as it did during the depression. Nothing was built into the machine—no regulator, no invisible hand—to ensure that it would call on just the precise number of people available.

What to do? The answer seems absurdly simple now. The government must raise the level of what people spend, or lower it if there is not enough output to match. It can do this through taxation and through putting extra money into the economy by leaving the budget unbalanced. It must induce businessmen to invest more, by subsidies or lower interest rates. Or it must simply invest more itself, through public works. Naturally, the whole scheme can be thrown into reverse. It is a matter of shuffling the figures in the national equation to keep the machine running at optimum speed.

The General Theory itself was a polemic designed to convince Keynes's fellow economists and in turn the British government. Classical economic theory had decreed a cut in wages as a depression remedy. First to get it in the neck, because they were closest to hand, were the nation's parsimonious teachers; they were followed by the unemployed, whose dole was cut. This helped balance the budget and maintain the gold standard. It didn't work. Ramsay MacDonald's Labor government went off the gold standard in 1931. This eased Britain's unemployment somewhat by making goods more attractively priced, especially in captive imperial markets. But when the Conservatives returned the same year, they refused to deviate from a balanced budget. The British Treasury's arguments against public works are something to behold; the mandarins opposed a road-building program because "who would use them?"

In the United States the New Deal acted more out of instinct than theory on Keynesian ideas that were already in the air. But without the underpinning of *The General Theory*, Roosevelt was eventually forced to bend to the classical economists and balance the budget. When he did this in 1937, unemployment rose at once. Keynes and the President had met in the White House in 1934. Although Roosevelt wrote Felix Frankfurter that he had "had a grand talk with K and liked him immensely," he did not put Keynes's ideas systematically into effect, especially the vital technical ones on deficit finance and credit as a positive (rather than accidental) cure for slack demand. This did not happen until John Kennedy was reluctantly persuaded that it was necessary by his economic advisers, all carefully schooled Keynesians.

Keynes admitted that he deliberately overstated his doctrine because he demanded action, quickly and sensibly. "Words ought to be a little wild, for they are the assault of thoughts upon the unthinking." His book is extremely difficult to read and almost impossible to use in a classroom; the mathematical hocus-pocus went well (if slowly) in the trade. Paul Samuelson of M.I.T., whose internationally used college textbook on Keynesian economics shows an admirable grasp of capitalist enterprise—the professor has made a fortune on it—once described his master's chef-d'oeuvre thus: "It abounds in mares' nests or confusions . . . In it the Keynesian system stands out indistinctly, as if the author were hardly aware of its existence or cognizant of its proportions. An awkward definition suddenly gives way to an unforgettable cadenza. When finally mastered, its analysis is found to be obvious and at the same time new. In short, it is a work of genius." Keynes knew it. On New Year's Day in 1935 he wrote Bernard Shaw: "I believe myself to be writing a book on economic theory which will largely revolutionize—not, I suppose, at once but in the course of the next ten years—the way the world thinks about economic problems."

So now the Keynesian revolution has been completed, and like any other, even one launched out of such a gentle and humane tradition, it has begun to devour itself. By demonstrating how to manipulate large forces in the economy, Keynes unwittingly drew the blueprint for an economic juggernaut that must eventually, if it has not done so already, kill the individual values and personal variety he passionately sought to preserve.

Like Freud's, Keynes's sensible ideas have been transported across the Atlantic and turned into a fake philosophers' stone of precise formulas for the supposed prediction of human behavior; statistical practitioners of his theory claim it cuts as fine as—what shall we say?—a guillotine? What has been constructed is a different kind of economic machine, but a machine nevertheless. It could hardly have been a benign intelligence—if it was any intelligence at all—that organized such unfettered production and wasteful competition by a selfish mass that cares not a sou for the legitimate economic needs of the poor in the ghettos. This same intelligence has assigned the shift of the control of investment—which is simply the control of economic creation—from the individual to the managerial elite, aptly described by Norman Mailer as "locked in common-law marriage with the government for thirty-five years."

As a descriptive social scientist, Keynes saw this coming, but he encouraged it as the only way to keep capitalism going. It seemed self-evident to him that the creators of economic wealth would cooperate with their political rulers in its proper distribution. He explained how to use idle resources, but not misdirected ones; that

was a task for simple intelligence. His system of short-term economic management is essentially static, like his very special society. Nothing in it allows for technological disruptions such as
automation, nor for the huge concentrations of economic power
that can fix the prices for goods or labor almost at will, nor for
geometrical progression of ordinary human wants. (In *The General
Theory* he suggested that after a few years of full employment
ordinary people might be so satisfied with their lot that a zero interest rate would be necessary to halt saving and boost spending.)
Keynes provided the economic rationale for public investment in
something as vague and rewarding as the pleasant English concept
of public amenity—parks, schools, planned housing. He provided
equally for public expenditure out of pure decency toward the forgotten, and significantly, nonconsuming parameters. But the will
to do this is not necessarily comprehended in Keynes's system,
only in his aristocratic soul. By invoking the state as a *deux ex
machina* to extract the capitalists from their own contradictions, he
assumed that the state would be beneficial, paternalistic, and sensible, if only it could shake off "a failure of intelligence."

But where in the world today can one find such a government of
disinterested Whigs? Governments now are the major actors in the
economic drama, seizing delightedly on the tools of taxation, investment, and credit that Keynes fashioned for them. Like the
Renaissance princes who clipped the coinage, they now know how
to manage the modern economy to suit their own purposes.

In the totally new type of economy created through Keynes—an
economy neither of scarcity nor glut but of previously unimagined
abundance—the master himself may be turning into a defunct
economist. The size, complexity, and sheer force of modern productive power are proving less and less amenable to the fine-tuning of
Keynesian levers. The economic managers have instead been
forced to start swinging meat axes to chop off vigorous but unwanted growths in an economy of such heterogeneity as Keynes
never imagined. These heroic weapons are becoming distressingly
familiar and less effective, partly because the motives of those
who swing them are distrusted. Credit crunches work indiscriminately; businessmen damn the interest rate and invest even more
fanatically. Across-the-board shifts in taxation only stimulate a
new rush of money into goods, before they become even more expensive. A situation in which everyone expects rising prices pro-
motes an irrational swirl that can eventually destroy the necessary
interplay of the market; for it to operate, buyers who believe prices

will go up must balance against sellers who believe they will go down. (Keynes himself was not too worried about inflation. He looked back across the centuries and associated the rentier's profits with periods of great cultural achievement, the inflation bestowing "freedom from economic cares" upon the governing classes.)

This is not to blame Keynes for the cornucopian monster his followers have created. He had a secure faith in the forces of the market, but also a sensible awareness of their destructive potential. "For my part," he wrote in 1924, "I think that Capitalism, *wisely managed* [my italics], can probably be made more efficient for attaining economic ends than any alternative system yet in sight, but that in itself it is in many ways extremely objectionable. Our problem is to work out a social organization which shall be as efficient as possible without offending our notions of a satisfactory way of life." Later he came to realize that wise management was not as easily attained as good, or even green. In an essay on "My Early Beliefs," read to his old Bloomsbury friends in the Memoir Club, he wrote: "We were not aware that civilization was a thin and precarious crust erected by the personality and the will of a very few, and only maintained by rules and conventions skillfully put across and guilefully preserved. . . . I still suffer incurably from attributing an unreal rationality to other people's feelings and behavior (and doubtless to my own, too). . . . The attribution of rationality to human nature, instead of enriching it, now seems to me to have impoverished it. It ignored certain powerful and valuable springs of feeling." That was in 1938, just after his heart attack. But Keynes had already devised his system. It was too late to change mental habits to fit in with his new and perhaps darker beliefs.

During his final years Keynes was deeply involved in managing Britain's wartime economy and was given a peerage for it. He negotiated with the United States over the form of the postwar economic system and England's subsidiary role in it. He proposed the equivalent of a world-wide central bank to regulate the financing of world trade, and an international currency that would have downgraded gold ("a barbarous relic"). The idea, a product of sheer intelligence, might have averted the world monetary crisis we periodically face. The United States refused to accept anything but a watered-down version in the International Monetary Fund, lest this entail yielding too much of its newly won power to the embryo world authority that Keynes's central bank would have become. After surveying the faces of the American bankers, busi-

nessmen, and bureaucrats arrayed around the table at the Bretton
Woods Conference in 1944, he remarked to a friend: "They look
like knees." It was a look into a faceless future. In March, 1946,
Keynes went to the founding meeting of the International Monetary Fund in Savannah and was reduced to quibbling over the
location of the Fund's headquarters and its directors' salaries. "I
went to Savannah expecting to meet the world, and all I met was a
tyrant," he said. A month later he was dead.

Keynes had outlived his time, but surely not his usefulness. What
he had missed about communism was that love of money would
turn into love of power; and about capitalism, that the managerial
elite, whether in business or government, would be suborned by
the same thing. But capitalism could not have done without
Keynes, and the question it now faces is what to do *with* him. His
techniques may be subject to revision, but his essential idea of man
controlling his economic destiny cannot be. The problem of capitalism is no longer economic, it is political. Success of this tremen-
dously creative system now depends on whether we can bend the
juggernaut to our social will. The key ideas now are not the elitist
concepts of management but democratic planning and personal
participation. If Adam Smith's invisible hand was, in a way, actually created and made visible by Keynes, it now must be connected
to those deeper springs of feeling he divined late in life. I do not
know what the mechanism should be. But I do know that it demands new democratic institutions to deal with economic com-
plexities. They probably must be drawn on a more intimate scale,
but they must also reach far beyond the intellectual elite that
Keynes believed was the repository of wisdom. If the ensuing
dialogue entails a loss of economic efficiency, then so be it. Economists, Keynes was fond of saying, should be technicians "like
dentists." He regarded members of his profession as "the trustees,
not of civilization, but of the *possibility* of civilization." Today his
intellectual heirs manipulate their slide rules and chortle, "We are
all Keynesians now." Keynes would have shuddered at the expression, and if he were alive, I doubt he would be one.

While anthropologists have reported and analyzed in detail the family organization and social behavior of many primitive peoples, we are still curiously ill-informed about many facets of the evolution of the European family. J. H. Plumb here emphasizes the paucity of our knowledge with regard to the changing status of childhood. He lists various factors that, over several hundred years, tended increasingly to isolate children from the adult world. He might have stressed also the brutality with which children were commonly treated even within the confines of the family, as Dickens among many others so eloquently testifies. It seems that the great alienation of youth came with industrialization and the factory system, which involved the absence from the family during crucial hours of the day first of the father and then frequently of the mother also. The problem is admittedly a complex one and Mr. Plumb's discerning essay touches many aspects of it which call for further investigation and study.

THE GREAT CHANGE IN CHILDREN

J. H. PLUMB

Within the family circle the affections binding parents and children seem so natural that one assumes these relationships are a part of our humanity. Certainly some aspects are. Mothers protect, look after, and feed children. One can see the biological urge of motherhood at work whenever one glances at animals or even birds. But once one moves away from this biological fact, one moves into a world of change, of varying social attitudes of remarkable diversity. And certainly our own attitudes toward children not only differ widely from our fathers' and grandfathers' but differ immensely once we push back into the early nineteenth century and beyond. The world that we think proper to children—fairy stories, games, toys, special books for learning, even the idea of childhood itself—is a European invention of the past four hundred years. The very words we use for young males— boy, *garçon*, *Knabe*—were until the seventeenth century used indiscriminately to mean a male in a dependent position and could refer to men of thirty, forty, or fifty. There was no special word for a young male between the ages of seven and sixteen; the word

Until comparatively recent times, children were considered to be small-scale adults, and were so dressed; witness this French pair.

Mary, Queen of Scots, with her son, the future James I of England, who is garbed in the cap and ruff worn by babies and old men alike.

"child" expressed kinship, not an age state.

About the ancient world's attitude toward children we know next to nothing, though we are somewhat better informed about the training and education of youths in Greece, and especially in Sparta. For classical China the situation is similar: deep reverence for parents, particularly the father, was insisted upon, but we know very little of what was thought of childhood as a state. The common pattern of attitudes toward children among most primitive peoples, and there are discernible relics of this pattern in most advanced societies, is this: they are regarded as infants until seven years of age; little differentiation is made between the sexes, indeed, they are often dressed alike; at seven infancy goes and the boys begin to follow men's activities—herding cattle, hunting for food, working on the farm. Usually they are not men in two important aspects, the making of love and the making of war.

The entry into full manhood is customarily marked by intricate ritual, almost always painful. Spartan boys were viciously flogged, Arabian boys were circumcised without anesthetic. Nuer boys had their foreheads incised to the bone. The boys undergoing this operation were regarded as being of the same tribal age. They remained "classmates" for the rest of their lives, although their actual ages might vary by as much as four or five years. Most of them, however, would be unaware of their own precise age—indeed, this is true of the majority of men and women in medieval Europe.

Again, it is very rare to find children depicted as children before the beginnings of the modern world, at the time of the Renaissance. In Chinese paintings, as in medieval manuscripts, they are usually shown as small adults, wearing the clothes, often having the expressions, of men and women. The Greeks paid little attention to childhood as a special state, and there are no Grecian statues of children. It is true that in the late Roman Empire there is the hint of a change. There are a few remarkable heads of young boys, ten or twelve years of age, very lifelike and obviously individual portraits; most of these seem to come from funerary monuments. They display a quite extraordinary sense of age, of the young and growing child, which was not to be found again in Western art until Renaissance times. And there was Cupid, who fluttered in and out of frescoes, who as Eros was sculptured again and again during Hellenistic times. He is the ancestor of the naked *putti* that flit through the pictures of so many European artists from the fifteenth to the nineteenth century, mischievous, impudent, and sentimental. But Eros was a stylized symbol, not a child. Similarly, toward the close of the Middle Ages, angels appear in illustrated manuscripts, singing and playing musical instruments, and they are quite obviously neither infants nor adults, but children. Yet they, too, like Cupid, fulfill a special function. And they do not lead to the portrayal of actual children. One has only to look at the church monuments of Elizabethan England to see how distant the concept was of childhood as a separate state. There, lined up behind the father are three or four little men, all dressed like himself in the formal clothes of the age, and behind his wife kneels a group of little girls wearing the habits of women. Only infants are clothed differently. They are shown either tightly bound in their swaddling clothes or dressed in the long robes worn by both girls and boys alike until they were "about seven."

Fortunately, enough records survive for us to be able to state with confidence that pictorial representation is but a reflection of a social attitude. And we can trace the slow evolution of our modern concepts of childhood over the past four hundred years. The journey, though slow, was immense—the development of a separate world of childhood. This seems so natural to us that it is difficult to conceive of any other.

First, we must remember that infants died more often than they lived. "All mine die," said Montaigne casually, as a gardener might speak of his cabbages. And until they had reached the end of infancy, between the ages of five and seven, they scarcely counted. A character in Molière, when talking of children, says, "I don't count the little one." Men and women of the sixteenth and seventeenth centuries would not have regarded the exposure of children by the Spartans, Romans, and Chinese as callous. Indeed, it is likely that the poor of Renaissance Europe treated unwanted infants with a similar brutality. Life was too harsh to bother overmuch about an infant who probably would not survive anyway. At that time the attitude was much nearer to the instinct of an animal—immense concern to feed and protect the infant while it lived, indifference after it was dead, and death was expected.

A new sensitivity toward infant mortality can be discerned near the end of the sixteenth century, when dead children began to be represented on their parents' tombs. The fact that they were dead, not living, children is made grimly clear. They either have skulls in their hands, or kneel upon one, or have one hanging above their head, and even tiny infants are depicted, still in their swaddling clothes, which indicates that they were probably younger than two years of age. Children, even babies, were ceasing to be anonymous; yet if this was the beginning, the dawn of a new attitude toward childhood, its fulfillment was still far in the future.

Certainly there was no separate world of childhood. Children shared the same games with adults, the same toys, the same fairy stories. They lived their lives together, never apart. The coarse village festivals depicted by Bruegel, showing men and women besotted with drink, groping for each other with unbridled lust, have children eating and drinking with the adults. Even in the soberer pictures of wedding feasts and dances the children are enjoying themselves alongside their elders, doing the same things. Nor need

A detail from Bruegel's Peasant Dance *pictures children enjoying themselves in the midst of the lively revels of their elders.*

we rely on paintings alone, for we have a wonderfully detailed record of the childhood of Louis XIII. His physician kept a diary, recording each day what the young dauphin did. From this, we can perceive how his father, Henry IV, and the court treated him. It gives one an insight into aristocratic attitudes toward childhood, and into middle-class attitudes as well, for we have corroborative sources, though none so rich, for this period just before some of the most momentous changes in adults' attitudes toward children were about to take place.

Like the peasant children painted by Bruegel, the young prince was involved in adult life to an outstanding degree. At four Louis was taking part in adult ballets, once stark-naked as Cupid; at five he enjoyed hugely a farce about adultery; at seven he began to go to the theatre often. He started gambling at the same age. By seven he was also learning to ride and shoot and hunt. He relished blue stories, as well as fairy stories, with a group of courtiers of all ages: fairy stories did not belong exclusively to children; courtiers, particularly the ladies, loved them. Similarly, the games he played —Hide-and-seek, Fiddle-de-dee, Blindman's Buff—were all played with adults and adolescents as well as with his child companions.

Although the adult and childhood worlds intermixed intimately, there were some differences, particularly before the age of seven. The dauphin when very young played with dolls, rode a hobby-horse, and rushed about the palace with his toy windmill; these were specifically the activities of infants. Before he was breeched, he was often dressed up as a girl. More surprising, however, was the amount of open sexuality permitted. The dauphin and his sister were stripped and placed naked in the king's bed, and when the children played sexually with each other, Henry IV and the court were hugely amused. The queen, a pious and rather austere woman, thought nothing of seizing his genitals in the presence of the court, and the dauphin often displayed himself, to the amusement of his staid middle-aged governess. He acquired the facts of life as soon as he could talk. At seven, however, all was changed. He was severely reprimanded for playing sexually with a girl his own age, and the need for modesty was constantly impressed upon him. The importance of this very detailed evidence from the dauphin's doctor, who saw nothing odd in it, stresses that the world of children and the world of adults were deeply involved. Children, even infants, were not thought of as requiring a special environment, special entertainments, special clothes; nor was it considered necessary
to keep them apart from the sophistications and ribaldries of adult

life. There were, however, some distinctions: actions that could be permitted, even joked about, in very young children had to stop as soon as they left infancy and became young adults.

In some ways the court was old-fashioned, for by 1600 there was growing up a new conception of childhood. This had been developed by the Schoolmen of the fifteenth century, and adopted and adapted by the educationalists of the Renaissance, especially Erasmus, Vives, and Mosellanus. It became the stock in trade of the Jesuits, who were to dominate the education of the aristocracy and the richer middle class of seventeenth-century Europe. This new attitude was based on the concepts that childhood was innocent and that it was the duty of adults to preserve this innocence. The child, surely, was a prey to passion and to irrationality, but just as innocence could be preserved, so passions could be repressed. The protected child could be guided by remorseless effort into the world of rational behavior; innocence could be transmogrified into adult morality. So even while the dauphin was playing with his naked sister to the ribald amusement of the court, the Jesuits were purging schoolbooks of indecencies and the religious at Port Royal were editing Terence so that he might be read at school. In many educational establishments discipline was becoming extremely stringent and the dangers of childish sexuality legislated against—boys were no longer put two or three to a bed, and there was a steady separation both of the sexes and of age groups.

Parallel with this developed the cult of the Infant Jesus, which symbolized childish innocence. One of the most common devotional prints of the seventeenth century showed Christ summoning the little children to his knee. Increasingly, the child became an object of respect, a special creature with a different nature and different needs, which required separation and protection from the adult world. By 1700 for a child of middle-class family to be outwardly licentious would have been deeply shocking, to have been allowed to gamble for money at six would have appeared outrageous. By then, too, the child possessed his own literature, books carefully pruned of adult sophistication or broad humor, but also especially written for the young mind. The period between seven and adolescence was becoming a world of its own.

In the eighteenth century this new vision of childhood became the accepted social attitude of the affluent classes. Among the poor the old attitudes lingered on—poverty bred proximity, and so forced adults and children to share the same world. In villages and in slums children and adults still played games together, listened to the same stories, lived lives much more closely bound together, lives that could not be separated.

Nor was it only in the areas of manners and morals that changes took place in the lives of children between 1600 and 1800. This period also witnessed a revolution in the attitude toward the education of children—and many of the assumptions that we regard almost as belonging to human nature itself were adopted during this time. For example, everyone assumes that the processes of a literate education should develop with the developing child: reading should begin about four or five, writing follow, and then gradually, more sophisticated subjects should be added and become more complex as the child grows. Education now is tied almost inflexibly to the calendar age of children. In the modern world, at least in Europe and America, a class of children at a school will all be nearly the same age—a few months, perhaps, on either side of the average, but rarely as much as a year.

As with manners and morals, there were for a very long time two worlds of education: one belonging essentially to the Middle Ages, which persisted among backward people for a long time; and the other, basically our own, which took centuries to achieve its final organization and definition. The medieval child usually learned his letters with the local priest or a monk from a nearby monastery, more rarely in the singing schools attached to cathedrals, but the age at which he started his primary education would be dictated by his personal circumstances. Often, a boy would not start to learn Latin, without which all but the most basic learning was impossible, until he was in his teens, sometimes even twenty or older, simply because his economic situation prevented it. In the seventeenth century Girardon, the French sculptor, worked at home until he was sixteen; then his father, prosperous at last, sent him off to begin his studies. Still not unusual in Girardon's day, this practice had been customary in the fifteenth century, when old men, young men, adolescents, and children could all be found sitting in the same classroom, learning the same lessons. They turned up for classes, but no one cared about the rest of their lives. Sometimes, as we learn from Thomas Platter's story of his school days in the early sixteenth century, groups of students ranging in age from the early twenties to a mere ten would wander in search of learning from France to Germany and back again. A young boy would be bound to an older boy, beg for him, be beaten by him, and might occasionally be taught by him, but always he would be fed and protected. Occasional jobs would enable them to attend classes and lectures; but usually they begged, and education proceeded by fits and starts. They lived like hippies and wandered like gypsies, begging, stealing, fighting; yet they were always hungry for books, for that learning that would open the doors of the professions. Platter was nineteen before he could read fluently, but within three years his hunger for learning led him to master Latin, Greek, and Hebrew. And in the end he became rector of Basel's most famous school.

Even in Platter's day, however, times were changing. The late Middle Ages witnessed the proliferation of colleges, particularly at Oxford and Cambridge and the University of Paris. Students entered the university at an early age—usually at fifteen, sometimes as young as twelve, though there was, of course, no bar to the very mature. Residence in colleges fixed them in one place, and parents could be certain that their sons would be subject to discipline, sent regularly to lectures and classes, and protected from the excesses of drink, the temptations of fornication, and the dangers of gambling. College rules became very strict; obedience was insisted upon, and whipping frequent for delinquency. Inexorably a world of learning, quite separate from the adult world, indeed carefully protected from it, was created. In the sixteenth and seventeenth centuries all Etonians were taught in one large room. The boys were divided up into groups in accordance with the progress of their studies, and the usher and master would go from group to group. At this time few grammar schools had more than one master and one usher.

This system began to change at the end of the eighteenth century, and by the early part of the nineteenth century a new system had been established. Schoolrooms were divided up or added, boys of the same age were moved steadily from class to class, and as the numbers swelled, fees grew and so did the number of masters employed. Yet much of the adult world lingered on, even in the boarding schools, which were becoming increasingly popular in England. We know that at Eton, Harrow, Rugby, and elsewhere there was drinking, smoking, fighting with local boys, a great deal of gambling, and a considerable amount of surreptitious wenching. But reform went relentlessly on, creating a separate world of childhood and early youth. Even the leisure and amusements of schoolboys were differentiated. Organized team-games replaced casual, personal sporting activity; innocence was insisted upon and incessantly preached about; sex before entry into the adult world came to be regarded as a social crime; literature was even more carefully censored—the headmaster of Harrow in the mid-century would

251

not allow the reading of any novel, for fear it would corrupt the reader; naturally gambling was forbidden and alcohol banned. Even food became different—far plainer than adult food and dominated by milk and suet puddings, which you may still hear an old-fashioned Englishman dismiss as nursery food. And school clothes changed, too. In the seventeenth century two ribbons at each shoulder marked a child's dress, otherwise it was the same as an adult's. In the eighteenth century children were frequently clothed in semi-fancy dress—sailor's costume, the kilt and bonnet of the Scottish Highlander, Vandyke dress for special occasions— rather as if society were searching for difference. Greater freedom was permitted to the child, and children were allowed trousers long before adults would wear them. But gradually, two basically separate forms of costume for children and adults evolved. By the early twentieth century boys between infancy and puberty wore short trousers, and their clothes were always far drabber than adults'— confined to grays and blues and blacks. At school children were clamped into uniforms as socially distinct as those of soldiers or prisoners.

In the European upper classes children in the nineteenth century were even excluded from adult society *in the home.* The children were forbidden most of the house and lived in day and night nurseries with nurses, governesses, or tutors, visiting the rest of the house and their parents only for very short periods. Indeed, the difference between the life of a sixteenth- and a late-nineteenth-century child is so vast as to be almost incomprehensible. Three centuries had created a private world for children.

Although this new attitude toward children developed in the middle classes, it seeped down into society as time passed. The pictures of working-class children of Victorian London or Paris show them still dressed as adults, usually in their parents' worn-out and cut-down clothes, and we now know that they participated in every form of adult life—indeed, they physically had no escape from it. But as affluence spread, the working class, too, was caught up in the system of mass education, and working-class children began to have a separate world forced upon them. Social legislation also took a hand. In the nineteenth and twentieth centuries children were excluded from public houses, forbidden to gamble or buy tobacco, and their sexual lives were regulated by the concept of the "age of consent"; for it was assumed that they would be innocent, and prefer innocence, unless a corrupt society forced sex upon them. So by World War I, speaking broadly, there were three ages

—infancy, which had been shortened to the age of four or five; childhood, which ran from the end of infancy to late puberty for the lower classes and to early manhood for the rest; and adulthood. And no child anywhere in the Western world was expected to share the tastes, the appetites, the social life, of an adult.

And then the revolutionary change came. The change from medieval to modern had taken more than three centuries, but the revolution that frightens modern society is scarcely a decade old. To understand it, one must know why children had gradually been separated from the adult world, and their lives and education carefully regulated.

The short answer is social need: after 1500 the Western world grew ever more complex, demanding more skilled and trained men for commerce and the professions. And for these activities boys rather than girls were needed, which is why attitudes toward the young male changed most of all. Also, the great empires—the French, the British, the Spanish, and the Dutch—required men with the habit of authority. The proconsuls of empire had to be stamped with the image of a gentleman, aware of obligations as well as privileges. Discipline, best enforced by regular schooling, proved the most efficacious mold for the colonial bureaucrat.

But society is never still, and even as the new attitudes toward childhood were becoming fully fledged, there were countermovements in social structure that were to make even profounder changes. Science and technology invaded more and more of economic and social life. From 1880 onward they increasingly dominated the activities of Western society. Their growth demanded a longer and longer education. Before World War I sixteen or seventeen was a not unusual age for a middle-class boy to leave school either in America or Europe. After World War II huge segments of the population, female as well as male, remained in the educational system to twenty-one and beyond, and the number increases every year. Such a vast social change must necessarily have affected our attitudes toward childhood and youth, but there were other complex social forces at work as well. The great European powers lost their empires. Their need for conformity to a middle-class pattern weakened. America filled up, became urban, and its accepted social images of youth became blurred and confused at the same time. The whole purpose of education, other than the learning of crafts and skills, became entangled in debate. Add to this the psychoanalytical attacks on the Victorian concept of childish innocence, and the social confusion about how to treat childhood is easy to comprehend.

There were other muddying factors. The middle classes grew much richer, and the pressures on their children toward economic and social goals eased, too. They were pressurized neither to be Christian gentlemen nor Horatio Algers. And yet in spite of a myriad of warning signs that attitudes toward children needed to be changed, the attitudes belonging to an earlier and simpler world were still enforced. Children were not allowed to drink; parents and educators insisted on old patterns of overt deference and unquestioning obedience. Behavior, clothes, and hair styles had to conform to archaic standards; juvenile reading was still censored; sex was regarded as belonging to the adult world and certainly not to be practiced by those being educated. Repression, conformity, discipline, and exclusion were until lately the historically bred attitudes of most educationalists and parents.

Kept out of the adult world, the adolescents naturally created a world of their own choosing—one that incorporated their own music, their own morals, their own clothes, and their own literature. And they, of course, began naturally to capture the minds and imagination of the children who, though younger in age, nevertheless lived with them in the same basic educational territory. In consequence, during the past few years the period between infancy and adolescence has been sharply reduced, and may be reduced even further in the future.

Social movements and tensions in the adult world can be adjusted by politics, but adolescents and children have no such mechanism for their conflicts with the exclusive world of adults. And so the result has been, and must be, rebellion. That rebellion, however, is not due to the mistakes or difficulties of the last few years. Rarely do we look far enough into the past for the roots of our present problems. This revolution of youth has been building up for decades because we forced the growing child into a repressive and artificial world—a prison, indeed, that was the end product of four centuries of Western history, of that gradual exclusion of the maturing child from the world of adults. We can now look back with longing to the late medieval world, when, crude and simple as it was, men, women, and children lived their lives together, shared the same morals as well as the same games, the same excesses as well as the same austerities. In essence, youth today is rebelling against four centuries of repression and exploitation.

Modern youth in revolt: an antiwar demonstration.

It is truly ironic that Soviet historians, more than fifty years after the event, have as yet been unable to produce a satisfactory account of one of the major overturns in history, their own great revolution of 1917. In large part this is due to the fact that the name of Leon Trotsky, next to Lenin the most important artisan of the revolution and its savior in the following period of civil war, has been taboo ever since Stalin outmaneuvered and defeated him in the great political struggle that followed Lenin's death. I had the privilege of spending two afternoons with Trotsky in his Mexican exile within a year of his assassination, and I still retain a most vivid impression of a dynamic personality, of a man with genuine charisma. If in the world of today the spirit of Trotsky is still alive and increasingly influential, it is because he was the dedicated proponent of world revolution and was unwilling to settle for less in the conflict with more "practical" men. Edmond Taylor, a veteran among foreign correspondents and a student of Russian affairs, writes brilliantly of one of the truly brilliant leaders of the twentieth century.

THE RISE & FALL & RISE OF LEON TROTSKY

EDMOND TAYLOR

"Of late," declares a recent British anthology of contemporary revolutionary thought, "a spectre has begun to haunt the Communist parties in Europe: Leon Trotsky. The [pickaxe] that killed Trotsky did not succeed in killing his ideas, and a revival of the theories advocated by Stalin's most powerful and consistent opponent is now seen by many as a Marxist alternative to Stalinism."

At first glance, neither the theme nor the rhetoric seems particularly original. Ever since the exiled Bolshevik leader's assassination in 1940, his loyal disciples—the handful that remained—have been predicting the relatively imminent triumph of their martyred prophet's revolutionary doctrines, and paraphrases of the *Communist Manifesto*'s famous opening sentence crop up periodically in Trotskyist literature. But in an abstract and purely ideological sense the Trotskyist mystique of "Victory in Defeat"—the title of Isaac Deutscher's closing chapter in his classic three-volume biography of Trotsky—has long had some rational foundation.

Trotsky in 1924, the year of Lenin's death. In the ensuing power struggle, Trotsky, the heir-apparent, was outmaneuvered by Stalin. 257

As Deutscher himself remarks, a certain substratum of Trotskyism, if rarely the same kind of Trotskyism, can be found in the policies, teaching, or revolutionary leadership of Khrushchev, Mao, Tito, Castro, and other prominent Communists of the post-Stalin era. Mao and Castro, for example, both preach the doctrine of ceaseless revolutionary struggle against capitalism and imperialism on a world-wide basis that underlies Trotsky's theory of the Permanent Revolution—the very cornerstone of Trotskyism—though both deviate from Trotsky's classic Marxist internationalism in their preoccupation with the industrially underdeveloped areas of the world. Conversely, while it is hard to detect much Trotskyism in Khrushchev's stress on peaceful coexistence between the capitalist and Communist nations or in the nationalist-bourgeois tendencies of Tito's Yugoslavia, all the "revisionist" Communist leaders have echoed Trotsky's theme of the Revolution Betrayed —another basic Trotskyist dogma—in their criticism of Stalinist despotism.

Trotsky wrote with equal fire and conviction as an apostle of revolution and as the critic of a revolution gone wrong, as a champion of the dictatorship of the proletariat and as the censor of a totalitarian bureaucracy established in its name. It is natural that every variety of Marxist revolutionary, and some who are more revolutionary than Marxist, have found inspiration in his voluminous, often contradictory, writings.

The really new development is the resurgence of Trotskyism as an actual revolutionary movement, with considerable and growing support among the young. Though still a minority within the revolutionary minority, the Trotskyists count in their ranks a number of the most brilliant and dynamic leaders of the New Left. A representative of the new trend—which seems to worry official Communist leadership in Europe even more than it does the defenders of bourgeois law and order—is Alain Krivine. As the outstanding leader of the Trotskyist Jeunesse Communiste Révolutionnaire, he played a key role in the French student revolt of May, 1968. In the French presidential elections the following year, Krivine, then doing his military service, ran as the candidate of the Communist League, a new Trotskyist organization, and though he was careful to explain that his candidacy was merely a kind of revolutionary put-on to bedevil the bourgeois establishment, he rolled up more than 236,000 votes.

Active, and in some cases strong, Trotskyist groups exist today in Europe, Canada, and the United States, throughout southern, middle, and southeast Asia—notably in Ceylon and Burma—in a number of African countries, and in Latin America. What for convenience can be termed the orthodox ones are affiliated with the Fourth International, created in 1938 in opposition both to the Socialist Second International and to the Communist Third International, by then completely under Stalin's control.

From the first, a number of Trotskyist groups in various countries refused to merge with the national sections of the International, either because of personal feuds with their leaders or because the whole idea of a new International seemed unrealistic to them in the existing world context. Others broke loose or were expelled because they were unwilling to follow the rigid party line that the leadership of the International sought to impose in regard to such issues as coexistence, de-Stalinization, the Sino-Soviet rift, support of the Castroite regime in Cuba, or the Soviet occupation of Czechoslovakia. As a result, in most countries today outside the Soviet and Chinese orbits there are several dissident or independent Communist organizations whose competing claims to represent the true principles and spirit of Trotskyism can scarcely be evaluated by outsiders.

Nearly everywhere, it is the student Trotskyists, less concerned with doctrinal quarrels than the veterans are, who are stimulating and leading the general resurgence of Trotskyism. In the process, they are also making a substantial contribution to the student unrest that afflicts most Western nations. "Trotskyist militants . . . were at the origin of the first Western European demonstrations for Vietnam," asserts Pierre Frank in his essay on the Fourth International (of whose secretariat he is a member). "They were in the forefront of the struggle at Berkeley and in the whole anti-war movement in the United States . . ." This somewhat sweeping claim is supported by a liberal British expert on left-wing political affairs, Brian Beedham, in *The Crisis of Communism:* "The student rebellions of the past couple of years—in Paris, Berlin, London, New York—have been led by a curious assortment of people: Maoists, anarchists, and some others who can only be described as fascists of the left. But the most important are the followers of Leon Trotsky."

To avoid attaching undue importance to the conspiratorial aspect of the Trotskyist movement, and thus adopting what Trotsky himself called the "police theory of history," it is well to remember that during their years of wandering in the revolutionary wilderness many Trotskyist groups got into the habit of bolstering their

Messianic faith by working within left-wing organizations of greater worldly scope and claiming the results achieved by the host bodies as so many victories for Trotskyism. This glory-by-association technique is too often taken at its face value by official police and intelligence agencies. Moreover, there is a tendency, particularly among youthful Trotskyists, to hail anyone whose political vocabulary is radical, internationalist, and even vaguely Marxist as an ideological brother. Some Trotskyists almost appear to regard Mao as a Trotskyist, although the label would no doubt be indignantly repudiated by the Chinese leader himself. "Che" Guevara is not only a hero to young Trotskyists (as he is to virtually all young radicals today) but is seen by them as an authentically Trotskyist hero—mainly, it seems, because of his militancy and revolutionary ardor.

Whether Trotsky himself, if he were alive, would recognize as his ideological disciples such romantic Marxists as Guevara, and whether he would acknowledge all the victories for Trotskyism claimed by his latter-day adherents, is doubtful but not really material. Clearly, it is not the strict canon of Trotskyist doctrine— if there is such a thing—that captivates the imagination of contemporary youth; even among students who call themselves Trotskyists it seems likely that only a minority have read their master's chief theoretical works.

What, then, explains the current Trotskyist revival throughout the world? Do students and militant young workers admire Trotsky for what he was, or despite what he was? Because of the ideas he stood for, or because of those they *imagine* he stood for?

Some of these questions are relatively easy to answer. Trotsky's historical achievements alone would suffice to elicit the admiration of anyone who professes a revolutionary philosophy. Most objective historians today regard him as the direct artisan of the 1917 October Revolution in Russia. He also created the Red Army, without which the Soviet experiment would almost certainly have ended in disaster. Unquestionably, Trotsky was one of the giants of modern history.

Unlike some giants, moreover, he possessed a number of particularly attractive virtues as a human being: courage, integrity, fortitude, intellectual honesty, compassion on occasion, and at least intermittently, a sense of chivalry—along with several all too human failings: vanity, intellectual arrogance, and excessive pugnacity. He was a great writer, a great orator, and a great revolutionary leader. Like Churchill, he made, and wrote, history with an

equal sense of style: passionate, intelligent, and a little flamboyant.
Politician, scholar, administrator, professional conspirator, writer, historian, social philosopher, distinguished literary critic, brilliant polemicist—Trotsky was probably the nearest the twentieth century has come to producing a universal genius (his chief intellectual weakness was a naive, almost endearing, unawareness of his limitations). His mind was intensely creative, constantly erupting with original ideas, bubbling with energy, magnificently untroubled by its own contradictions.

Other aspects of Trotsky's complex personality and many-sided world outlook seem less calculated to arouse the enthusiasm of young rebels against twentieth-century industrial society. Trotsky was a stern disciplinarian, with himself and with others. An exceptionally devoted and generally faithful husband—at least to his second wife, Natalya Sedova—he was an authoritarian, at times despotic and heartless, father. He was a born rebel, and in theory an ardent lover of human freedom, but repression never troubled his conscience if he felt the success or safety of the revolution was at stake: he slaughtered the anarchist sailors of the Kronstadt naval base in 1921 as ruthlessly as he had earlier slaughtered the White Guards. Though he excoriated Stalin's personal tyranny for years, he believed as strongly as Stalin did, not only in the dictatorship of the proletariat, but in that of the Bolshevik party.

Trotsky was an unabashed militarist, a bureaucratic martinet, a fanatic believer in the virtues of industrialization, and a staunch upholder of Western cultural tradition. He preached—and practiced—the revolutionary virtues of clean appearance, clean living, and clean language. "The struggle against 'foul language,'" he once wrote, "is an essential condition of mental hygiene, just as the fight against filth and vermin is a condition of physical hygiene."

Though some young Trotskyists may be happily ignorant of the "square" and authoritarian elements in their prophet's teachings, it does not seem too farfetched to suggest that a larger number are positively attracted by these elements and are therefore unconsciously revolting against the current permissiveness of Western society rather than against its imagined repressiveness. There is a similar but even stronger case for thinking that the unavowed, sometimes inverted, romanticism of Trotsky's life and character accounts for much of his appeal to a certain type of contemporary young rebel. Trotsky was often accused of being a romantic Marxist; there is no doubt that to the end of his days he remained a Marxist romantic.

Revolutionaries commonly grow up in families that are either harshly exploited or else overprivileged, and romantics spring more often from a decadent or dispossessed elite than from an ascendant social milieu. Trotsky—originally Lev (Leon) Davidovich Bronstein—was born, however, on a farm in the southern Ukraine of parents who had started poor but were making it, by their own efforts. They were Jews, but they lived as independent, landowning peasants—a rare thing among Russian Jews at that time—and were largely free both from the trammels of custom that Jewish society imposed upon itself and from the restrictions or vexations that the czarist state imposed upon Russian Jewry.

Life in the Bronstein family when Leon was born, in 1879, was not very different in many respects from what it might have been had the family lived at the same period in Kansas or Nebraska. They had clay floors in two of the rooms, several hundred acres of good wheatland, and a free horizon. Leon's father, David Leontievich, drove himself and his family as hard as he drove his workers. He eventually set up a prosperous flour mill in addition to his farm and was respected by his peasant customers for being honest and tightfisted.

When he was nine, Leon was sent to school in Odessa. He lived with middle-class relations of his mother named Spentzer. They were cultivated and mildly liberal Jewish intellectuals, who recognized Leon's exceptional gifts from the start and systematically helped him to develop them. He became regularly the top boy in his class, but got into trouble more than once for defying school regulations or being rude to his teacher.

Young Bronstein moved to the Black Sea port of Nikolayev for his last year of secondary school. It was there he first got caught up in the student revolutionary movement. What pushed him into it is not wholly clear. The sympathy with the underdog that was later to become one of his ruling passions seems at that time to have manifested itself only fitfully. Probably the deep-rooted emotional allergy to authority that he manifested all his life was activated by the general climate of rebellion then prevailing in Russian student circles, itself a reaction to the intensified despotism that had characterized the reign of Nicholas II during its first years.

Whatever his initial motivations, Bronstein's revolutionary career began under appropriately romantic auspices. He was introduced by school friends into a radical discussion group conducted by a self-educated Czech gardener named Franz Shvigovsky. Though the group's subversive activities were limited to tea drinking and talk, Shvigovsky was regarded as a dangerous conspirator by the czarist police, and therefore had immense prestige in the eyes of the students.

One member of the group was a young woman, several years older than Bronstein, named Alexandra Sokolovskaya. Alexandra —who later became Bronstein's first wife—was a Marxist. Bronstein, like his mentor, Shvigovsky, thought of himself as a Narodnik, a socialist-populist of the old-fashioned, idealistic, warmhearted Russian sort. "A curse upon all Marxists, and upon those who want to bring dryness and hardness into all the relations of life," he exclaimed in a defiant New Year's toast, addressed with adolescent boorishness to Alexandra herself. She walked out of the room, and a few months later he became a convert to Marxism.

This incident illustrates the basic dichotomy in Trotsky's nature. There were to be occasions in his career as an adult revolutionary when the Marxist zealot or windy theorizer would seem, in fact, to have forgotten his native humanity, not to mention his common sense. (In 1919 Trotsky proposed conscripting workers to lay the basis for a socialist economy in Russia, and in what a few years later would have seemed a typical example of Stalinist cynicism, denounced the "wretched and miserable liberal prejudice" that forced labor was always unproductive.) More often, perhaps, Trotsky's Marxism would serve as a focusing lens to the somewhat diffuse ardor of his temperament, magnifying both his virtues and his faults to a heroic intensity, ultimately enabling him to personify better than any other figure in modern history the twentieth-century myth of revolution.

Young Bronstein went to jail for revolutionary agitation for the first time a few months after his eighteenth birthday. (He had briefly attended the University of Odessa—where his professors had predicted a brilliant future for him as a pure mathematician— and then dropped out to return to Nikolayev as an underground agitator.) He spent two years in various prisons before being sentenced to exile in Siberia. After another two years he escaped, getting away from Siberia on a false passport—in which he had written, for the first time, the name Trotsky—and leaving behind a wife and two baby daughters. (He had married Alexandra Sokolovskaya in prison while still a minor.)

Sent abroad as the delegate of the Social Democratic underground in Siberia, Trotsky, then twenty-three, joined the émigré circle around Lenin in London and began contributing to Lenin's paper, *Iskra*. A priority objective of Marxist revolutionaries in

In 1902 young Leon Bronstein first used the name Trotsky on this forged passport, which enabled him to escape from exile in Siberia.

those days, as now, was to discredit liberals and moderates, especially in the eyes of the young. Trotsky, with his youthful verve and insolence, his bent towards sarcasm, and his genius for invective, excelled in this activity, particularly as an orator addressing various Social Democratic gatherings.

Soon, however, the young iconoclast turned the cutting edge of his tongue and pen against Lenin himself. Trotsky believed in a centrally controlled revolutionary party and recognized the need on occasion for conspiratorial methods, but he criticized Lenin for trying to centralize too much control in his own hands and for substituting professionalized conspiracy for mass action. Relations between the two men became ambivalent, each esteeming but censuring the other, and remained that way until 1917, when Trotsky finally accepted Lenin's primacy as a revolutionary leader. In the quarrel between Bolsheviks and Mensheviks that split the Russian Social Democratic party after 1903, Trotsky most frequently adopted an independent position, more extremist—in the revolutionary sense—than that of the Mensheviks, but more democratic than that of the Bolsheviks.

264   Trotsky slipped back into Russia as the Revolution of 1905 was

beginning, and it catapulted him to fame, at least within the revolutionary movement, at the age of twenty-six. No other Marxist
émigré, not even Lenin himself, and few underground militants
assessed the situation so fast and so accurately, or manifested so
much "revolutionary intuition"—to use Trotsky's own term—in
exploiting it. Elected to the St. Petersburg Soviet (Council) of
Workers' Deputies, Trotsky almost immediately became its dominant figure. He simultaneously made himself popular with the
mass of Petersburg workers as a rabble-rousing balcony orator and
kept a tight rein on the hotheads in the soviet who deluded themselves with the hope of storming some czarist Bastille or dreamed
of a heroic death on the barricades.

When the czar's police finally moved against the soviet, Trotsky,
who was chairing its last meeting, instructed his fellow delegates to
break the hammers of their revolvers before surrendering, gave the
floor to the police commander so that he could read out the war-
rant of arrest, and then told the baffled official to keep quiet while
the meeting wound up its agenda. The performance was pure
Trotsky—and wonderful revolutionary theatre.

While in prison awaiting trial, which led to a new deportation to
Siberia and shortly afterward to a new escape abroad, Trotsky
wrote a pamphlet outlining a radical, and to some, heretical, innovation in Marxist doctrine: the theory of the Permanent Revolution, which became the cornerstone of Trotskyism. Briefly sum-
marized, the theory stipulated: (1) that despite Russia's industrial
backwardness, the country's relatively small proletariat could and
should impose its leadership on the peasant majority in the revolution against czarism; (2) that because of the dominant role of the
proletariat this revolution would finally turn into a socialist one,
drastically shortening, if not skipping over, the bourgeois-demo-
cratic phase predicted by most orthodox Marxists at the time; (3)
that the Russian proletariat would not be able to remain long in
power without the massive support of the European proletariat,
thus implying revolution in Europe; and (4) that the Russian
workers by their example and by throwing Russia's "colossal"
power into the scales of the class struggle abroad could initiate a
successful world-wide socialist revolution or series of revolutions.

The global aspects of the theory of Permanent Revolution seem
most pertinent, if still questionable, today; they have undoubtedly
influenced revolutionary leadership in China, Cuba, and elsewhere
in the Third World. In 1906, however, it was the assumption that a
revolution led by the working class was possible and desirable in

Russia that startled, and frequently shocked, European Marxists. Indeed, Trotsky's pamphlet marked an important date not only in Marxist but in world intellectual history. It was the bluntest, if not the first, repudiation by a Social Democrat of the traditional Marxist revolutionary credo that the workers should seek to seize power only when they had become a majority of the nation. Lenin himself had not yet moved so far on the road that was to lead from the dictatorship of the proletariat to the dictatorship of the Communist party and finally of the party's apparat.

After the triumph of the Bolsheviks, Trotsky's theory of the Permanent Revolution furnished in large measure the ideological background for the split between him and Stalin. Overshadowed at first by personal antagonisms and quarrels over more immediate issues of policy, the Permanent Revolution eventually became in Stalin's eyes his adversary's major heresy. Perhaps it was the only point of pure doctrine in dispute between him and Trotsky in regard to which the cynical Georgian had any deep convictions.

What mainly caused the trouble was not Trotsky's overoptimistic expectation that the Russian revolution would start an almost immediate and irresistible chain reaction of revolution in Europe— most of the other Bolshevik leaders shared this delusion—but the corollary that Trotsky derived from the eventual exposure of his malcalculation. The revolutionary timetable would have to be revised, Trotsky admitted, but the long-range promotion of socialist revolution throughout the world should remain the basis of Soviet policy. True socialism could not come into being in Russia until the whole world was socialist. To put world revolution out of one's mind and concentrate on building socialism in one country would inevitably produce "bureaucratic deformations" that betrayed the Marxist ideal.

As the foremost champion and theorist of Socialism in One Country, particularly with the collapse of the German and Chinese revolutions after the First World War, Stalin naturally found Trotsky's viewpoint abhorrent. As the rift between them widened, Stalin worked up an elaborate demonology that portrayed Trotsky as a secret saboteur of the revolution and Trotskyism as the predestined counter-revolutionary fruit of his alleged original "Menshevism."

On Trotsky's side, the doctrine of Permanent Revolution gradually merged with his criticisms of the Soviet state bureaucracy and his protests against the stifling of internal democracy within the Communist party; together, they would lay the foundations for his

almost equally metaphysical dogma of the Revolution Betrayed.
Stalinism, as he finally came to view it, was not a personal aberration but the epitome of those very "bureaucratic deformations" inevitably generated by the victory of Socialism in One Country over the Permanent Revolution. Of course, Trotsky could not—or at least, did not—foresee the emergence of Stalinism when he formulated his theory of the Permanent Revolution in 1906. If he had, he might have theorized somewhat more cautiously about the desirability of attempting to establish the dictatorship of the proletariat in a country that had just begun to produce a working class. (That any kind of dictatorship tends sooner or later to degenerate into a personal despotism never seems to have occurred to him.)

Trotsky was still in exile (in New York at the time) when the March Revolution overthrew the czarist regime in 1917. He rushed back to begin mobilizing the Russian, and world, proletariat for the final struggle. In Petrograd he met Lenin, by now converted to the doctrine of the Permanent Revolution, or something very similar, and the two men patched up their fifteen-year-old feud. After a few weeks Trotsky joined the Bolshevik party and became the chief executor of Lenin's insurrectionary program, though the politico-military strategy of the insurrection seems to have been largely his own. Elected president of the Petrograd Soviet in September, Trotsky brilliantly exploited his official position to organize the armed Bolshevik uprising behind a smoke screen of revolutionary oratory that bemused both the Kerensky government and a number of his brother socialists.

The most vivid and detailed account of Trotsky's role in the October Revolution is that given by Trotsky himself in his two masterpieces, *My Life* and *The History of the Russian Revolution*. In both books he seems much of the time to be occupying the front of history's stage, but on the basis of all the available evidence, he had every right to put himself there. He is frank, at moments cynical, in revealing the deception and covert manipulations that lay behind the Bolshevik coup (". . . an insurrection . . . develops better, the more it looks like self-defense").

The insurrection, however, as it emerges from the magic of Trotsky's prose, was no mere *Putsch*. It had to be conspired, but it was not simply a conspiracy. It was largely a military stroke, but the soldiers of the Petrograd garrison who carried it out had already been won over by the "proletarian vanguard." What Trotsky means is that Bolshevik agitators had systematically subverted the loyalty of the garrison with revolutionary propaganda; he himself 267 was the party's foremost agitator, and his volcanic oratory almost literally mesmerized the crowds, civilian or military, that were exposed to it. No doubt he mesmerized himself.

In plotting successfully to seize power from Kerensky, Trotsky did not consider that he and Lenin had themselves made a revolution; he insisted—not always convincingly—that they had merely helped one to be born, acting as midwives to history. And what history was bringing forth with their aid was not just a Russian revolution but the Russian prologue to a world revolution that was destined almost overnight to transform the human condition. The Permanent Revolution was theory in 1906; by October, 1917, it had become Messianic mystique.

Consciously, or almost consciously, Trotsky came to regard himself as the prophet of this revolutionary mystique, uniquely qualified—especially after Lenin's death—to interpret its revelation. At a deeper level of his mind, especially in moments of supreme crisis, when there was no time for rational analysis and "revolutionary intuition" took over, he seemed rather to be identifying himself with the hero of some epic myth of revolution that his own imagination had conceived. He became charged with elemental energy; it was as if invisible sparks were incessantly crackling from his heavy mustache, his defiantly satanic goatee, and his wild shock of hair.

The attitudes he struck took on not merely a theatrical but an archetypal quality. His actions had an exemplary and an almost ritualistic, as well as a practical, dimension. When he spoke on certain particularly dramatic occasions, he became the voice of the revolution itself. "To the dustbin of history!" he shouted at the old Menshevik leader Theodore Dan, who was protesting in the Congress of Soviets against the Bolshevik insurrection, and it was all the young, impatient, implacable todays since the beginning of time shouting down the tired, timid, old yesterdays.

The element of heroic myth in Trotsky's career was no less marked during the Russian Civil War, when as the Soviet Commissar for War he lived for more than two years in his famous armored train (usually only the locomotive was armored), dashing from one threatened front to another. His personal contribution to the formation of the Red Army and to its victory on several decisive battlefields was undoubtedly immense, but his contribution to revolutionary legend was even greater.

Trotsky's train was a rolling liaison office between the Soviet government in Moscow and the fighting fronts, plus a communications center, emergency supply depot, and psychological-warfare unit. In the economic breakdown and general chaos that prevailed throughout Russia after the civil war erupted, following the October Revolution and defeat in the war with Germany, it was a brilliant administrative improvisation. Trotsky's personal role as an ambulatory war minister was not purely that of a civilian administrator, however, and his constant visits to the front lines or outposts, accompanied by members of his own bodyguard, wearing leather jackets with distinctive brass insignia, were more dramatic than the usual VIP morale-building battlefield tours.

At one particularly critical moment in czarist General Yudenich's offensive against Petrograd, which narrowly failed to capture the former capital, the commander of a Red regiment, hard pressed by the advancing Whites, ordered an injudicious withdrawal that put the neighboring units in jeopardy. Trotsky, who happened to be visiting that sector at the time, recognized the danger. Leaping on a horse that was standing nearby, he galloped forward to countermand the order for retreat, rounded up the stragglers who were continuing to flee, and—still mounted on his providential charger —led the regiment back to its original position under enemy fire.

The chapters in *My Life* on the civil war almost give the impression at times that it was won by sheer heroism and force of will, with Trotsky as a revolutionary Prometheus inspiring the soldiers of the Red Army to defy all "pusillanimous historical fatalism"— an odd phrase from the pen of a Marxist writer. The same romantic subjectivism that colored Trotsky's writing as a military historian undoubtedly distorted his judgment as a revolutionary strategist on occasion. In his preoccupation with morale and psychological impact (Trotsky was one of the master propagandists of his age), he tended to overlook Napoleon's "big battalions." As the chief Soviet negotiator at Brest-Litovsk, he wanted to reject the outrageous German peace terms and adopt a policy of "no peace and no war." Though fine revolutionary propaganda, the policy, as Lenin realized, would probably have resulted in the replacement of the Soviet regime by a German military government.

What Lenin termed Trotsky's "excessive self-confidence" likewise tempted him sometimes into rash courses of action. He was by no means, however, the irresponsible hothead that Stalinist critics have made him out to be. He was more prudent and realistic than Lenin himself, for example, in opposing the march on Warsaw during the war with Poland in 1920. Despite his obsession with the Permanent Revolution, Trotsky argued that the Polish masses would not welcome the invaders and that in the absence of local political support, attempting the military conquest of Poland would be a reckless adventure. The disastrous outcome confirmed his prescience.

Trotsky was seldom too much the revolutionary doctrinaire to reject a favorable tactical alliance with one ideological enemy against another: he was probably the chief Soviet sponsor of the Rapallo policy of an entente with German nationalism against the Versailles powers. His usual reaction in the face of overwhelming force, however, was to avoid a suicidal confrontation while waging an incessant war of harassment and psychological attrition against the adversary, at the risk of provoking disastrous reprisals. (The same strategic pattern can be detected in the permanent war that present-day Trotskyists wage against bourgeois society. So far, the results have not been particularly brilliant—except, perhaps, to those of Trotsky's spiritual heirs for whom the struggle is its own reward.)

A normal post-revolutionary career as bureaucrat and statesman in the Soviet Union might have dimmed to some extent the revolutionary glamour that surrounds Trotsky's name today. Stalin saved Trotsky from this fate by outmaneuvering him in the power struggles within the Bolshevik party that followed Lenin's death in 1924 and by eventually banishing him from the USSR. The personal dictatorship Stalin established likewise furnished Trotsky with the subsidiary myth—the Revolution Betrayed—that helped insulate his central myth of world revolution from too brutal exposure to historical reality. Finally, by sending an assassin to Mexico to strike down his exiled enemy in 1940, Stalin unwittingly supplied the last touch needed to consecrate in the minds of Trotsky's disciples, and of disciples to come, the image of the mythological hero fulfilling his tragic destiny.

It would be a distortion of contemporary history, as well as an affront to the memory of a great man, to imply that the romantic and mythological elements in Trotsky's life, and the element of mystique in his doctrine, suffice to explain the present revival of Trotskyism among young people throughout the world. (Its genuine internationalism is certainly part of its appeal.) But perhaps among today's crop of young Trotskyists, and no doubt other rebels, there are a certain number whose unconscious need for a hero to worship is even stronger than their conscious attachment to the cause of revolution. That is a disturbing thought from one viewpoint, but a reassuring one from another.

There has probably never been a society without its critics, moralists, and prophets of doom. But they seem to have become more numerous and strident in the past two centuries. The phenomenal growth of population in that period, together with the concurrent industrialization, have profoundly altered the conditions of human life. On the one hand, men have moved increasingly from the land to the already overcrowded cities; on the other, labor has become largely mechanized, which in turn has meant more and more regulation and control.

George Orwell's book 1984 is one of the more recent cries of alarm about the course of social development, warning insistently of the threat of collectivism from both the right and the left and foretelling the inevitable menace to the individual and his freedom. Mr. Malkin here discusses the trends that seemed so ominous to Orwell when he wrote more than a score of years ago. If, within the next dozen or so years, Orwell's worst forebodings have not materialized, it will be at least in part because of the emphasis laid on the problem by him and other critics.

HALFWAY TO 1984

LAWRENCE MALKIN

I never think of 1984, either the book or the year, without a slight shudder of foreboding. This can be no accidental idiosyncrasy. George Orwell set out to shock by the juxtaposition of fact and fancy. He combined the stylistic skills of the modern polemicist with the wry detachment of the classical moralist. He stood the year of the book's completion on its head to sum up his negative vision of the future in a single stroke. He had considered entitling it *The Last Man in Europe*, which lacks the stinging immediacy of his final choice but gives a stronger clue to his humanist aspirations. Had he been less a propagandist (and he said every artist was a propagandist for his own vision of life), I would not be writing this now. This curious, uncomfortably honest, and painfully decent man wanted to reach his readers primarily for political purposes; by the end of his life as a writer he had come to believe that people didn't make aesthetic judgments at all, only political ones. He wanted to be a popular author without surrendering his particular vision of the world. In all this he succeeded. Since World War II no political book, whether fiction or nonfiction—and the essence of Orwell's success is that no one is ever sure whether *1984* is one or the other—has passed more thoroughly into the English language and the popular consciousness of the Western world than Orwell's dark masterpiece.

Various insights expressed in this short, prophetic tract (Orwell described it as "a Utopia in the form of a novel") have secured a hold on individuals and groups of amazing diversity. *Life* published the first excerpts in 1949 with cartoon illustrations by Abner Dean; readers were offered the interpretation that "in the year 1984 left-wing totalitarianism rules the world." Michael Harrington wrote that Orwell had discovered that a technology of abundance would disenfranchise the victims of poverty and racism to maintain a permanent menial class. The John Birch Society of Westchester County offered *1984* for sale, and its Washington branch adopted 1984 as its telephone number. Writers of the Budapest Petöfi Club read *1984* before the 1956 Hungarian uprising, and the BBC's Overseas Service receives reports of the book's continuing popularity in eastern Europe. Various members of Congress have invoked the image of Big Brother against wiretapping, government personality-testing, and plans for a computerized central data bank. The liberal critic Harold Rosenberg said *1984* had set the tone of the postwar imagination by first describing the organization man as "the victim of the dehumanized collective that so haunts our thoughts."

The message that these and many, many others most commonly extract from *1984* lies in its most obviously frightening level: the totalitarian threat to individual freedom from collectives of the right or left. Any book that becomes such common intellectual currency risks being turned into debased coinage, especially when minted by such a critical and nonsystematic intelligence as Orwell's. But equally, any book that can strike such a responsive chord among such natural enemies must say something about the world in which they all live.

What the Orwell cultists cannot take in is his description of the most pervasive development of postwar political thought: the bankruptcy of liberal rationalism. Most of us have been raised on the comforting meliorist belief that if only the weight of human institutions is more equitably distributed, man will at last behave decently and rationally. We may disagree, as Mr. Rosenberg, say, disagrees with the John Birch Society, on where the balance of equity lies. But we still believe that ideas can make a more perfect society. Orwell says this simply is not true, or at the very best it is not possible. We have been schooled to believe that the best defense against totalitarian invasions of the privacy of the human spirit must be centered around rationally perfectible institutions. Orwell maintains they are no defense. He warns that the rationalist spirit of progress represents in fact the first step toward the very thing it aims to prevent, because it means giving me the power to enforce my ideas on you.

According to Orwell's timetable, by 1984 institutions of social and political control will have been invented that could, if those guiding them only desired it, solve the problems of mankind by issuing a few orders of the day. But those in power simply refuse to do so. "Sensible men have no power," Orwell said in dismissing the dream of a well-ordered world government. "The energy that actually shapes the world springs from emotions—racial pride, leader-worship, religious belief, love of war—which liberal intellectuals mechanically write off as anachronisms, and which they have usually destroyed so completely in themselves as to have lost all power of action." Orwell wrote those lines in 1941 in an attack on the utopianism of H. G. Wells. Had he lived into another generation, and watched the rise and sometimes tragic fall of American political dynasties with their attendant courts of pundits and professors, I doubt that he would have concluded the sentence as he did. No one could accuse the Kennedy Mafia or Johnson's Texans of forgetting race, leadership, religion, or war. Their overriding concern, however, was the pursuit of political power for its own sake, a pursuit followed at the cost of their sense and their sensibilities. Orwell's most important discovery was that the managers of our society, far from being sensible men, share the irrational drives of their fellows, and these include power. This is really what frightens us as we watch the liberal imagination turn into a totalitarian nightmare.

As a novel, *1984* is not particularly good. It is more fable than fiction and more fantasy than both. Big Brother is the only character anyone seems to remember, and he probably doesn't even exist. This is quite proper. Big Brother is the symbol and apex of an all-embracing and self-perpetuating state machine called the Party. It is split into an Inner Party (the decision makers) and an Outer Party (middle management). The mass of citizens, called the proles, simply do not count at all in the political scheme. Their lives are dominated by work and poverty, but their emotions are still free.

The plot of *1984* concentrates on the life of Winston Smith, a member of the Outer Party who cannot bear his job of rewriting the past to conform to the Party's directives and simply wants to be left alone. This desire for privacy is, of course, a crime; in every Party member's home stands a two-way telescreen to regulate his behavior and his thoughts. Winston is the last in a consistent line of Orwell's anti-heroes, starting with Flory in his novel *Burmese Days*, who said, "Be as degenerate as you can. It all postpones Utopia." Winston's degeneracy consists first in keeping a diary of his private thoughts, then in having a love affair. In *1984* hate is the common emotion; the Two Minutes Hate against the Party's enemies, real or imagined, is a daily ritual. Nevertheless, Julia, a dissident member of the Junior Anti-Sex League, makes clandestine contact with Winston, and they fall in love. All this is watched by the Thought Police. The guilty couple are tricked into a mock conspiracy against the state by O'Brien, a member of the Inner Party and a supremely rational ideologist. He finally tortures Winston into betraying Julia, and at the book's end, into loving Big Brother instead.

Winston's pitiful retreat into privacy, his blowzy love affair, his melodramatic detection, torture, and extinction as even a pallid individual by the apparatus of the Party, are unworthy of second-rate science fiction. Yet here we are more than halfway to 1984, and the book is still selling in the tens of thousands each year. To find a literary parallel, one would have to reach back beyond the nineteenth-century English novel with its romantic conception of man as a problem solver and into the eighteenth century, where life is larger than man and the world is a wicked place. Winston is a descendant of that almost faceless traveler in strange lands, Lemuel Gulliver.

The book tells us more, much more, about the quality of modern life than about the people in it. Orwell's style, a mixture of ideological fantasy and grubby realism, grows naturally from his beliefs. He confronts ideas with the rough edge of fact. He once wrote of Shakespeare: "he loved the surface of the earth and the process of life," and he could have been writing about himself. By 1984 life has been streamlined to a drab uniformity and the surface of the earth has been paved over, although not without cracks. People have been turned into mere ciphers in a topsy-turvy equation of ideas. The state is organized for war, but War is Peace. A fantastic communications system has been developed (even a "speakwrite" machine), but the Party uses it only to disseminate its own ideas, so Ignorance is Strength. Society has been organized into an immutable hierarchy that frees the individual from even considering his position in it, so Freedom is Slavery. These are the slogans of

Oceania. People live by them with an unthinking drudgery. The plastic food has stirring names ("Victory Coffee"). Clothing has no style. Houses are collapsing, and people are crowded into them. Most important, the past is being systematically expunged as part of a process of controlling thought; without human experience, ideas thus can exist in a vacuum. Privacy, individuality, history, tragedy, have vanished. As Winston realizes:

> The terrible thing that the Party had done was to persuade you that mere impulses, mere feelings, were of no account, while at the same time robbing you of all power over the material world. When once you were in the grip of the Party, what you felt or did not feel, what you did or refrained from doing, made literally no difference. Whatever happened you vanished, and neither you nor your actions were ever heard of again. You were lifted clean out of the stream of history. And yet to the people of only two generations ago, this would not have seemed all-important, because they were not attempting to alter history. They were governed by private loyalties which they did not question. What mattered were individual relationships, and a completely helpless gesture, an embrace, a tear, a word spoken to a dying man, could have value in itself. The proles, it suddenly occurred to him, had remained in this condition. . . . they were loyal to one another. . . . The proles had stayed human.

This is not a very helpful view of society for those trying to order it to some predetermined outline. It has never been fashionable for the modern intelligence to consider such human qualities as important *by themselves*. For Orwell, they were the main reason for living. For modern social engineering, human feelings represent unfortunate variables that somehow must be fitted into projections of gross national product (which sound increasingly like those phony figures of rising standards of living blared over the loudspeakers in *1984*); conditioned politically and psychologically for ideological wars in some obscure corner of the world (in *1984* the telescreen carries gruesome pictures of carnage from Malabar and announcements of victories that never bring peace any nearer); adjusted willy-nilly for the huge structures of human beings organized to produce, to dwell, and to play together (and you better like it and look the part, for by 1984 you may be guilty of an offense known as "facecrime").

Orwell deliberately ignored the two major areas of the social sciences where the twentieth century has made its strongest advances (if that is what they are): economics and psychology. "Economic injustice will stop the moment we want it to stop, and no sooner," he wrote in *The Road to Wigan Pier*, "and if we genuinely want it to stop, the method adopted hardly matters." Richard

Rees, a friend and colleague for twenty years, never once heard
Orwell mention Freud, Jung, Kafka, or Dostoevsky. He was not a
modern man, and he abhorred systematic (which is not to say
critical) thought. By his own admission, he liked gardening, cheese,
and even English food. He liked the combination of stolidity and
irreverence that marks the English working class, although he
never felt at home with them. He was half Eric Blair of Eton and
the Imperial Burmese Police, and half down-and-out tramp revolu-
tionary-socialist, a literary propagandist and apocalyptic allegorist
who became known as George Orwell. His friends addressed him by
the name under which they had first known him; he always meant
to change his name legally but never got around to it. In the same
way he never really decided who he was, although there was no
doubt that his loyalties lay on the left. This constant confrontation
of values, shaped by a personal honesty that is unique in modern
letters, made Orwell what he was. In a way the nagging dilemma
came to a head during World War II, when the pacifist and intellectual left revolted him and the rest of England got out and fought.
He wrote in 1943: "As to the real moral of the last three years—
that the Right has more guts and ability than the Left—no one
will face up to it." Indeed, an uncomfortable man to know.

Because *1984* appeared when the postwar Labor government
was on its last legs, and because the society it describes lives under
a system of government called Ingsoc, the book is often interpreted
as the pained protest of a disillusioned socialist. Admittedly, the
postwar world of London, with rationing, shortages, and the endless exhortations of the first ideological government England had
ever known, provided much color for the book. But Orwell was a
far more complex man than that. "I am not a real novelist," Orwell
once wrote his friend Julian Symons. "One difficulty I have never
solved is that one has masses of experience which one passionately
wants to write about . . . and no way of using them up except by
disguising them as a novel."

Orwell got the idea for *1984* while working on wartime propaganda for the BBC. He was appalled by the entanglement, perversion, and eventual swallowing up of ideas in the BBC bureaucracy
and described the place as "a mixture of a whoreshop and a lunatic
asylum." He resigned in 1943 to recover his freedom as a political
commentator; just before quitting he wrote a friend: "At present
I'm just an orange that's been trodden on by a very dirty boot."
(O'Brien says in *1984*: "If you want a picture of the future, imagine a boot stamping on a human face—forever.") The BBC can-

George Orwell, 1943.

teen, windowless and underground, was a model for the *1984* cafeteria in the Ministry of Truth (i.e., the propaganda ministry). A wartime colleague tells me that while Orwell survived the stale fish and cabbage smells with less grumbling than most, his imagination dwelt on what the BBC would be like if it were run by a Stalin instead of the liberal muddlers of Broadcasting House.

Orwell was dying of tuberculosis when he wrote the book; the disease killed him in January, 1950, seven months after *1984* was published. It was reviewed on the BBC by Malcolm Muggeridge and Tosco Fyvel, two friends and sometime literary colleagues. Discussing the climactic scene in which Winston breaks down and betrays Julia under threat of having his face chewed by rats, they compared it to the worst imaginings of a pair of prep-school boys trying to scare each other after lights-out. Orwell was listening in his hospital bed and laughed out loud. But Orwell refused to accept the thesis of another friend, Arthur Koestler, that political reformism springs from infantile neurosis. Orwell's strength lies in his insistence that politics rests on a moral foundation outside the individual and that truth rests in experience outside any system the individual can construct. An individual's search for truth in political life is not purely a function of intellect but of something with an old-fashioned name. The English call it character.

It is no accident that after a lifetime as a political essayist and a writer of starkly realistic novels, Orwell suddenly shifted to allegory in *Animal Farm* and *1984*. It is the literary form best suited to pointing up the contradictions between idea and reality. For Orwell it became the vehicle for explaining the major intellectual event of the first half of this century, the failed utopia—in Russia and elsewhere. The raw material consists of the curiously dated sectarian quarrels of the left in the 1930's, which Orwell freezes forever in the brilliant amber of *Homage to Catalonia*. But the issue described there is still real: freedom vs. power. In a time of social change, how much freedom can be allowed the individual to adjust to it, and at what rate must he adjust? His own or theirs? Totalitarianism insists on controlling the speed of change without reference to individual needs and finally must insist on trying to mold those very needs to fit its predetermined utopia.

Winston, in his subversive notebook, casts utopia aside and insists on following the instincts of his senses—"stones are hard, water is wet"—and finally: "Freedom is the freedom to say that two plus two make four. If that is granted, all else follows." But the catch phrase becomes perverted into the symbol of his humiliating subservience to the Party beyond the bounds of common sense. O'Brien forces him to admit that if the Party decrees it, "two plus two make five." This innumerate slogan has a revealing genesis. In *Assignment in Utopia*, which Orwell read soon after its publication in 1937, at the height of the Soviet purge trials, Eugene Lyons reports that electric signs were affixed to Moscow buildings with the slogan "$2 + 2 = 5$," exhorting the populace to work hard and complete the then current five-year plan in four years.

"The real answer," Orwell once wrote, "is to dissociate Socialism from Utopianism." The myth of utopia lies as deep in Western culture as that of the Garden of Eden, but it did not come alive politically until Thomas More added topical realism to it in the sixteenth century. As an early humanist, More raised the question of whether utopia could be transferred from the next world to this. As a Christian, he realized that after the Fall and before salvation the answer would have to be no. A utopia of happiness and boredom was literally no place, because of the nature of man and his exposure to the Christian experience—but by 1984 rational idealism has eradicated experience. All ideologies are to some degree utopian, from Pauline Christianity to Bolshevism to the Great Society. To the extent that they are rational and programmatic—and they cannot escape that any more than water can escape being wet—they are subject to disillusion and to perversion by power for its own sake. When More's *Utopia* is translated from the original Latin into modern English, it contains more than a hint of *1984*. Here is a random passage: "whatever you are, you always have to work. There's never any excuse for idleness. There are also no wine-taverns, no ale-houses, no brothels, no opportunities for seduction, no secret meeting-places. Everyone has his eye on you, so you're practically forced to get on with your job, and make some proper use of your spare time." More finally concludes: "Pride would refuse to set foot in paradise, if she thought there'd be no under-privileged classes there to gloat over . . . ."

More was a humanist trying to preserve Christian values, Orwell a socialist trying to preserve libertarian values. Later utopians, especially those late Victorians bemused by the deceptively liberating potentialities of technology, were not so wise. They failed to realize that human experience and philosophical perfection are incompatible. Orwell did, and he turned utopia into "dystopia." Like that other eccentric and pseudonymous English allegorist of modern life, Lewis Carroll, he stepped through the looking glass and parodied rational beliefs to their logical conclusions. Technology, especially the new technology of communications and management, becomes a tyrannical instead of a liberating force in *1984*.

The utopia from which Orwell borrowed most closely was Evgeny Zamyatin's *We*. Zamyatin, a Russian novelist, underwent the enlightening experience of being imprisoned by the czar's police in 1906 and by the Bolsheviks in 1922—in the same corridor of the same prison. He seems, however, to have looked all the way back to Bakunin, the father of anarchism. "I do not want to be I, I want to be We," Bakunin said, alluding to the anarchist's sense of community as a defense against centralized state power. Zamyatin foresaw the collapse of even the community into the state. His book was written in 1923 and set in the year 2600. People have numbers instead of names, and "The Benefactor" rules the "United State." The narrator, D-503, is the mathematician-designer of the first spaceship, soon to be launched carrying the message: "Long live the United State. Long live the Numbers. Long live the Benefactor." D-503's only problem in this well-ordered state is that he suffers from the serious mental disease of imagination. Eventually, after committing the crime of falling in love with beautiful young I-330 and joining her in a rebellion against the "reason" of the United State, he is forced to submit to X-ray treatment that removes the brain center responsible for imagination. He then betrays I-330. Afterward, this chastened number writes: "No more delirium, no absurd metaphors, no feelings—only facts. For I am healthy—perfectly, absolutely healthy . . . I am smiling." In the end D-503 throws in his lot with law and order: "I am certain we shall win. For Reason must prevail."

Orwell first read Zamyatin's book in 1945, when he was already making notes for *1984*. "What Zamyatin seems to be aiming at," Orwell wrote in a review, "is not any particular country but the implied aims of industrial civilization. . . . It is in effect a study of the Machine, the genie that man has thoughtlessly let out of its bottle and cannot put back again." Aldous Huxley also seems to have borrowed from *We* for his *Brave New World*. Zamyatin's, Huxley's, and Orwell's books all make similar assumptions about a technological utopia—that it has at last become possible, but that it also will be collectivist, elitist, and incompatible with the ideas of freedom.

In none of these dystopias is physical force the effective agent of control. It is, of course, the ultimate threat—as it must be even in a truly democratic state—but not the proximate one. In the first two the citizens are held down largely by a sort of synthetic happiness, a myth of contentment reinforced by material well-being. For this they have exchanged their freedom. By 1984 the citizens of Oceania have not only lost their freedom but have not even gained happiness for it. Those who wish to retrieve their freedom are subjected to humiliation, loss of identity, and in the last resort, pain. "We shall meet in the place where there is no darkness," O'Brien tells Winston, as he tricks him into disclosing himself as a rebel. This promised utopia turns out to be the torture chambers of the windowless Ministry of Love.

In Orwell's dystopia the proximate agent of control is language. The myths of freedom and peace are kept alive by a hollow language that has completely lost its meaning. In Newspeak, Orwell's most brilliant and culturally incisive creation, language, like personality, has been leached of all flavor. It is "objective," without the subtlety or irony that reflects experience. Newspeak is a caricature of C. K. Ogden's Basic English, in which the inventor hoped to compress the English language into 850 words. Orwell at first became interested in it as a possible corrective to official euphemism and as a cleansing agent at a time when, he said, most political writing consisted of phrases bolted together like a child's erector set. But he later realized its sinister possibilities when the British government bought the world rights. Syme, a compiler of a Newspeak dictionary in *1984* (he is a bit too clever and is eventually vaporized), knows what it is all about. His team is destroying words by the hundreds every day: "Don't you see that the whole aim of Newspeak is to narrow the range of thought? In the end we shall make thoughtcrime literally impossible, because there will be no words in which to express it. . . . Every year fewer and fewer words, and the range of consciousness always a little smaller." Newspeak accomplishes this, as Orwell explains in an appendix, by divorcing language from thought. Such words as remain express acceptable ideas or condemn unacceptable ones out of hand. Even by 1984 the process has not been completed, but it is well under way. I have before me a 1970 release of the "Headquarters, U.S. Military Assistance Command, Vietnam" describing activities of the month. It is interesting to note that the enemy often "attacks" but the "Free World" forces never do; they go on "search and destroy" missions. As usual, the demotic variant, ugly as it may be, is more forceful and more accurate; to "zap." I think Orwell, with his dedication to plain speech, would have been pleased by it.

In truth, everything in 1984 is controlled, ordered, managed. But who shall guard the guardians? In 1984, as ever, no one. Although the concept of an Inner Party can be traced back to Plato, Orwell's most immediate source was the American writer James Burnham and his book *The Managerial Society* (1941). It provided the ideological stalking horse for *1984* by predicting the rise of a new managerial class that would not be different from one superstate to another. (Milovan Djilas calls it the New Class in the Communist world.) Burnham foresaw the division of the world into power blocs centered around Europe, Asia, and America, another concept Orwell took over. These managers are described in the theoretical center of *1984*, the book-within-a-book that describes the principles of Ingsoc. Naturally this work is forbidden, as is any truthful book. It says of this managerial class:

The new aristocracy was made up for the most part of bureaucrats, scientists, technicians, trade-union organizers, publicity experts, sociologists, teachers, journalists, and professional politicians. These people, whose origins lay in the salaried middle class and the upper grades of the working class, had been shaped and brought together by the barren world of monopoly industry and centralized government. As compared with their opposite numbers in past ages, they were less avaricious, less tempted by luxury, hungrier for pure power, and, above all, more conscious of what they were doing and more intent on crushing opposition.

It would be invidious to put names on this rogues' gallery of twentieth-century types; I should imagine that for any casual student of the daily newspapers no names would be needed. The essence of Orwell's quarrel with Burnham, and he explains it in two detailed essays, is not that Burnham's description is incorrect but that, having worked it out, he has become fascinated by it and has accepted it as inevitable and therefore even desirable. Orwell labels this, with a kind of political prophecy, "realism." Burnham for a time accepted Nazism as a viable social order—until it began to lose. In England Orwell found that the middle-class managers accepted the Soviet regime, but only *after* it became totalitarian: "Burnham, although the English Russophile intelligentsia would repudiate him, is really voicing their secret wish: the wish to destroy the old, equalitarian version of socialism and usher in a hierarchical society where the intellectual can at last get his hands on the whip."

It is not surprising that when success finally came to Orwell, it was far from sweet and did strange things to this critic of the modern world. After his wife died suddenly in 1945, he retired with their adopted child to the barren and primitive Hebrides to write *1984* in surroundings simpler and more stark than the intellectual hothouse of London liberal society. The move helped break his health.

And he never bothered to conceal his views; quite the contrary, he exaggerated them to the point of personal abrasion. Michael Ayrton, then a young artist, recalls that whenever Orwell, wrapped in his old raincoat and scarf, appeared in the local pub, the young people would bemoan the arrival of "Gloomy George." But he loved to entertain friends in his flat for a high tea with English jams and pickles, and when he struck pay dirt with *Animal Farm* (1946), he told his publisher: "At last I can take you out to lunch." Before his death this committed socialist was in the process of turning himself into a limited company to escape England's high income-tax rates.

Animal Farm, the anti-Stalinist satire in which Orwell said he had for the first time managed to fuse artistic and political purpose, had "a hell of a time" finding a publisher. Victor Gollancz, the epitome of the left-wing British intellectual between the wars, refused to publish it although Orwell was under contract to him. "We couldn't have published it then," Gollancz told me several years ago. "Those people were fighting for us, and they had just saved our necks at Stalingrad." T. S. Eliot turned it down for Faber, but on the debatable critical ground that Orwell had failed to bring off the satire. Some Nice Nelly at the Ministry of Information or the publisher Jonathan Cape, Orwell wasn't quite sure which, objected to the use of pigs as a symbol for Bolsheviks. Ironically, Frederic Warburg, no less a middle-class, Oxford-educated Jewish liberal intellectual than Gollancz, took on *Animal Farm* and became Orwell's publisher and friend. In the United States Orwell's last books encountered initial misunderstanding that has dogged them ever since. Dial Press wrote Orwell that *Animal Farm* would not do for the American market because it is "impossible to sell animal stories in the USA." A year later, after Harcourt, Brace had accepted it, Dial wrote back and said someone had made a horrible mistake.

Going through the original reviews of *1984* seems to justify the complaint of the Trotskyite historian Isaac Deutscher: "The novel has served as a sort of an ideological super-weapon in the cold war." Scores of American newspaper reviews hailed it as a warning of the menace of "creeping Socialism." In the more liberal big-city press there was an almost grudging admission that tyrannies other than left-wing ones might be involved. Saddest of all is the *New Republic*'s review. "The only thing to guard against is taking it too seriously," wrote Robert Hatch, who refused to believe—and this, in the same decade as Hitler's gas chambers—that men could sink to such depths as to be unable to solve their problems by reason. The English reviewers, less hysterical, more thoughtful and questioning, got closer to the book's human values. They may be summed up by V. S. Pritchett's remark: "The heart sinks but the spirit rebels as one reads Mr. Orwell's opening page."

I don't think Orwell was the least surprised by such massive misunderstandings. ("Of course not," Warburg comments. "He regarded the world as a wicked place.") Orwell meant the book to go into the political arena like all his works and was quite prepared for it to take its lumps there. From his hospital bed he fought back as best he could. He wrote a friend: "I am afraid some of the US

Republic papers have tried to use *1984* as propaganda against the Labor Party, but I have issued a sort of démenti which I hope will be printed."

On June 15, 1949, Warburg dictated a memo containing a statement that Orwell approved. It begins by saying that *1984* is a parody; Orwell does not believe that its details will come true in the Western world, but "something like 1984 *could* happen." It continues: "This is the direction in which the world is going at the present time, and the trend lies deep in the political, social and economic foundations of the contemporary world situation. Specifically, the danger lies in the structure imposed on Socialist and Liberal capitalist communities by the necessity to prepare for total war with the USSR and the weapons, of which of course the atomic bomb is the most powerful and most publicized. But the danger lies also in the acceptance of a totalitarian outlook by intellectuals of all colors. The moral to be drawn from this dangerous nightmare situation is a simple one: *Don't let it happen to you. It depends on you.*" The memo then cites the dangers of superstates and adds: "The superstates will naturally be in opposition to each other or (a novel point) will pretend to be much more in opposition than they in fact are . . . it is obvious that the Anglo-Americans will not take the name of their opponents and will not dramatize themselves on the scene of history as Communists. The name suggested in 1984 is of course Ingsoc, but in practice a wide range of choices is open. In the USA the phrase 'Americanism' or '100 per cent Americanism' is suitable and the qualifying adjective is as totalitarian as anyone can wish."

As a prophet of specific events, Orwell has a less than perfect record, but only those who want to turn him into the original anti-Communist ideologue could complain of that. Orwell had long before written off the Communist experiment as a brutal failure. He was more immediately concerned with preserving deeper individual values. Ingsoc does not rule the English-speaking world, and we have not been smothered by a blanket of collective thought, at least not yet. Even in the Communist world the plants of individualism keep putting up flowers, if only to be tragically lopped off as soon as they bloom. In any society Orwell's message is what carries the relevance: it still "depends on you" whether or not 1984 comes true. I prefer to think of Julia as the precursor of the slogan that helped ignite a generation: "Make love, not war."

It is comforting to feel that more than halfway to 1984 we have no real Big Brother. London today is not the shabby metropolis of

1984. It has given birth to a species of pop culture that, although it may be excessively channeled into the pleasures of personal adornment and self-expression, has at last turned its back on the pretentious mock-aristocratic manners of the middle class that Orwell detested.

On a cool and luscious June day I visited No. 27B Canonbury Square; Orwell's fifth-floor wartime walkup there was the model for Winston Smith's "Victory Mansions." Poor Winston would never have recognized it. The neighborhood is festooned with greenery. Trees line the streets. Children play in the square; old folks sun themselves in it. Across the street, in a beautifully proportioned eighteenth-century mansion rented from the Marquis of Northampton, lives the London correspondent of the New York *Times*. The garden, the brickwork, and even the plumbing of Orwell's old house are in excellent order. Around the corner is an outdoor pub, a rarity in London. It is frequented by a mixture of working-class couples and the chic middle class (Orwell avoided the place because it used to be a hangout for Stalinist intellectuals). The whole neighborhood is urban landscape at its best, but of course property values have skyrocketed. I met a delightful London type tending the garden who could have been the model for the singing prole woman hanging her washing on the line in *1984.* Of course she remembered Mr. Blair, the writer; she used to work as a housekeeper for the woman who eventually became his second wife. Now she was a pensioner, and her chief worry was that the building had just been sold to some faceless property company. She hadn't even been told its name, and she was afraid she would be evicted and housed in some anonymous government redevelopment scheme far from her old neighborhood. So perhaps Big Brother, unseen as always, is not so distant from Orwell's old back yard after all.

It is easy to draw pictures of bogeymen; the caricature is too quickly adopted as imminent reality, and that is what has happened to Orwell's *1984.* I think Orwell underestimated the strength of European culture in resisting the encroachments of the machine age. The shared experiences that the Party would rub out in 1984 are still very much alive. Surely his own country still contains the sanest, kindest, and probably the most civilized people in Europe or possibly anywhere. Their mature self-awareness expresses itself in an articulate culture that exalts the individual and tolerates his eccentricities. Despite the erosions of two world wars, they cling to a hierarchic social order that encourages self-development, but

285

only within boundaries so comfortably defined that everyone knows the rules of the game stop at the actual winning of it.

But the threat of 1984 has roosted, like a vulture in a tree, most firmly in the American consciousness. The myths of our competitive culture are coming up against the rough edge of human experience, and the culture itself is shuddering under the strain. The sleek society of managers, the streamlined men whose values lie in sheer accomplishment by control of their environment, has dehumanized itself as Orwell foresaw. Values imposed by work have tended to transcend and sometimes obliterate those that grow naturally from human contact. The community is a place to *do* something—to work, to play, to sleep—rather than to *be* someone. Synthetic personal contacts through the telescreen are more real than everyday life.

The trouble with literary dystopias is that they are essentially negative. Orwell says that "hope lies with the proles"—hope lies with human experience—but it will take a long time. To find a more concrete way out one has to look elsewhere in Orwell's work. It will not do to try to turn Orwell into a prophet of anti-Communism or some kind of New Conservative. He simply refuses to get into bed with the left or the right, or any other programmatic apostle. Just before leaving Spain in 1937 he wrote Cyril Connolly: "I have seen wonderful things and at last really believe in Socialism, which I never did before." If his words mean anything, Orwell remained a socialist to his death. But to him socialism was not a programmatic ideology of social and economic change. It dwelt more deeply in the transcendent values of justice, liberty, equality, and the community of feeling (the brotherhood perverted into Big Brother) in which material values play their role alongside human ones. Its primary motives are surely neither rational nor public. Life is held together by family, community, and the shared values and experiences that constitute culture. For the rest of his life Orwell stressed the human and individual quality of this type of socialism. His critics find him gloomy because he returned to classical stoicism and abandoned progress. But without the relativism of ideology to organize human affairs, only the stark absolutes of human character remain. What Orwell is saying is that, now or in 1984, they are the things that really matter.

Juan Genovés, Beyond the Limit, *1966.*

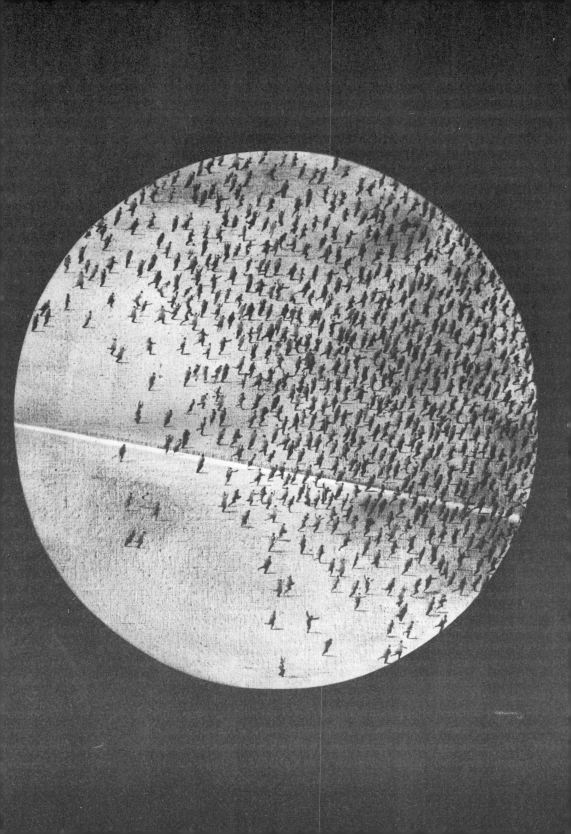

PICTURE CREDITS

74 75 76 9 8 7 6 5 4 3